"Bergman argues that preventing unjust wars requires more people with the moral strength to resist the lure of power and illusory success that war often promises. He presents social, philosophical, and religious grounds for the right to selective conscientious objection to unjust wars, and he shows the importance of communities that nurture those with the depth needed to say no. A valuable and timely book. Read it."

—**David Hollenbach, SJ**
Georgetown University

"Bergman's fine book addresses how to prevent unjust war by issuing three challenges: 1) to the pacifist tradition and its absolute presumption against any just use of violent force; 2) to the just war tradition and its historical deference to political authority rather than the conscience of the individual; and 3) to the Catholic Church as a moral educator forming consciences. His exploration of these challenges will leave readers better informed citizens and wiser disciples."

—**Kenneth R. Himes, OFM**
Boston College

"Finally, with Roger Bergman's nuanced and careful treatment of the problem of unjust war, we have an accessible and academic resource for Catholics and others that *integrates* a serious account of the just war tradition and a sympathetic appreciation of pacifism and nonviolence. Although not the final word, of course, this book offers an inclusive and constructive way forward for just peacemakers and peacebuilders."

—**Tobias Winright**
Saint Louis University

"*Preventing Unjust War* is excellent—highly readable and aimed right at the great challenge today for Catholicism and war: how to shape a culture where citizens and citizen-soldiers are able to refuse participation in an unjust war. I've taught 'Ethics of War and Peace' for years and this text will be a great addition to my class."

—**David DeCosse**
Santa Clara University

"This scholarly book with deep personal roots puts the question of the formation of conscience front and center. Bergman made a name for himself a decade ago with a book on Catholic social *learning*—which the documents of Catholic social teaching blithely ignore. With this new book, he challenges Catholic educators to breathe life into the teaching of selective conscientious objection to war. In brief, we must consider: How was someone like Franz Jägerstätter possible?"

—**Bernard G. Prusak**
King's College, Wilkes-Barre, Pennsylvania

Preventing Unjust War

Preventing Unjust War

A Catholic Argument for Selective Conscientious Objection

ROGER BERGMAN

Foreword by Drew Christiansen

CASCADE *Books* · Eugene, Oregon

PREVENTING UNJUST WAR
A Catholic Argument for Selective Conscientious Objection

Cascade Books
An Imprint of Wipf and Stock Publishers
199 W. 8th Ave., Suite 3
Eugene, OR 97401

www.wipfandstock.com

PAPERBACK ISBN: 978-1-5326-8665-8
HARDCOVER ISBN: 978-1-5326-8666-5
EBOOK ISBN: 978-1-5326-8667-2

Cataloguing-in-Publication data:

Names: Bergman, Roger (Roger C.), author. | Christiansen, Drew, foreword.

Title: Preventing unjust war : a Catholic argument for selective conscientious objection / Roger Bergman ; foreword by Drew Christiansen.

Description: Eugene, OR : Cascade Books, 2020 | Includes bibliographical references and index.

Identifiers: ISBN 978-1-5326-8665-8 (paperback) | ISBN 978-1-5326-8666-5 (hardcover) | ISBN 978-1-5326-8667-2 (ebook)

Subjects: LCSH: War & Conflict Studies. | Conscientious objection. | Conscientious objectors. | Selective conscientious objection. | Jägerstätter, Franz, 1907–1943.

Classification: UB341 .B47 2020 (print) | UB341 .B47 (ebook)

DECEMBER 9, 2020

This book is dedicated to the memory of
two twentieth-century martyrs of the faith

Blessed Franz Jägerstätter (1907–43)
*"I cannot and may not take an oath in favor
of a government that is fighting an unjust war."*

Saint Óscar Romero (1917–80)
*"No soldier is obliged to obey an order
contrary to the law of God."*

The wise man will wage just wars....
For, unless the wars were just,
he would not have to wage them,
and in such circumstances
he would not be involved in war at all.

—SAINT AUGUSTINE, *CITY OF GOD*, 19.7

There are two reasons why men especially deviate from justice.
The first is because they defer to important persons.
The second is because they defer to the majority.

—SAINT THOMAS AQUINAS,
COMMENTARY ON THE BOOK OF JOB, 34.2

Contents

Foreword

Drew Christiansen, SJ

Terrence Malick's film *A Hidden Life* meditates on the heroic witness of the Austrian farmer Franz Jägerstätter against Hitler's wars of aggression. For Malick, Jägerstätter is an existential hero; true to his conscience, he stands alone. Misunderstood by his family, he is patronized by his pastor and bishop, who counsel him to do his patriotic duty and swear allegiance to the *Führer*. Rejected and derided by his fellow parishioners, he moves resolutely toward his death. Ironically, the only character who is touched and troubled by his convictions is Judge Lueben, the president of the court that sentenced him to death by guillotine.

Jägerstätter's stand was a "solitary witness," the title the late Gordon Zahn gave to the biography that first brought Blessed Franz's story to the world. He had no companions in his witness, though his wife Franziska, despite her incomprehension, loved him as she could, laboring to eke out a living on their mountainside farm. She toiled like a beast of burden alongside the bullocks and horses to cultivate and harvest the fields. Her fidelity and suffering, in the midst of incomprehension, make Franziska also a hero of the film.

But Malick makes Franz in his solitariness too inarticulate to reveal the strength of his faith and the clarity of his convictions. For in his diaries, reflective musings, and final testament, Franz, who had only an eighth-grade education, was exceedingly articulate about his faith, about the evil of Hitler's wars, and about his conscientious refusal to be inducted into the German army. He had a rich inner life, a clear mind, and keen judgment. Malick, however, prefers the loneliness of the steely, tight-lipped martyr to the thoughtful man of faith, better to fit his model of the German romantic hero destined to die.

The figure of Blessed Franz hovers over Professor Roger Bergman's elaboration of the principle of selective conscientious objection. There were very few Catholic resisters in Hitler's Germany. To gain insight into what it is like to be so convicted by conscience that one stands against the state, Bergman lets us hear the voices of other men of conscience from Shakespeare to veterans of America's recent wars. Not all are conscientious objectors. Most are warriors, but all testify to the power of conscience on the battlefield—and after. Especially remarkable is Bergman's treatment of those who suffer from "moral injury," the post-war psychological condition in which the pangs of conscience for what soldiers have done or what they have witnessed of the savagery of war assault them as veterans in civilian life. From their suffering Bergman extracts an acute sense of the centrality of conscience to human integrity, and its power to convict the soul—and trouble the mind—even when military training, church, and society legitimate the violence in which the soldier has engaged in the name of the state. For that disturbing, sideways view of conscience alone, *Preventing Unjust War* is worth the price of the book.

Bergman's stories stirred up memories for me of Joshua Casteel, a young Army interrogator at Abu Ghraib, whose experience led him to espouse nonviolence and to enter the Catholic faith. A talented writer, Joshua, like many of those Bergman names, made his witness through his writings and public appearances. To my knowledge, Joshua did not suffer from moral injury in the technical, psychiatric sense. Instead, he met an early death in a succession of painful cancers he attributed to the military trash fires he was assigned to manage at Abu Ghraib. Joshua was just as surely a victim of that unjust war as those suffering PTSD and moral injury.

Drawing on Gordon Zahn's sociological analysis of the failure of German Catholics to dissent from Hitler's wars, Bergman contends that dissent is made possible by identification with another community outside the mainstream that adheres to an alternative set of values. For Jägerstätter, he suggests that community was the communion of martyred saints of the past. For Joshua Casteel, it was the Catholic Worker, the Catholic Peace Fellowship, and a band of loyal friends led by his mother.

Bergman's ambition is high. He would like to make the Catholic Church, and particularly the American Catholic Church, embrace conscientious objection as the vanguard of a campaign to prevent unjust war. He provides a history of the right to objection from Augustine in the fifth century, for whom there was none, to the 2004 *Compendium of Catholic Social*

Doctrine. It wasn't until Aquinas's recognition of the right of the people to rise up against unjust rulers (*Summa theologiae* 2a IIae, art. 43), however, that the first glimmers of the right to conscientious objection might be seen to emerge. The right of subjects to exemption from combat for reasons of conscience, however, is a later development still. Some four centuries later John Calvin allowed that possibility only for lesser magistrates, and the Spanish scholastic Francisco Suárez would impose on the king's commanders the obligation to true counsel, though not the exemption from obedience in battle.

Before and after Aquinas, though there were exceptions, the presumption in favor of established authority remained strong right up through the pontificate of Pope Pius XII. Judging from Shakespeare's *Henry IV, Part I*, however, discussion about the crimes of war was already fare for common soldiers as well as for statesmen in Elizabethan England. The play opens with a debate between the young Henry and his bishops about the justice of the king's cause in France. Throughout the play, the argumentative Welsh sergeant Fluellen, a kind of "common man," protests violations of the laws of war from the English siege of Harfleur to the vengeful slaughter of the baggage boys by the French after they have fled the field of battle.

Most of all, in a vivid conversation the night before the battle of Agincourt, Henry in disguise engages in serious banter around a campfire with ordinary fighting men over whether obedience exonerates the common soldier from the crimes of war commanded by kings. After he departs, the men go on to speculate on the fate of kings on the other side of death for their pursuit of unjust wars.

> But if the cause be not good, the king himself hath a heavy reckoning to make, when all those legs and arms and heads, chopped off in battle, shall join together at the latter day and cry all "We died at such a place;" some swearing, some crying for a surgeon, some upon their wives left poor behind them, some upon the debts they owe, some upon their children rawly left. I am afeard there are few die well that die in a battle . . .

Bergman's arguments are especially pertinent today when President Trump flouts every imaginable norm. He has made resignation in protest and selective conscientious objection matters of urgent concern for the US military and defense analysts in military service. For a time it seemed as if the military could hold the line against the president's transgressive urges; but in the last year he has repeatedly come out against good order and discipline in the military and reversed decisions of court martials and review boards. He has taken retribution against those who, like Lt. Col. Alexander Vindman, testified to Congress against him, and he has stiffened his open opposition to international humanitarian law and the laws of armed combat.

Some parts of the military, at least, take those norms seriously. They educate their personnel in the laws of war and just-war theory, assign JAG officers (military lawyers) to participate in war-planning and targeting exercises, and courts martial try at least the most egregious violators of international standards. Even those in top command positions practice refusing to implement illegal orders. How long, then, can the military's moral culture withstand abuse from the commander in chief? Bergman quotes Aquinas to the effect that people sin either out of deference to authority or by succumbing to popular opinion. He missed a third motive, namely, even a hardened soldier may buckle under the relentless pressure of bullying superiors.

Under current circumstances, the formation of conscience and the building of communities of moral discernment to support potential conscientious objectors are both sorely needed. At a time, moreover, when new technologies necessitate defending old norms and devising new ones, faith communities have a special role to play to provide support and guidance for those in military service.

Like Pax Christi International in its promotion of Just Peace, Roger Bergman is looking for the hierarchical church to take leadership in this area. Pope Francis is said to be preparing a document on peace. It is fair to assume that in keeping with his 2017 World Day of Peace Message, "Nonviolence: A New Style of Politics," Francis will make Just Peace one of his principal themes. He has also told Pax Christi in response to the demands of radical pacifists among its members that he will not condemn the Just War. While the strict pacifists may chafe at that decision, many Christian ethicists who believe Just War is still a useful tool for curbing the violence of war will be exceedingly relieved. Their concern is how Just War may be made effective as a tool to limit violence in the name of the state. Bergman's answer is by making conscientious objection more common and more public. If the pope's projected statement elaborates on his support for selective conscientious objection, it would be a positive contribution to a chastened just-war teaching. For, sadly, the Just War tradition has been more often used to rationalize unjust war than to curb it. As long as there is unjust war,

Christians, who allow war only by exception, are obliged to resist it. Affirming selective conscientious objection, making it a more common option, would be a way to give the Just War Tradition the effective restraints it has so often lacked.

At the same time, we might find ourselves disappointed if we put our hope primarily in church officials and official church structures. National episcopacies are divided internally on issues of war and peace, and bishops' conferences differ depending on the strategic situation of their own countries. In the United States, at least, the infrastructure for social teaching and social action has sorely diminished from its peak in the 1980s. Cost-cutting as a result of the sex-abuse crisis and the great recession led to significant reductions by dioceses in social programs and social-action offices. Under Pope Francis and Cardinal Turkson, however, the Holy See is reaching out to collaborate with lay groups like Pax Christi and the Community of Sant' Egidio, with universities like Georgetown and Notre Dame, and with men and women of goodwill like Naomi Klein and Dr. Klaus Topfer who assisted in preparing and publicizing *Laudato Si'*.

When we say "the Church" will be the base for purifying just-war thinking and preventing unjust war, the program might find greater traction if we look at communities of faith who discern the Signs of the Times together as well as at formal church structures. Pope Francis has embraced the teaching of Blessed Paul VI on the responsibilities of communities of faith to discern the Signs of the Times with a view to social transformation. Even under Saint John Paul II bishops recognized that engaging the church did not necessarily mean the official structures of dioceses and parishes. The Synod for America, for example, defined the parish as "a community of communities and movements," affirming that smaller sub-communities and both informal and formal ecclesial movements could be centers of discernment and pastoral action. So, we should look to Catholic NGOs like Pax Christi, Pax Romana, and the Catholic Peace Fellowship, to Catholic universities, to prayer groups, faith-sharing circles, and affinity groups, say, among military personnel, defense specialists, and veterans, to take on the promotion of selective conscientious objection, as well as to formal church structures like bishops' conferences, dioceses, and parishes.

In addition, in "A Call to Action" Paul VI envisaged social action as a "big-tent" affair embracing men and women of other Christian churches and other religions, extending further to embrace "men and women of good will," those of no formal faith but with moral discernment and commitment. Pope Francis took this "big tent" approach in preparation and dissemination of *Laudato Si'*, and he made a methodological case for it in *Evangelii gaudium*. I think too of Pope Emeritus Benedict XVI's interpretation of the parable of the mustard seed that grows into "a tree where all the birds of the air make their home." He allowed that in the Kingdom of God many dwell who do not belong to the visible church. The campaign to prevent unjust war will prosper when we understand the church in these broader ways, invest in small grassroots groups, and build networks with other activists. The hierarchical church has an essential role to play, but as Saint John Henry Newman wrote, the church is at its best when it is "a conspiracy of bishops and faithful" working together. Just so, supporting selective conscientious objectors on a scale that prevents unjust wars will have better prospects of success when it becomes a broadly ecumenical cause advanced by the diverse groups, inside and outside the visible church, stirred up by the one Divine Spirit, who is active both in the baptized and in the world. *Spiritus spirat ubi vult.*

Introduction
Setting the Ecclesial Context[1]

"AN APPEAL TO THE Catholic Church to Re-Commit to the Centrality of Gospel Nonviolence," the statement from the 2016 conference sponsored by the Pontifical Council on Justice and Peace and Pax Christi International, rightly acknowledges the dangers of misguided use of "just war" language. But, in calling for jettisoning that tradition, the statement endangers the just-peace it hopes to promote.

The US Catholic Bishops' pastoral letter of 1983, *The Challenge of Peace: God's Promise and Our Response*, embraces a hopeful but realistic eschatology (the kingdom of God is "already but not yet,"[2] inaugurated but not fulfilled) and takes nonviolence seriously in that context. It teaches a strict interpretation of the just-war tradition, of the right of nations to defend themselves against aggression, and places a high responsibility on personal conscience, endorsing pacifism, but also selective conscientious objection, the right of soldiers to refuse participation in wars judged unjust.

I find the richness of this perspective missing from the Appeal. No Catholic should take exception to the call "for our Church to be a living witness and to invest far greater human and financial resources in promoting a spirituality and practice of active nonviolence and in forming and training our Catholic communities in effective nonviolent practices."[3] If even a minority of Catholics were to take up this challenge, it would make a difference. But it's more complicated than that.

---

1. This introduction is based on Bergman, "Jettisoning Just War," which appeared in *National Catholic Reporter*, and also draws on Bergman, "Jesus, Scripture," which appeared in *Creighton Magazine*. Both are used with permission of the editors.

2. NCCB, *Challenge of Peace*, #58.

3. Pax Christi, "Appeal," 1.

Pope John Paul II, in his 1991 encyclical letter *Centesimus Annus*, declared, "No, never again war, which destroys the lives of innocent people, teaches how to kill, throws into upheaval even the lives of those who do the killing and leaves behind a trail of resentment and hatred, thus making it all the more difficult to find a just solution of the very problems which provoked the war."[4] Having lived under the totalitarian oppression of both the Nazis and the Communists, John Paul II can hardly be described as naïve about worldly realities. Rather, one of the contemporary realities that seems most to have impressed the Pope, as recorded in *Centesimus Annus*, is the decisive role nonviolence played in bringing down communism in Europe.[5] His own role in the fall of the regime in his Polish homeland is justly celebrated. The Catholic Church can also take credit for playing a significant role in the nonviolent ouster of the dictators Marcos in the Philippines and Pinochet in Chile.

Nonetheless, the pope also favored humanitarian *military* intervention in Bosnia, East Timor, and Central Africa to disarm the aggressors and to establish peace. His attitude toward force is obviously complex. It would not be inappropriate to call John Paul II a "just-war pacifist." While not absolutely ruling out the use of force as a last resort in defense of human life, he might well now be thought of, in retrospect, along with Gandhi, Dr. Martin Luther King Jr., Archbishop Desmond Tutu of South Africa, and the Dalai Lama, the last three Nobel Peace Prize recipients, as one of history's most ardent advocates of nonviolent resistance.

The most compelling statement I have ever come across about war and peace is that "after Hiroshima, just war can never be the same, and after Auschwitz, pacifism can never be the same."[6] But what would that look like? Just-war pacifism is, strictly speaking, a logical contradiction. One cannot simultaneously endorse, in one agent, an absolute *and* a relative presumption against the use of force. On the other hand, perhaps what John Paul II is pointing us toward is a third alternative that is only beginning to emerge in the examples, such as the Solidarity movement in Poland, chronicled in *A Force More Powerful: A Century of Nonviolent Conflict*,[7] both the book and the three-hour PBS documentary series by the same name. As much planning, preparedness, discipline, and courage would be required

4. Pope John Paul II, *Centisimus Annus* #52, in O'Brien and Shannon, 512–13.

5. Pope John Paul II, *Centisimus Annus* #23, in O'Brien and Shannon, 488–89.

6. Author unknown.

7. Ackerman and DuVall, *Force More Powerful*.

to wage nonviolent resistance as now goes into military operations. Such a transformation obviously represents a long-term vision. In the meantime, the just-war tradition provides Christian citizens and all people of good will with a substantial ethical perspective by which to engage public debate about US military policy and conduct.

I must take exception to the assertion of "An Appeal to the Catholic Church to Re-Commit to the Centrality of Gospel Nonviolence," "that there is no 'just war.' Too often the 'just war theory' has been used to endorse rather than prevent or limit war. Suggesting that a 'just war' is possible also undermines the moral imperative to develop tools and capacities for non-violent transformation of conflict."[8] The obvious counter-example is the Allied war against the Axis Powers in the 1940s. Certainly Hitler's wars were not just, so to oppose them militarily, since no other effective means were available, was eminently just. However, the Allied bombing of German and Japanese cities, even apart from the atomic bombing of Hiroshima and Nagasaki, was, to cite Vatican Council II, "a crime against God and man himself... [and] merits unequivocal and unhesitating condemnation."[9] But defeating Hitler's racist, totalitarian imperialism by discriminate and proportionate means was of the highest moral imperative. Do the authors of the conference statement believe that could have been done nonviolently? Do they think such a threat could never arise again?

No doubt just-war language has been used improperly, even cynically, when it has been used at all. That all wars are unjust on at least one side does not mean that all sides in all wars are unjust. And maintaining that war can be undertaken as a last resort does not necessarily detract from the imperative to avoid war whenever possible, and to develop means to do so effectively. But it is the recommendation of the conference statement that the Catholic Church "no longer use or teach 'just war theory.'"[10] So how will the Church evaluate future wars? Even pacifists must make an argument if they want to be taken seriously in public debate, as condemning all wars is not likely to get traction when innocent citizens are under attack.

There are other weaknesses in the document, especially its treatment of the Bible. First, the New Testament does not require jettisoning the just-war tradition that arose in post-biblical times. While the teaching of Jesus

8. Pax Christi, "Appeal," 2.

9. Vatican II, *Gaudium et Spes* #80, in O'Brien and Shannon, *Catholic Social Thought*, 233.

10. Pax Christi, "Appeal," 2.

does not explicitly provide a warrant for using force to defend neighbors against attack, neither does it prohibit using force when other means are lacking. Love of enemies is not necessarily incompatible with participation in just war. On the other hand, refusal to defend the innocent, by force if necessary, may be incompatible with *agapē*.

Second, Jesus's self-sacrifice does not require abandoning just war. His example of not using force to defend himself (a bilateral situation) does not tell us what he would have done if he came across an aggressor attacking an innocent victim (a multilateral situation).[11] What would the Good Samaritan have done had he arrived during the beating, not after?[12] What if all nonviolent attempts at intervention failed? What if coming between the aggressor and the victim would have led to two deaths instead of one? At what point does the commitment to nonviolence become complicity in violence? Jesus defended the woman caught in adultery with wit, word, and gesture, but what if the mob had not responded as it did? Could Jesus have prevented her death by his self-sacrifice?

Beyond scriptural concerns, I would argue that the prevention of unjust war is the most pressing issue, and that abandoning the just-war tradition would harm the cause. What if citizens refused to support unjust wars and members of the military refused to fight them? Is that more likely to happen because of widespread conversion to pacifism or because citizens and soldiers learn to take the just-war tradition seriously? The conference statement points to successful nonviolent campaigns as suggesting a credible alternative to opposing injustice militarily. Nonviolence has indeed had triumphs in combating tyranny in the twentieth century, but few if any are examples of stopping international aggression. The Danes resisted Hitler non-militarily, but they did not defeat or expel him. The Allied militaries did that.

The US Bishops got it right in 1983: we should simultaneously develop strategies of nonviolence *and* hold to a strict understanding of when war can be justified, *and when it cannot*—but we should not jettison the tradition until it is genuinely obsolete. Pope John Paul II and the US bishops denounced or expressed deep skepticism about the 2003 invasion of Iraq before it began. Was the problem the tradition, or was it the reluctance of Catholic citizens and soldiers to abide by it? *Uncritical* social conformity,

11. I owe this analytic distinction between the ethics of bilateral and multilateral situations to Mott, "After All Else."

12. This question was famously posed in relation to war by Ramsey, *Just War*, 142–43.

patriotism, and obedience to authority are the problem, not the just-war tradition itself. As we will see in what follows in this book, the specific problem is the conventional view that warriors have no responsibility to judge the justice of the wars they are asked to fight. I applaud the call for Pope Francis to issue a deeply researched encyclical on these matters. He could do worse than modeling such a teaching on *The Challenge of Peace*.

THE BOOK AHEAD

Why do unjust wars litter human history? No doubt because of the ambition of rulers, but also because soldiers are expected to fight whether the war can be morally justified or not. "Our obedience to the king wipes the crime of it out of us" (Shakespeare's *Henry V*) captures the tradition as begun with Augustine. Chapter 1 presents in depth the counter-exemplary story of Blessed Franz Jägerstätter, as far as I know the only officially recognized martyr of the just-war tradition. In that same chapter, sociologist Gordon Zahn's analysis of Jägerstätter's refusal to serve in Hitler's army offers a germ of what I'm arguing for in the book as a whole but especially in chapter 5. Chapter 2 outlines the developing Catholic history of the question. Selective conscientious objection, or objection to unjust wars, has been endorsed by the US Catholic bishops since Vietnam, and by the Vatican, in 2004. But no attention has been paid in Catholic culture.

Because conscience is at the heart of this argument, chapter 3 focuses on the principal source of Catholic teaching on the primacy and structure of conscience in Saint Thomas Aquinas, with special attention to the foundation of conscience in what the medieval schoolmen called *synderesis*, for which there is no translation, for reasons that will become apparent. Chapter 4 will relate this conception of conscience to the attention currently paid to combat-induced moral injury. As one 3-star general has lamented, being ordered to fight in an unjust war (without legal recourse to refuse) is the "ultimate moral injury." This book is a just war argument for the prevention of unjust war, and to that extent, for the prevention of moral injury. A related Excursus: "Lord, Deliver Me from My Necessities!" explores the relationship, in Augustine and in a modern interrogator's experience, between public duty, torture, sin, and moral injury.

Chapter 5 acknowledges that the key to making this argument for SCO realistic is philosopher Jeff McMahan's critique of the moral equality of combatants (contra Michael Walzer's endorsement, which lays the conceptual groundwork for making widespread SCO untenable) and especially McMahon's proposal for an international court to judge the justice of new wars. With the authority of such a court in place, under Catholic auspices, SCO would be possible not only for the rare martyr like Blessed Franz. An appendix on three historical precedents for such a court follows, as does an appendix on a precedent for the implementation of SCO in the military—from a surprising source. A fifth appendix to chapter 5 reflects on the relationship of selective conscientious objection to civil disobedience.

Chapter 6, in the framework of contemporary research into psychological development (cognitive, moral, and identity) recounts my course on Christian ethics of war and peace as an example of what can be done in the classroom to promote the stance of selective conscientious objection. It responds to the complaint that most warriors are too immature to make responsible decisions about matters such as going to war. Chapter 7 addresses the scholarly debate over the presumptions of the just-war tradition by setting it in the dynamic context of eschatology, ecclesiology, and ethics. The focus is on the tension between legitimate authority and the primacy of the conscience, and the role the Church might play in addressing that tension. The American war in Vietnam, as portrayed in The Pentagon Papers, provides a case study of legitimate authority gone awry. Imagination gets the last word, in the form of an epilogue that explores the wonderful poem of Seamus Heaney, "From the Republic of Conscience." No ambassador of conscience is ever relieved from her post; we are all ambassadors of conscience.

1

Toward an Ecclesiology of Conscience

The Example of Franz Jägerstätter
and the Legacy of Gordon Zahn

There are two reasons why men especially deviate from justice. The first is because they defer to important persons. The second is because they defer to the majority.

—Saint Thomas Aquinas[1]

Those who want to find the right way to eternal well-being should not walk with the majority of people who are usually timid about making sacrifices, and they should not entrust themselves to leaders whose actions differ from their words.

—Blessed Franz Jägerstätter[2]

1. Aquinas, *Commentary on Job*, 34.2.
2. Putz, *Franz Jägersttätter*, 215.

INTRODUCTION

ON FEBRUARY 22, 1943, Franz Jägerstätter, a thirty-five-year-old peasant farmer living in the Catholic village of St. Radegund, Austria, received his military induction notice from Adolf Hitler's Third Reich. On March 2, he refused induction for reasons of conscience and was imprisoned in Linz, where he had previously sought the counsel of Bishop Joseph Fliesser regarding this very matter. As had his parish priest, the Bishop advised him to think of his wife and three daughters (six, five, and three years of age), and to do his duty for the *Vaterland* in a time of great national peril. On May 4, Jägerstätter had a hearing before the Military Tribunal in Berlin; on July 6, the Tribunal sentenced him to death for undermining military morale.[3] He was executed by guillotine on August 9, 1943, the Feast of the Transfiguration. On October 26, 2007, Pope Benedict XVI beatified Franz Jägerstätter as a martyr of the Catholic faith.[4]

This recognition of Blessed Franz sixty-four years after his death came to pass only because of the discovery of the Jägerstätter story by the American Catholic sociologist Gordon Zahn in the process of researching his classic account, *German Catholics and Hitler's Wars*.[5] Otherwise unknown, and unheralded even in his native village, Jägerstätter was introduced to the world through Zahn's second classic book, *In Solitary Witness: The Life and Death of Franz Jägerstätter*. As that title suggests, Jägerstätter was one of only a handful of Catholics throughout Germany and Austria to refuse induction into Hitler's army. His costly refusal, if not unique, was exceedingly rare. Although a peasant farmer with only an eighth grade education, Jägerstätter, *unlike the entire Catholic leadership of Germany and Austria*,[6] saw clearly the murderous injustice of Hitler's imperialist wars and acted on his conscience accordingly. He would not sin against the Fifth Commandment and damn himself to Hell.

I have taught *In Solitary Witness* twice. The first time I paired it with Charles Curran's excellent collection of essays, *Conscience*. To my

3. Forest, *Franz Jägersttätter*, xxiii.

4. For a chronology of Franz Jägerstätter's life and the history of the Third Reich, see Putz, *Franz Jägersttätter*, 249–52.

5. For his earliest account of his discovery of Jägerstätter, see Zahn, *In Solitary Witness*, 4–7.

6. "With the exception of Bishop Preysing of Berlin, who carefully refrained from any support of Hitler's wars, all German bishops until the very last days of the conflict called on the faithful to do their patriotic duty." Lewy, *Catholic Church*, 232.

astonishment, I discovered that only one of the fifteen essays by prominent Catholic moral theologians addressed even indirectly the obvious questions raised by Zahn's two books: how could almost the entire Catholic leadership and population of Germany (and Austria) capitulate to the Nazi war machine, and how could a solitary Austrian peasant go so boldly against that machine and his own religious leadership? The essays in the Curran collection, despite the fact that the editor himself and many of their authors in other contexts demonstrate a strong commitment to Catholic social teaching, simply do not address the sociological dimension of the formation and functioning of conscience. Instead, they are almost uniformly preoccupied with the question of the relationship of personal conscience to magisterial teaching. Dissent within the church, not faithful witness over against the secular culture and the state, is the agenda-setting issue.[7] Given the stakes made abundantly evident by the carnage of World War II—and the tarnishing of Catholic moral credibility during that period—this is an omission of considerable significance.

I attempted to address this omission the second time I taught the Jägerstätter story by replacing the Curran collection with Zahn's own sociological analysis of Catholic complicity in Hitler's wars, as presented in his first book. It became clear to me that in these two books, Zahn had contributed substantially to that sociological understanding of conscience so conspicuously absent in the Curran collection. Yet another book by Zahn, *War, Conscience, and Dissent*, a collection of his essays, contributes further to this understanding. The publication in 2009 of *Franz Jägerstätter: Letters and Writings from Prison* makes possible a deeper analysis of Jägerstätter himself and thereby of Zahn's presentation of him. As far as I

7. As will be made clear later in this chapter, Jägerstätter's disagreement with his bishop was not at the level of doctrine nor even of church teaching about the ethical criteria for a just war. The questions over which they disagreed were whether a Christian could in good conscience fight in *Hitler's* wars, and more fundamentally, whether a layman had the responsibility to make such a moral discernment. All the German and Austrian hierarchy answered yes to the first question and no to the second; Franz and a very few others answered no and yes. (See notes 47 and 68 below for further if brief discussion of Jägerstätter's obedience to church teaching.) There is no evidence, as Zahn ("In Celebration of Martydom," 9) insists, that Franz did so as a pacifist. As will become evident, he was a *selective* conscientious objector to an unjust war, not a conscientious objector to all wars. That seems to me to make the value of his witness more significant, not less. As Brian Wicker ("Significance," 385) points out, "democratic governments can accommodate pacifism, as long as it remains a minority option. . . . On the other hand, refusal by individuals to take part in a particular war they think is unjust presents any government with a much more difficult predicament."

am aware, there has been no scholarly attempt to analyze and synthesize Zahn's writings as they relate to the question of formation and functioning of conscience in the Catholic tradition. This describes the occasion for this chapter. A celebrated voice of Catholic conscience himself and a co-founder of Pax Christi USA, Professor Zahn died in 2007,[8] just two months after the beatification that probably would not have happened without his book and persevering advocacy of Jägerstätter's cause. This chapter will first offer a narrative analysis of Jägerstätter's life and writings and then elaborate Zahn's "sociotheology" of conscience.

THE EXAMPLE OF FRANZ JÄGERSTÄTTER

> Duty and interest are perfectly coincident, for the most part in this world, but entirely and in every instance if we take in the future and the whole, this being implied in the notion of a good and perfect administration of things. Thus they who have been so wise in their generation as to regard only their own supposed interest, at the expense and to the injury of others, shall at last find that he who has given up all the advantages of the present world rather than violate his conscience and the relations of life, has infinitely better provided for himself and secured his own interest and happiness.
>
> —Bishop Butler[9]

From Ruffian to Religious Resister

Nothing in Franz's very ordinary background and early life suggests a saint-in-the-making. He was a better-than-average student and became an avid reader, but ended his formal schooling on his fourteenth birthday.[10] It could not have been a very formidable education as the St. Radegund school had one room and one teacher for seven grades and fifty to sixty students.[11]

8. For a fine eulogy of Zahn by a longtime friend and colleague, see Hovey, "Man of Peace," 6.

9. Butler, *Five Sermons,* 45.

10. Zahn, *In Solitary Witness,* 24.

11. Forest, "Introduction," xii. Forest draws on Putz's biography of Jägerstätter, which is not available in English, to report some details, such as these about his school, not included in Zahn's earlier work.

At least until his mid-twenties, his religiosity seems to have been conventional at best. If anything, he was remembered by villagers as something of a popular, fun-loving "ruffian" and girl-chaser. Indeed, at age twenty-five and unmarried, he fathered a child with whom he developed a caring relationship and for whom he provided materially for the rest of his life.[12] Perhaps in part due to regret over the illegitimacy of this birth, around the time of his marriage to Franziska Schwaninger (not the mother of his first child), which took place on April 9, 1936, Franz seems to have undergone a religious conversion. Atypically for couples from St. Radegund, the newlyweds honeymooned in Rome, where they received a papal blessing in a public audience with Pius XI, and where Franz may have been impressed particularly by the many memorials to the Christian martyrs.[13] As he wrote in a letter to his godson, apparently sometime in 1936, "Since the death of Christ, almost every century has seen the persecution of Christians; there have always been heroes and martyrs who gave their lives—often in horrible ways—for Christ and their faith."[14] In this same godfatherly exhortation, in language that would mean something quite different just several years later, Franz wrote that "we must do everything in our power to strive toward the Eternal Homeland and to preserve a good conscience."[15] But in 1936, the frame of reference for moral integrity was the sixth, not the fifth commandment: "For it often happens that a man risks his temporal and eternal happiness for a few seconds of pleasure. . . . This much I can tell you from my own experience."[16]

The intensification of religious devotion that came over Franz was so dramatic that many of his fellow villagers thought he might be mentally deranged.[17] That this exceptional fervor was the source of his subsequent refusal to accept induction as a soldier, as every other inductee of the village had done, led those same villagers to regard his execution, which left his family without a husband, father, and provider, as a senseless tragedy.[18] In 1940, however, he became sexton of his local church, evidence that the pastor thought him "thoroughly sound in his approach to religious matters,"

12. Zahn, *In Solitary Witness*, 32.

13. Forest, "Introduction," xiv.

14. Zahn, *In Solitary Witness*, 34.

15. Zahn, *In Solitary Witness*, 34.

16. Zahn, *In Solitary Witness*, 34.

17. Zahn, *In Solitary Witness*, 37, 40–42.

18. Zahn, *In Solitary Witness*, 38.

although that didn't mean Franz shied away from criticizing the pastor for too much emphasis in his homilies on the virtues of military life.[19] Indeed, the villagers indicated to Professor Zahn that Franz's religious conversion and his outspoken opposition to the Nazi regime arrived in tandem.[20] He was remembered as answering the usual "Heil Hitler!" with "Pfui Hitler!" as a gesture of disrespect for the *Führer*. When the local peasants' organization weakened its opposition to the Nazi movement, Franz withdrew.[21]

A Solitary Vote and a Troubling Dream

But the most clear-cut early expression of Franz's opposition to the Third Reich was his vote in the plebiscite of April 10, 1938, just a month after the *Anschluss* of March 11. Asked to render public approval of Hitler's bloodless takeover of Austria,[22] Franz cast the only dissenting vote[23] in St. Radegund, despite the encouragement of the Austrian hierarchy to do otherwise. Across the nation, the vote was almost unanimously positive at 99.08 percent,[24] in celebration of which Cardinal Innitzer, head of the Church in Austria, signed a declaration under the words "Heil Hitler!"[25] Five years later, in 1943, Franz made a startling comparison: "I believe that what took place in the spring of 1938 was not much different from that Maundy Thursday nineteen-hundred years ago when the Jewish crowd was given a free choice between the innocent Savior and the criminal Barabbas."[26] Franz, in opposition to the religious authorities and to the multitudes, had voted for Jesus. From this time on, he refused to contribute to or benefit from the various Nazi relief programs that came to St.

19. Zahn, *In Solitary Witness*, 44–45.

20. Zahn, *In Solitary Witness*, 39.

21. Zahn, *In Solitary Witness*, 46.

22. "On April 10, 1938, the German people at the polls were handed a ballot that read, 'Do you pledge yourself to our Führer Adolf Hitler and therewith to the reunification of Austria with the German Reich carried out on March 13?'" Lewy, *Catholic Church*, 216–17.

23. Although Putz's chronology (*Franz Jägerstätter*, 249) indicates a "no" vote, according to Zahn "he cast an intentionally invalidated ballot, thereby voting neither for nor against the measure" (*In Solitary Witness*, 888). Still, such a vote was singular within St. Radegund and clearly a dissent from the national near-unanimity.

24. Lewy, *Catholic Church*, 217.

25. Forest, "Introduction," xvii.

26. Zahn, *In Solitary Witness*, 47.

Radegund, although there is no evidence that he refused to cooperate with agricultural production regimens; he continued to farm as usual until his induction notice arrived.[27] The Jägerstätters' three daughters were born just before or during this period, in 1937, 1938, and 1940.

Sometime in 1938, Franz had a now-famous dream. He described it four years later, in 1942:

> All of a sudden I saw a beautiful shining railroad train that circled around a mountain. Streams of children—and adults as well—rushed toward the train and could not be held back. I would rather not say how many adults did not join the ride. Then I heard a voice say to me, "This train is going to hell." Immediately it seemed as if someone took me by the hand, and the same voice said, "Now we will go to purgatory." And oh! So frightful was the suffering I saw and felt, I could only have thought that I was in hell itself if the voice had not told me we were going to purgatory. . . . Then I heard a sigh and saw light—and all was gone. . . . At first this traveling train was something of a riddle to me, but the longer our situation continues, the clearer the meaning of this train becomes for me. Today it seems to me that it is a symbol of nothing but National Socialism, which was then breaking in (or better, creeping in) upon us.[28]

At least in retrospect, this nightmarish image became for Franz a lens through which to interpret what was happening in Germany and Austria, in the Catholic Church, and in his own conscience: "I believe that God has clearly spoken to me through this dream or appearance and placed it in my heart so that I could decide whether to be a National Socialist or a Catholic!"[29] Presenting such a stark and fateful choice, Franz's dream would seem to have had direct bearing on his eventual refusal to serve in the Nazi military. Yet despite his great dismay at the capitulation of the Austrian hierarchy, he does not reproach the bishops, for "they are human beings of flesh and blood as we are, and they can be weak."[30] He adds (I don't think he means it ironically), "Maybe they have been too poorly prepared to take up this struggle and to make a choice between life or death."[31] As for himself,

27. Zahn, *In Solitary Witness*, 48–49.
28. Zahn, *In Solitary Witness*, 111–12.
29. Putz, *Jägerstätter*, 175.
30. Putz, *Franz Jägerstätter*, 175.
31. Zahn, *In Solitary Witness*, 114.

"If God had not given me the grace and strength even to die for my faith if I have to, I, too, would probably be doing the same as most other Catholics."[32]

But since these reflections were written four years after the dream itself, one might wonder about its significance at the time. Zahn dates the dream to the summer of 1938,[33] Putz to January of that same year.[34] That is, what Zahn translates as summer, Putz translates as January. Not knowing German, I asked Dr. Olaf Bohlke, professor of German at my university, if the words for summer and January were so similar that translators working from a hand-written text might read the word differently. That is not the case, according to Dr. Bohlke. In fact, he found the hand-written text on-line and reported that the problem was that the original word was crossed out and another written above it. Apparently, Franz himself corrected his own first memory of the date of the dream. Dr. Bohlke could not make out either the rejected word or its replacement. But I don't think that leaves us stranded, for in the same journal entry in which Franz describes his dream he goes on to say, "Just *prior* to the dream, newspapers reported that 150,000 young Austrians had recently entered the Hitler Youth and hence had joined the N.S. Party." Putz's footnote to this sentence indicates that "*after* Austria's plebiscite on April 10, 1938, the Reich required all youth between the ages of ten and eighteen to belong to the Hitler Youth."[35] So the dream, according to Franz, occurred *after* the entry of those 150,000 Austrians into the Hitler Youth, which took place *after* the plebiscite of April 10. The dream must have occurred in the summer of 1938, as Zahn indicates, and not in January, as indicated by Putz.

What difference does this dating make? Since the dream occurred after Franz learned about the Hitler Youth movement in Austria, it stands to reason to see that actual event as the provenance of the particular imagery of the dream: "streams of *children*—and adults as well—rushed toward the train and could not be held back" (emphasis added). Franz's dream, however much a grace and a revelation, was also historically informed. It was a symbolically accurate depiction of what was going on in annexed Austria, with adults and children alike unable to resist the shining train that was National Socialism. It is perhaps a moot point whether the dream helped Franz see his context clearly or whether Franz's clear vision of his context

32. Zahn, *In Solitary Witness*, 128.

33. Zahn, *In Solitary Witness*, 111.

34. Putz, *Franz Jägerstätter*, 173.

35. Putz, *Franz Jägerstätter*, 173; emphases added.

informed his powerful dream. Either way, Franz saw National Socialism for what it was in a manner that few of his fellow German and Austrian Catholics did. So that even before his induction notice arrived, Franz could write (in 1942), "I would like to call out to everyone who is riding on this train: 'Jump out before the train reaches its destination, even if it costs you your life!'"[36]

From Religious Resister to Conscientious Objector

> Other people, arrayed against us, also pray to God and implore victory. God is indeed in the same manner the father of all people, but he is not, at one and the same time, the advocate of justice and injustice, of honesty and falsehood.
>
> —Franz Josef Rarkowski, Army Bishop of Germany, 1940[37]

But even after the dream of 1938, and even after Hitler's occupation of Czechoslovakia and invasions of Poland, France, and the Low Countries, in June of 1940 Franz reported for military training at Branau am Inn as ordered. He was released a few days later, as farmers were as needed for the war effort as were soldiers, only to be recalled to training as an army driver in October, this time not to be returned to his farm for six months, in April of 1941,[38] when he became sexton of the St. Radegund church. According to Zahn, it was during his military training that "the incompatibility between his opposition to the Nazi regime and his service in the Nazi forces first became clear to him."[39] (Remember that the dream occurred before the beginning of Hitler's wars and that it makes no reference to fighting.) Franz reports[40] that on the Feast of the Immaculate Conception (December 9, 1940) he was accepted into the Third Order of St. Francis, although he does not mention that the original rule prohibited the possession or use of deadly weapons.[41] Just less than three weeks later, he reports, "Today I

---

36. Zahn, *In Solitary Witness*, 113.
37. Quoted in Lewy, *Catholic Church*, 239.
38. Forest, "Introduction," xviii.
39. Zahn, *In Solitary Witness*, 56.
40. Putz, *Franz Jägerstätter*, 47.
41. Forest, "Introduction," xviii.

practiced my sharpshooting during the afternoon. Again, I had good luck with this."[42] This argues against describing Franz's position as pacifist.

Nonetheless, as Zahn insists, Franz "returned to St. Radegund with the firm conviction that if he were ever called to service again, he would have to refuse."[43] He made this abundantly clear to anyone he talked to in the village, especially his pastor, Fr. Karobath, who was sympathetic to his anti-Nazi views but nonetheless counseled him against conscientious objection to a war Franz was certain was unjust, a conviction whose validity the pastor did not dispute.[44] Franz also approached the pastor of a nearby village, who asked him to put his thoughts in writing, which he did. According to this priest, as reported to Zahn, these several pages "set forth in detail a position against serving in an unjust war—a position which he could only describe as unchallengeably [sic] sound in theory and logical development. Nevertheless, he, too, gave the man the same advice: he should report for service as ordered."[45] Unfortunately, this early statement of conscience does not seem to have been preserved.

In February 1943, Franz visited Bishop Joseph Fliesser of Linz, who reported after the war that he "knew Jägerstätter personally, since he spent more than an hour with me before his scheduled induction. To no avail I spelled out for him the moral principles defining the degree of responsibility borne by citizens and private individuals for the acts of the civil authority. I reminded him of his far greater responsibility for his own state of life, in particular for his family."[46] As explained by Jim Forest, this was "an answer any Catholic might have heard from any bishop in any country at the time: if not a doctrine found in any catechism,[47] it was widely be-

42. Putz, *Franz Jägerstätter*, 50.

43. Zahn, *In Solitary Witness*, 56–57.

44. Zahn, *In Solitary Witness*, 57.

45. Zahn, *In Solitary Witness*, 57–58.

46. Zahn, *In Solitary Witness*, 58.

47. In his 1956 Christmas Message, Pope Pius XII "stated that a Catholic could not cite conscientious disagreement with the legitimate leaders of a state as a reason to refuse participation in war. In this he echoed the views of his recent predecessors" (Himes, *Christianity*, 329). This raises the question of whether Jägerstätter, in so refusing, *knowingly* went against not only the counsel of his pastor and his bishop but also against the teaching of the popes who ruled during his lifetime. In the one context in which this teaching would seem most likely to come up—his interview with Bishop Fliesser, as recounted by Fliesser himself, as cited by Zahn (*In Solitary Witness*, 165)—neither the current pope, nor his predecessors, nor this teaching is mentioned. If Jägerstätter had known of this teaching, it seems very unlikely that he would not have struggled

lieved that any sins you commit under obedience to your government are not your personal sins but are regarded by God as the sins of those who lead the state."[48] (The following chapter takes up the history of this question in detail.) But in the months prior to his meeting, Franz was already clear in refuting this position, as evidenced in a journal entry: "I do not agree with the view that an individual soldier bears no responsibility for the whole [war] and that this responsibility belongs to only one individual [i.e., Hitler]."[49] Franz had written a list of eleven questions he hoped the bishop could answer. They indicate clearly how sharpened his thinking had become on the morality of Hitler's wars and the ordinary Catholic citizen's responsibility to oppose them. For example,

> 3. What kind of Catholic would venture to declare that these military campaigns of plundering, which Germany has undertaken in many lands and is still leading, constitute a just and holy war? . . .

> 8. If we can declare the German-speaking soldiers, who have relinquished their lives in the fight for the N.S. [National Socialist] victory, to be heroes and saints, how much more highly should we regard the soldiers in the other lands who were intent on defending their homelands after they were suddenly attacked by German-speaking soldiers? . . .

> 11. Who can succeed in simultaneously being a soldier of Christ and also a soldier for National Socialism?[50]

Although posed as questions, the powerful rhetoric reveals Jägerstätter's deep convictions. It is no wonder that even a leader of the Church he deeply respected could not persuade him otherwise. As Franz wrote, echoing St.

---

with it in his writings, but there is no evidence of this. This raises a further historical question that cannot be answered here: how well known generally was the papal teaching prohibiting conscientious objection to war when waged by legitimate authority *before* the best-known example of it, the Christmas Message of Pope Pius XII in 1956. In short, it does not seem that Jägerstätter *knowingly* went against papal teaching on obedience to the state during wartime. We can only speculate on what he *would* have done had he known of this teaching.

48. Forest, "Introduction," xx. To the extent that such wartime sins are also war crimes, this principle was repudiated by Nuremburg Principle IV: "The fact that a person acted pursuant to order of his Government or of a superior does not relieve him from responsibility under international law, provided a moral choice was in fact possible to him."

49. Putz, *Franz Jägerstätter*, 200.

50. Putz, *Franz Jägerstätter*, 207–8.

Peter in the Acts of the Apostles (5:29), "The important thing is to fear God more than man."[51]

From Conscientious Objector to Martyr

By April 1941, Jägerstätter's basic stance toward military service had been solidified, but he continued to think about the issues; most of his writings come from this two-year period before his death. In a reflection "On Humility" in Notebook I (Summer 1941–Winter 1942) Franz states a fundamental insight: "But it may sometimes happen that we must not obey this world's leaders and lawmakers because we judge that in obeying them we may in fact act incorrectly, wrongly." The model and authority for such resistance is "Christ himself who taught the greatest obedience, even in relation to this world's authorities. He was obedient until death, even until death on a cross."[52] "Therefore," as Franz writes in a subsequent reflection, "let us take the cross upon ourselves and not complain about it."[53] And this is a model not only for the exceptional few: "Things would be no worse today for genuine Christian faith in our land if the churches were no longer open and if thousands of Christians had poured out their blood and their lives for Christ and their faith. This would have been better than now watching silently as there is more and more acceptance of falsehood."[54]

Franz has no doubt as to Germany's guilt, and, foreseeing his probable induction, contemplates what action he must take—and what the consequences would be: "Is it not more Christian for someone to give himself as a sacrifice than to have to murder others who possess a right to life . . . ?"[55] Better to suffer unjust death than to inflict it. In sum, "I can never and shall never believe that we Catholics must make ourselves available to do the work of the most evil and dangerous anti-Christian power that has ever existed."[56] And yet, "our spiritual leaders, on whom we rely the most and should rely, now remain silent. Or they tell some of us even the opposite of

51. Zahn, *In Solitary Witness*, 66.
52. Putz, *Franz Jägerstätter*, 153.
53. Putz, *Franz Jägerstätter*, 160.
54. Putz, *Franz Jägerstätter*, 175.
55. Putz, *Franz Jägerstätter*, 190.
56. Putz, *Franz Jägerstätter*, 190.

what we should do if we are to be rescued from this dangerous stream [of National Socialism]."[57]

A Final Discernment: To Whom Do You Belong?

Conscience does not kneel before authorities but before the truth.

—Dean Brackley, SJ[58]

Franz's great clarity about what he was called to do was complicated, once he was imprisoned, by the possibility that he could accept induction but avoid actual fighting in an unjust war: "I am ready to serve as a military medic, for in this work a person can actually do good and exercise Christian love of neighbor in concrete ways. Doing this would not disturb my conscience."[59] Indeed, this was the path taken by no less an exemplar than Bernard Häring, the preeminent Catholic moral theologian of the twentieth century: "I had decided to forego public conscientious objection, although I admired those who made it their cause. My preference was to be with the sick and wounded, to try to heal in the midst of horror."[60] Franz's wife believed this possibility was denied him by military authorities.[61] However, as Franz came to realize, becoming a military medic would still have required him to take the Wehrmacht Oath of Loyalty: "I swear before God this sacred oath that I will render *unconditional* obedience to the *Führer* of the German nation and *Volk*, Adolf Hitler, the Supreme Commander of the armed forces, and that, as a brave soldier I shall be ready at all times to stake my life in fulfillment of this oath."[62]

Whether or not the authorities made this medical corps option available to Franz, the oath would seem to have been an insurmountable obstacle: "If I cannot uphold and obey everything that I promise in this oath, then I commit a lie. I am of the mind that it is best to tell the truth, even if it costs me my life: I cannot obey [the oath] in all of its aspects." Thinking of his duties as a father does not alter his conviction: "For it is because of

---

57. Putz, *Franz Jägerstätter*, 198.

58. Brackley, *Call to Discernment*, 170.

59. Putz, *Franz Jägerstätter*, 86.

60. Häring, *Embattled Witness*, 51.

61. Putz, *Franz Jägerstätter*, 86, n. 9.

62. Zahn, *German Catholics*, 56; emphasis added.

my family that I am not permitted to lie, not even if I had ten children."[63] Furthermore, even if he were allowed to return to his family and his farm, on condition that he take the oath, he could not do it: "Does there exist a great difference between what would be demanded of . . . a farmer and what can be demanded of a soldier?"[64] It seems likely that the very last words Franz wrote were a crystallization of his position: "I cannot and may not take an oath in favor of a government that is fighting an unjust war."[65] By swearing unconditional obedience to Adolf Hitler, even a farmer caring for his young family would become an accomplice to murder, if not a murderer himself, and to so much else.

Over the objections of his wife, pastor, and bishop, and over against the imperial will of the powerful and the dutiful compliance of the multitudes, he refused. Strangely, Franz might have agreed with Roland Freisler, state secretary of the Reich Ministry of Justice, when he observed that "'Christianity and we are alike in only one respect: we lay claim to the whole individual'. . . . 'From which do you take your orders? From the hereafter or from Adolf Hitler? To whom do you pledge your loyalty and your faith?'"[66] Franz pledged himself to the hereafter.

THE LEGACY OF GORDON ZAHN

> Given the traditional doctrine of the Just War . . . then in the case of war between A and B there are only three possibilities: A is in the right; B is in the right; A and B are in the wrong. If A is in the right, then the Catholic subjects of B have an absolute duty to resist the commands of their own government; if B is in the right the Catholics of A have a duty to resist; if both are in the wrong, then the Catholic subjects of both A and B have a duty to disobey the commands of their governments. It is clear from this argument that it makes no sense to say that we have grounds for presuming that the cause our own government commands us to support is just. The presumption is all the other way; and if to formal considerations we add the evidence of history, then the doctrine that we

63. Putz, *Franz Jägerstätter*, 236.

64. Putz, *Franz Jägerstätter*, 241.

65. Forest, "Introduction," xxiv.

66. Forest, "Introduction," xvi. In the foregoing sentence, I am quoting Forest, who is quoting Freisler, who puts some of his comments in quotation marks apparently to indicate they are not his alone but represent the position of the Reich itself. Thus, for accuracy's sake, there are quotation marks within quotation marks within quotation marks.

have a duty to presume that our own government is in the right in the matter of war and peace looks like a piece of insanity.

—J. M. Cameron[67]

We cannot say that we would not know of the example of Blessed Franz Jägerstätter were it not for Gordon Zahn, but in fact we *do* know about him principally because of Zahn. We certainly can say that Franz was fortunate to be discovered by such a sympathetic, intrepid, and gifted Catholic sociologist. We can say that all those who admire Franz and wish to see his witness against unjust war made less solitary should be grateful to Zahn not only for his telling of Franz's story but also for his compelling and courageous analysis of its ecclesial context. In the second major section of this essay, we move from a narrative interpretation of Jägerstätter himself toward a ecclesiology of conscience, as made possible by Zahn's analysis, first, of the sociological dynamics of German episcopal support for Hitler's wars, and second, of Jägerstätter's conscientious dissent. What made both possible?

German Catholics and Hitler's Wars

We begin this recounting of Zahn's analysis at the ecclesial level where we ended our presentation of the biography with the question, To whom do you belong? For the German bishops collectively as for the Austrian peasant individually, this was a question of "value selection" and the problem posed by two competing value systems.

> On the one hand, the [National Socialist] state claimed sole competence to determine and judge its own actions and objectives, holding that the individual citizen had no alternative but to render loyal and obedient service even to the point of offering his life in battle. In opposition to this, the Church in its "just war/unjust war" distinction at least *implied* a right and duty, first, to evaluate these actions and objectives according to a rather specific formulation of moral conditions, and, second, to refuse to serve in any war which did not meet these conditions. The heart of the whole [value] selection problem lay in the fact that both state and Church claimed ultimate jurisdiction over the individual's behavior.[68]

67. Cameron, "Foreword," xiii.

68. Zahn, *German Catholics*, 20; emphasis in original. As I indicated in note 47 above, Pius XII would strongly disagree with Zahn's assessment that the church's just/unjust war distinction at least implied a right and duty of the individual Catholic to question the

This competition for the individual's loyalty was heightened because "every secular value system embraces its own set of . . . myths which it invests with a kind of 'sacredness'; for the German, the most sacred of all are those designated by the terms *Volk*, *Vaterland*, and *Heimat*," which Zahn is reluctant to translate because the terms *people*, *fatherland*, and *habitat* do not convey to an English-speaker what the German terms convey to a member of the sacred *Volk*, to a citizen of the sacred *Vaterland*, and to a resident of the sacred *Heimat*.[69]

Furthermore, "from the critical core of the values represented by the *Volk-Vaterland-Heimat* myths there arises a set of secondary, or derived, values which have a more immediate relevance to the behavior of the individual citizen. . . . All of these good-citizenship values [i.e., self-sacrifice, loyalty, obedience, duty, and honor] take on a much greater intensity when they are converted into the soldierly virtues applying to men called into military service."[70] On the other hand, Zahn argues that

> all members of the Catholic religious community subscribe to a value system which requires them to refuse to co-operate with evil knowingly and willingly; [and that] since an unjust war would constitute such a moral evil, members of the Catholic religious community may be expected to refuse to contribute to or support such a war. In this context there would be no value-selection problem for the German Catholic who believed the Third Reich was conducting a just war. . . . But the German Catholic who believed the war was not a just war would be obliged to refuse to serve— even were such refusal to mean the martyr's death.[71]

This last sentence, of course, describes Jägerstätter's dilemma exactly.

However, despite this sharp (if implied) contrast between the National Socialist and the Catholic value systems in the specific matter of Hitler's wars, "in many respects the two systems are not only highly compatible, but, to a very significant degree, the religious value system specifically and intentionally supports the secular value system."[72] That is, self-sacrifice, loyalty, obedience, duty, and honor were sacred values for the German

---

moral legitimacy of a particular war. For an argument that this right and duty has been present in the tradition even before Pius XII, see chapter 2 of this book.

69. Zahn, *German Catholics*, 21–23.

70. Zahn, *German Catholics*, 23–24.

71. Zahn, *German Catholics*, 26–27.

72. Zahn, *German Catholics*, 27.

Catholic citizen as both German *and* Catholic, as both patriot *and* believer. The particular power of this convergence should be understood in historical context. Zahn points out that German Chancellor Bismarck's *Kulturkampf* (culture struggle) against the Church in the late nineteenth century "burdened it with something of an inferiority complex which continued long afterward to manifest itself in a compulsive drive to prove that Catholics *could be* good and loyal Germans, that they *were* good and loyal Germans, that, in fact, their religious formation made it certain that they would be the *best* and *most loyal* Germans of all."[73] The implication for the individual German Catholic might be put this way: Do self-sacrifice, loyalty, obedience, duty, and honor require him to serve in Hitler's army—or to refuse such service?

How did the German bishops answer this question? In brief, the legacy of the *Kulturkampf* "is evidenced throughout the wartime pastorals of the hierarchy."[74] Zahn explains more extensively that

> the German Catholic supported Hitler's wars not only because such support was required by the Nazi rulers but also because his religious leaders formally called upon him to do so; not only because the actions and opinions of his fellow citizens made him feel obligated to share the nation's burdens and sorrows but also because, by example and open encouragement, the Catholic press and Catholic organizations gave their total commitment to the nation's cause; not only because of deep-felt fears of the terrible price nonconformity would bring or the warm surge of satisfaction accompanying nationalistic or patriotic identification with the war effort, but also because his most cherished religious values had been called into play to encourage him to take his post "on the field of honor" in the "defense of *Volk* and *Vaterland*."[75]

To cite just one example of the many given by Zahn, in their 1941 pastoral letter the eight Bavarian bishops wrote that "if the commandment to love is always the greatest commandment of all, this is especially true in times of danger and need. . . . To be united is . . . the great commandment of this

---

73. Zahn, *German Catholics*, 189; emphasis in original.

74. Zahn, *German Catholics*, 189.

75. Zahn, *German Catholics*, 56. Carl Amery makes the same point: "Thus, for the church too, war meant the continuation of ecclesiastical politics—that is the politics of the Kulturkampf—by other means. In the liveliest possible way the authorities were shown that an intact and solid national Catholicism could not fail to serve their interests" (Amery, *Capitulation*, 81).

serious hour. To be united in love and in the service of the *Vaterland* is our wish, so that we may form one single community of sacrifice and effort for the protection of the *Heimat*."[76] By 1941, Germany had not only annexed Austria and occupied Czechoslovakia but also invaded Poland, France, and the Low Countries. Not to put too fine a point on it, in this serious hour, German Catholics were called to unity with their fellow Germans under the *Führer* but not with their fellow Catholics (and other human beings) unfortunate enough not to be German but Polish, French, or Dutch. According to Zahn, "nowhere in these Episcopal statements [of wartime Germany] does one encounter the question, or even a hint of any question, of whether or not the Hitler war effort met the conditions set for a 'just war.' ... Unquestioning service to *Volk* and *Vaterland* and the protection of the *Heimat* emerge as virtually the only two standards for determining the individual Catholic's obligations with regard to the war."[77]

What were the consequences? Zahn observes that "it is not possible to furnish accurate statistics as to the number of German Catholic men who actually did bear arms for the Third Reich, but it is clear that most of them who were called to the 'defense of *Volk* and *Vaterland*' answered that call."[78] Zahn learned of seven Catholics, of whom Jägerstätter was one, who openly refused military service.[79] This dramatic numerical contrast takes on a severe irony when Zahn observes that "one might interpret the virtual unanimity of Catholic support for Hitler's wars as prima-facie evidence that Catholics were convinced that these wars were just wars." This, however, may not have been the case. Zahn conducted a series of interviews with "knowledgeable and highly respected German Catholics" who reported "that few German Catholics considered it [a just war] even while World War II was in progress."[80] In those who were not convinced the war was just but who nonetheless supported the war effort, the power of the

76. Zahn, *German Catholics*, 61.

77. Zahn, *German Catholics*, 68.

78. Zahn, *German Catholics*, 54–55.

79. "It would be extremely unjust, however, to assume that these were the only cases of such refusal; far more likely is the interpretation that others who may have done the same went to their death with no record being made of their heroic sacrifice. Nevertheless, however great the total number may have been, it would still represent the merest handful when compared with the number of German Catholics who did accept service in the military forces" (Zahn, *German Catholics*, 54–55).

80. Zahn, *German Catholics*, 31.

Volk-Vaterland-Heimat myths to determine the practical meaning of self-sacrifice, loyalty, obedience, duty, and honor is tragically obvious.

Zahn argues that the Germany hierarchy not only did nothing to resist this dynamic in which nationalism trumped, co-opted, and corrupted religiously held values but actually contributed to it.[81] To the argument that to counsel resistance would have meant encouraging martyrdom, which the bishops in good conscience could not do, Zahn replies that such an explanation can be discounted "for the bishops did call for martyrdom on the part of German Catholics—but it was a 'martyrdom' for *Volk* and *Vaterland* and not for the religious values represented by the traditional morality of war."[82] Is it possible for the irony to become any more severe?

Zahn sums up his argument this way:

> *As a German citizen*, [the Catholic] was subject to the full range of secular social controls organized to induce him to conform to the demands of the war effort. . . . To stand alone against this flood, to reject the demands of this organized totality of social controls, would have required an extraordinary degree of heroic self-determination—and more. It would have required a sense of total commitment to some alternative system of values which, to one so committed, could claim precedence over those values of personal and national survival inducing support for the war. . . . *As a German Catholic*, our hypothetical individual was now subject to the full range of religious social controls directed toward this end [conformity to the demands of the national war effort]. . . . To stand alone against *this* flood [emphasis in original], to reject the demands of this totality of religious controls . . . would have required both clarity of judgment and an extraordinary degree of heroic *sanctity* [emphasis added].[83]

And that, of course, takes us back to Franz. How does a sociologist explain his solitary witness?

---

81. "This should not obscure the fact that the Catholic Church in Germany did show a strong and often effective resistance to certain Nazi policies and programs. . . . But the scope of resistance was most generally limited to those issues involving direct assaults upon Church rights and property or those government programs which in the eyes of the Catholic hierarchy clearly contradicted Catholic moral principles. Active participation in or other forms of support for Hitler's wars of aggression were apparently not recognized as such a contradiction of principle—indeed, quite a contrary view is indicated by the tenor of their wartime directives" (Zahn, *German Catholics*, 71, 77–78).

82. Zahn, *German Catholics*, 186–87.

83. Zahn, *German Catholics*, 177–79.

On Belonging to the Church of the Martyrs

Moral criticism in war is not performed in a social vacuum but from a position of connectedness to the past as well as to the future.

—Ruth Linn[84]

Although the term rings strangely in a layperson's ear, Zahn the scientist treats Jägerstätter as a social deviant: "when a sociologist uses the term 'social deviant' it refers to nothing more than an individual's failure to conform to behavioral patterns approved or prescribed within a given society at a given time."[85] It is a purely descriptive and not at all a term of moral judgment. In this sense, in the Jim Crow South, it was Rev. Martin Luther King Jr., and not Sheriff Bull Connor, who was socially deviant. Indeed, Zahn acknowledges that in regard to Jägerstätter, "we have been dealing . . . with what may properly be treated as a case of *extreme* social deviance."[86] The question then becomes, how does one explain such social deviance, especially such a dramatic, solitary, and noble case as that of Franz Jägerstätter? This requires the introduction of another scientific term. In what is not quite a tautology, Zahn observes that individual deviance is produced by conformity to deviant groups or communities—social collectives that fail to conform to behavioral patterns approved or prescribed within a given society at a given time. What from one perspective is social deviance is from another perspective social conformity, and vice versa. The difference can be described as "a shift of focus that relates most directly to reference group theory. The 'reference group' has been defined as one 'whose outlook is used by the actor as the frame of reference in the organization of his perceptual field.'"[87]

Needless to say, groups may compete with one another for pride of place in an individual's frame of reference. Formal, explicit expressions of membership and loyalty may be less important than tacit adherence to one frame of reference over another. And that makes all the difference, for how one sees determines how one acts:

> For once it is possible to introduce the possibility of adherence to . . . some "different culture" which can exist within and still

84. Linn, "Conscience at War," 353.
85. Zahn, *In Solitary Witness*, 182.
86. Zahn, *In Solitary Witness*, 183; emphasis added.
87. Zahn, *In Solitary Witness*, 190.

apart from the complex of our current attachments and obligations to the greater society in which we live, there become available to us "images formulating positive or negative commitments,
a set of hierarchically ordered prescriptions and proscriptions" *different* from those imposed by the secular culture. It then becomes
possible for us to internalize a partially or totally divergent set of
values to which we can conform and which will support behavior
that will be designated as "deviance" according to the standards set
by the state authority.[88]

As this quotation indicates, one of the chief competitions in certain forms
of society, such as Nazi Germany, will be between the secular, state culture
(with its sacred nationalistic myths) and that of a religious community: "that
the religious community can provide such a 'different culture' with norms
and values distinct from those of the secular culture should be obvious."[89]
The existential and even theological question, To whom do I belong?, has a
profoundly sociological dimension.

Unfortunately for him, "the harsh truth is that Jägerstätter had chosen
to take his stand at a time and a place where the religious community itself
had abandoned all pretensions to the traditions of protest and prophecy that
had marked its earlier history. Shepherds and flock alike had succumbed
so thoroughly to the temptations of conformism and accommodation . . .
that they had lost all sense of identity and purpose."[90] *Fortunately* for him,
there was a third alternative beyond *Volk-Vaterland-Heimat* and its bap-
tism by the German Catholic hierarchy. For Jägerstätter, the Church—one
is tempted to say *the one true Church*—"was represented by the martyrs,
the men and women who had taken their 'stand apart' when their secular
community and its rulers made demands that could not be reconciled with
the values of the religious community."[91] Zahn's sociological insight is that
"the key to Jägerstätter's deviance should be obvious to anyone who has
noted the content of his writings,"[92] as exemplified in these two selections:

88. Zahn, *War, Conscience and Dissent*, 279; emphasis in original.

89. Zahn, *War, Conscience and Dissent*, 279.

90. Zahn, *In Solitary Witness*, 173. Once again, Amery (*Capitulation*, 82) makes a
similar point: "In view of the zealously practiced patriotism [of the German Church],
what remained of the consciousness of being one body, of the common responsibility of
all Christians for one another in the conduct of war? Very little indeed."

91. Zahn, *War, Conscience and Dissent*, 280.

92. Zahn, *In Solitary Witness*, 192.

We are expected not only to offer sacrifices [to the state] but also to attack, rob, and even murder people so that a N.S. world empire [*Reich*] will come about. Nevertheless, people who decide not to obey the state's commands are accused of doing something seriously sinful. Wouldn't it be worthwhile to learn from the lives of the saints so that we would know how the first Christian would have responded to today's evil commands?

The first Christians encountered much suffering. Yet do we contemporary Christians no longer know that every hardship that God sends us can be very necessary for our eternal blessedness if we bear it with patience and out of love for God?[93]

Jägerstätter's "'reference group' . . . was the Church of prophets and martyrs that had been abandoned and rejected by those who constituted the acting Church in Nazi Germany and Austria."[94] It was this Church to which Jägerstätter conformed, as it was the Church of the bishops to which he was deviant: "he *believed* himself to be acting in full compliance with the norms and expectations of the *real* Catholic Church. To this extent Jägerstätter, too, though properly described as a 'resister' deviant in the objective context, may be said to have acted in conformity with the reference group which claimed priority in his eyes."[95]

This sociological insight leads to what might be called a sociotheology of conscience:

the point of immediate significance is the peasant's choice of a referent group out of the time-place context in which he was called upon to act. . . . [H]e was appealing to a past reference group and 'reactivating' a forgotten set of values, standards, and practices— or, in another sense, one might hold that his action was keyed to a *future* reference group in that he framed his aspirations in terms of enjoying eternal blessedness in the life of the hereafter.[96]

"Between the times," to borrow a well-known phrase of the US Bishops' pastoral letter, *Economic Justice for All*,[97] between the age of the martyrs and the hereafter, sociotheology becomes eschatology. In what might

93. Putz, *Franz Jägerstätter*, 210, 189.

94. Zahn, *In Solitary Witness*, 192.

95. Zahn, *In Solitary Witness*, 193–94; emphases in original.

96. Zahn, *In Solitary Witness*, 192–93; emphasis in original. "Sociotheology" is Zahn's term; see his *German Catholics*, chapter 12.

97. NCCB, *Economic Justice for All* #53.

appropriately be called Jägerstätter's vocational or life commitment, he made his position clear:

> Now anyone who is able to fight for both kingdoms and stay in good standing in both communities (that is, the community of saints and the Nazi Folk Community) and who is able to obey every command of the Third Reich [as demanded by the oath of loyalty to Hitler]—such a man, in my opinion, would have to be a great magician. I for one cannot do so. And I definitely prefer to relinquish my rights under the Third Reich and thus make sure of deserving my rights granted under the Kingdom of God.[98]

This sociology of conscience, as developed from Gordon Zahn's analysis of the WWII German bishops and of the martyr Franz Jägerstätter, can be encapsulated in five propositions:

1. Persons in complex societies are confronted by competing value systems.

2. Those competing systems offer competing interpretations of secondary values.

3. Selection of a value system and its interpretation of values is a matter of social deviance and conformity.

4. One may deviate from the dominant reference group by way of adherence to an alternative, ideal reference group.

5. Adherence to such an alternative reference group may empower one to resist the disvalues of the dominant system.

As far as Jägerstätter knew, his witness, however much he believed it to be in conformity with the Commandments of God as understood and practiced by the Church of the first centuries, was not just solitary but unique—and almost completely hidden. He had no contemporary models, much less imitators.[99] During his time in the Berlin prison, however, the Catholic chaplain, Dean Kreuzberg (or Kreutzberg, according to Putz) told him of a Pallotine priest, Fr. Franz Reinisch, who had died in the same prison for the same reasons the previous year. In a letter to his widow, the chaplain wrote, "I have seen no more fortunate man in prison than your

---

98. Zahn, *In Solitary Witness*, 193.

99. See Zahn, *In Solitary Witness*, Preface, for a brief reflection on Jägerstätter's influence on US Catholic peace activists during the Vietnam War.

husband after my few words about Franz Reinisch."[100] He was consoled as well as inspired by community, however insubstantial by worldly standards.

No one would have been more incredulous than Franz Jägerstätter himself had he been told before his death that one day he would be lifted up by a German pope, a former member of the Hitler Youth, as an example of faithful conscience and true obedience for all Catholics. He has joined the "community of saints" which was his standard of judgment, his referent group. Blessed Franz is the deviant to whom Catholics are now called to conform. "The stone the builders rejected has become the cornerstone" (Mark 12:10, quoting Ps 118:22). There is no full-bodied Catholic conscience without such a frame of reference to the innocent victim-resister of social injustice. This book is a testament to the enduring value of even a peasant's solitary and nearly invisible martyrdom of conscience, of refusal to participate in unjust war.

100. Forest, "Introduction," xxiv.

2

Conscientious Objection to Unjust War
From Augustine to John Paul II[1]

INTRODUCTION: THE CASE OF BLESSED FRANZ JÄGERSTÄTTER

AS FAR AS I am aware, Blessed Franz Jägerstätter is the only officially recognized martyr of the just-war tradition, beatified in 2007 by Pope Benedict XVI. That is, the Austrian peasant was not a pacifist in the manner of St. Martin of Tours in the fourth century, who famously proclaimed, while a Roman soldier but after a religious conversion, "I am a soldier of Christ and it is not lawful for me to fight."[2] Even Jägerstätter's pacifist biographer Gordon Zahn acknowledged that he was not a pacifist, not someone who understood his Christian faith to preclude participation in all war. Rather, Jägerstätter's refusal to accept induction into the German army in 1943 was selective conscientious objection—conscientious objection to a particular war, Hitler's war, which he understood to be unjust, and in which he therefore could not participate.

This chapter will examine the Catholic tradition from Augustine (fifth century CE) through Aquinas (thirteenth century), Vitoria, Suarez

---

1. This chapter first appeared under the same title in *Journal of Religion and Society* Supplement 14 (2017) 28–43.

2. Ellsberg, "St. Martin of Tours," 288.

(both sixteenth century), and Grotius (seventeenth century),[3] to Pope John XXIII's *Pacem in Terris* (1963), Vatican II's *Gaudium et Spes* (1965), the US bishops in multiple documents (1966–2002), and the *Compendium of the Social Doctrine of the Church* (2004), for evidence of justification for Jägerstätter's witness. However solitary his witness was and is, should it be understood to be within the normative tradition of the Church? It has been argued that support for what we now call selective conscientious objection has been a minority position—over against the majority position that argues that soldiers have no responsibility to make judgments about the justice of the war in which they are called to fight.[4] The soldier's only responsibility, according to this position, is to fight justly, obeying legal orders but disobeying illegal ones, such as targeting innocent civilians. *But is it possible to fight an unjust war justly?* That is the question before us, a question that has been posed by Catholic thinkers since at least Augustine in the early fifth century.

A pope prior to Vatican II would not have beatified someone like Jägerstätter. Yet, despite the fact that Pope Pius XII in 1956 stated that "a Catholic citizen cannot invoke his own conscience in order to refuse to serve and fulfill those [military] duties the law imposes,"[5] since 1968 the US bishops have been repeatedly on record in support of selective conscientious objection. Obviously, Pope John XXIII and the Second Vatican Council intervened between 1956 and 1968. Did *Gaudium et Spes* make the beatification of Franz Jägerstätter possible, even logically necessary? Is he a hero to be admired, or a model to be emulated? Might he become the first of many Catholic conscientious objectors to unjust war?

But perhaps I shouldn't assume that we are all considering a case like that of Jägerstätter in the same light, from the same perspective. As a way of laying out the basic parameters of the issue, let me suggest possible

---

3. The Dutch jurist and theologian Hugo Grotius (1583–1645) was not himself a Catholic but stood within the Catholic tradition of reflection on the morality of war.

4. Walters, "Historical Perspective."

5. Pope Pius XII, "Communism and Democracy," 225. The preceding sentence qualifies this prohibition thus: "If therefore, a body representative of the people and a government—both having been chosen by free elections—in a moment of extreme danger decides, by legitimate instruments of internal and external policy, *on defensive precautions*, and carries out the plans which they consider necessary, it does not act immorally" (emphasis added). The phrase I have italicized would seem to suggest that in fact Jägerstätter's refusal was morally justified—unless one judges Hitler's war to be defensive and therefore morally licit.

responses to this particular historical example of selective conscientious objection (SCO):

1. Jägerstätter was wrong because Hitler's wars were right and just; he was mistaken.

2. He was wrong even though Hitler's wars were unjust, because a citizen must serve his country right or wrong; he was unpatriotic.

3. He was wrong because it is wrong to disobey lawful authority (Rom 13); he was disobedient.

4. He was wrong because he had no authority or expertise to make such a decision; he was incompetent.

5. He was wrong because he betrayed his fellow citizens, especially those who accepted induction and risked their lives as soldiers on his behalf; he was a shirker.

6. He was wrong because he could have accepted induction and *then* avoiding killing; he was imprudent.

7. He was wrong because he could have accepted induction as an unarmed medic; he was a purist.

8. He was wrong because he left his wife without a husband, his three young daughters without a father, his widowed mother without a son, and all of them without a provider; he was selfish.

9. He was wrong even if he was right because his solitary witness would make no difference; he was a loser; he wasted his life.

On the other hand, one might take the position that:

1. Jägerstätter was right because he acted upon a sincere and well-formed conscience; he was true to himself.

2. He was right because Hitler's wars were wrong, and his church, his country, and his village were wrong in supporting Hitler's wars; he was courageous.

3. He was right because it is better to suffer injustice than to inflict it; he was noble.

4. He was right because it is wrong to swear unconditional obedience to any political authority, especially a tyrant (see #7); he was astute.

5. He was right because it is better to obey God than men (Acts 5:29); his soul was at stake.

This chapter takes the perspective that #1–5 in the second list supply the best response to the example of Franz Jägerstätter, and I take it that something like that perspective explains the church's recent beatification of him as a martyr of the Catholic faith. To be proclaimed a martyr means that Jägerstätter is one verified miracle away from sainthood, since martyrdom itself is considered the first of the two miracles required for canonization.

A BRIEF HISTORY OF CATHOLIC THINKING ABOUT SELECTIVE CONSCIENTIOUS OBJECTION

Augustine

But is this endorsement of SCO in the example of Franz Jägerstätter something entirely new in the Catholic tradition? What follows is an overview of that tradition, especially as regards the "minority report." Let us begin with St. Augustine, who is often referred to as the father or founder of Christian just-war ethics. Although Augustine wrote no systematic treatise on the ethics of war, and his occasional writings on the subject run to only twenty pages or so in most anthologies on the topic,[6] his influence has been enormous. For St. Thomas Aquinas, Augustine is far and away the most cited and authoritative source on this question. What does the bishop of Hippo say about a soldier's obedience in war? In *Contra Faustum* (22.75), Augustine writes,

> A just man, even if he fights under a sacreligious king, can lawfully fight when the king commands it—as serving the order of peace— if it is certain that what he is commanded to do is not opposed to the precept of God or if it is not certain whether or not it is opposed to divine precept. *Thus the iniquity of the one commanding makes the king guilty, but the order of serving makes the soldier innocent.*[7]

6. Holmes, *War and Christian Ethics*, 61–83; Reichberg, Syse, and Begby, *Ethics of War*, 70–90.

7. Quoted in Walters, "Historical Perspective," 204; emphasis added. For an alternative translation, see Swift, *Early Fathers*, 139. It is often pointed out that this Augustinian position can be found outside of properly ecclesial contexts, as in Shakespeare's *Henry V* (Act 4, Scene 1), when an English soldier proclaims, before the battle of Agincourt, "For we know enough, if we know we are the king's subjects: if his cause be wrong, our

There are at least six observations to make about this seminal statement. The *first* is the acknowledgment that a king may be "sacreligious" or "ungodly"[8] but still require obedience unless, *second*, the soldier judges with *certainty* that the command directed at him by his king is morally illicit. Notice that the judgment is put in the negative: if the command is certainly *not* opposed to the law of God, the soldier may obey. But, *third*, if there is doubt about the licitness of the command, the benefit of that doubt goes even to an ungodly king, and perhaps by this we can infer that Augustine has in mind a king engaged in an unjust war. *Fourth*, I take it that the phrase "as serving the order of peace" may refer to the internal peace of the kingdom, which is preserved by obedience to lawful authority, and not to the external peace, the preferred international order, that the king is presumed to pursue through war.[9]

But what is not addressed in this text is just as significant as what is said. Our *fifth* observation is that Augustine does not address explicitly the situation of the soldier who judges certainly that his king's order *is* opposed to the precept of God. However, as Louis J. Swift observes,[10] the right or even obligation to disobey an unlawful command would seem to be inferred, since otherwise there really is no moral judgment to be made by the individual soldier. If there are no times when he may or must disobey, there is no time when a judgment about obedience can be at issue, and for Augustine it clearly is. *Sixth*, Augustine seems to assume that the only judgment appropriate to the soldier is whether to obey an order on the battlefield, not whether he should go to *this* war in the first place, as if that initial command of the king could not be questioned. In other words, Augustine limits the soldier's moral responsibility to what many centuries later came to be called *jus in bello*, the law of the conduct of war, and this responsibility does not extend to *jus ad bellum*, the law governing the entry into war. This is the classic position on conscientious objection to war and essentially the counsel given by the Bishop of Linz to Franz Jägerstätter.[11]

---

obedience to the king wipes the crime of it out of us."

8. Swift, *Early Fathers*, 39.

9. Augustine observes that all wars, even wars of unjust aggression, seek peace, a peace more favorable to the war-making ruler than that which otherwise prevails. See *The City of God* 19.12–27, in Holmes, *War and Christian Ethics*, 71–74.

10. Swift, "Augustine on War," 371.

11. Zahn, *In Solitary Witness*, 58. Jim Forest ("Introduction," xx) observes that the Bishop's advice "was, in fact, an answer any Catholic might have heard from any bishop in any country at the time: if not found in any catechism, it was widely believed that any

But Swift also offers an alternative interpretation of Augustine on obedience to authority. When the emperor Julian (known as the Apostate) ordered his troops into battle, they obeyed, but when he ordered them to sacrifice to pagan deities, they refused. According to Swift, this is an example used by Augustine to illustrate his dictum that "any man who refuses to obey imperial laws that are enacted contrary to God's truth receives a great reward."[12] The disobedience praised by Augustine is not in reference to a command in warfare, but Swift suggests that the principle might by inference be applied to that context. But this speculative inference cannot be definitive. As Augustine plainly asserted, "The iniquity of the one commanding makes the king guilty, but the order of serving makes the soldier innocent"; the soldier's obedience to lawful authority is the norm. Had Jägerstätter fought in Hitler's wars, believing that it was not certain that these wars were unjust, as did nearly all his German and Austrian counterparts—and as did, apparently, all the German and Austrian bishops—his soul would not have been in jeopardy, as his bishop, as if channeling Augustine, informed him. In the Augustinian tradition, it is possible for a soldier to fight an unjust war justly and not be culpable. We can only speculate on what Augustine would have thought of selective conscientious refusal like that of Jägerstätter.

Aquinas

St. Thomas Aquinas, eight centuries later, drawing heavily on Augustine, provides the classic formulation of the Christian just-war tradition, although his writings on the topic are even more scant than his predecessor's: only six articles in the *Summa Theologiae* (about ten pages in modern anthologies such as Holmes and Reichberg) are addressed directly to the ethics of war, although other writings are related indirectly. As LeRoy Walters points out, although Aquinas did not address obedience in warfare, he did address an analogous issue, and his discussion was cited frequently

---

sins you commit under obedience to your government are not your personal sins but are regarded by God as the sins of those who lead the state. God would judge the leader, not those who obeyed his orders. But for Franz, it seemed obvious that, if God gives each of us free will and a conscience, each of us is responsible for what we do and fail to do, all the more so if we are consciously aware we have allowed ourselves to become servants of evil masters."

12. Swift, "Augustine on War," 372.

by subsequent just-war theorists. What should an executioner do if he is ordered to kill an innocent man? According to the *Summa*,

> He that carries out the sentence of the judge who has condemned an innocent man, if the sentence contains an inexcusable error, he should not obey, else there would be an excuse for the executions of martyrs; if however it contains no manifest injustice, he does not sin by carrying out the sentence, because he has no right to discuss the judgment of his superior; *nor is it he who slays the innocent man, but the judge whose minister he is.*[13]

This is nearly identical to the position of Augustine. Only if the command is certainly unjust is it to be disobeyed. Otherwise, the executioner himself has no moral responsibility to make a judgment; he is guiltless if in fact he kills an innocent man. Aquinas's influential argument for the primacy of conscience, trumping even the order of a religious superior[14] does not seem to add anything to his account of the executioner's dilemma. If one is confident in conscience that a command contains a manifest injustice, one must disobey the command. One may infer that this primacy of conscience would extend to the command to participate in war, and to refuse to participate in an unjust war, but Aquinas does not make this position explicit. He does make the argument that rebellion against a tyrant, who is in sedition against the common good, may be justified.[15] As Martin Luther King, Jr. famously pointed out in "Letter from Birmingham Jail," citing Aquinas, "An unjust law is no law at all" and so must be resisted.[16] Again, perhaps we can infer that such resistance could be extended to the command to participate in unjust war, but Aquinas himself does not make this argument. Nonetheless, Vincent Genovesi argues that Aquinas's general arguments about primacy of conscience are sufficient to establish "the individual's right and duty to refuse involvement in [an unjust] war."[17]

---

13. Quoted in Walters, "Historical Perspective," 204; emphasis added.

14. Aquinas, *Truth*, Question XVII, Article V, 335–37.

15. Holmes, *War and Christian Ethics*, 116–17.

16. King, "Letter From Burmingham Jail," 293.

17. Genovesi, "Just-War Doctrine," 511.

Vitoria, Suárez, Grotius

The majority or mainstream tradition we have traced first to Augustine and then to Aquinas finds fullest expression in the more systematic treatments of the ethics of war in two sixteenth-century Spanish theologians, Francisco de Vitoria and Francisco Suárez, often referred to as neo-scholastics, so firmly are they in the tradition of Aquinas. In the summary statement of LeRoy Walters, both "argued that the subject had no moral obligation to investigate the cause of a war; rather, he could participate in good conscience provided that the war was not clearly unjust."[18] Similarly, "both theorists agreed that as long as the justice of the war was in doubt, the subject was morally obligated to participate."[19] However, "the case is different when the war is manifestly unjust. . . . In such a case, they may refuse to serve, for to serve would endanger their souls more than refusing to obey their rightful sovereign."[20] The implications of this position are significant because the Spaniards are explicitly addressing the *jus ad bellum* question, not only questions of *jus in bello*. According to James Turner Johnson, Vitoria and Suárez "offer a *clear justification for individual conscientious objection to particular wars.* . . . It is emphatically the subject's responsibility to dispel any doubt that may confront him regarding the war in which he is commanded to take part, and if doing so results in certainty on his part that the war is unjust, he must in conscience refuse to abide by his prince's call."[21] A war judged to be unjust may not be fought justly by the soldier making that judgment. Neither Vitoria nor Suárez spell out how such refusal should be carried out by the subject or treated by the prince.

Within the Christian just-war tradition, "the most systematic spokesman for [the] minority strain"[22] regarding selective conscientious objection, over against the majority position of Augustine and Aquinas and its further development in Vitoria and Suárez, was the seventeenth-century Dutch jurist and Protestant theologian Hugo Grotius, who is often referred to as the father or founder of international law. He challenged the majority tradition in three ways. *First*, referring to the analogy of the soldier to the executioner first offered by Aquinas, Grotius argued "it is probable

18. Walters, "Historical Perspective," 204.
19. Walters, "Historical Perspective," 205.
20. Johnson, *Ideology*, 182.
21. Johnson, *Ideology*, 183; emphasis added.
22. Walters, "Historical Perspective," 205.

that even the executioner, who is going to put a condemned man to death, should know the merits of the case, either through assisting at the inquiry and the trial or from a confession of the crime, in such a degree that it is sufficiently clear to him that the criminal deserves death."[23] The presumption is no longer preponderantly in favor of the authority of the judge but in favor of the responsibility of the executioner to exercise his conscience. *Second*, Grotius differed not only with Augustine and Aquinas but also with Vitoria and Suárez in insisting that the just causes of war must be "clear and open," that such causes may not remain secret to the prince lest "skeptical solders lack enthusiasm for the war-effort."[24] *Third*, in what Walters calls "his boldest departure from tradition, Grotius launched a frontal assault on the majority view concerning doubtful causes."[25] Whereas Vitoria and Suárez argue that the benefit of the doubt should be given to the prince, Grotius wrote that "*disobedience* in things of this kind, by its very nature, is a lesser evil than *manslaughter*, especially than the slaughter of many innocent men."[26] As Walters observes, this does indeed stand the tradition on its head: the greater threat to a subject's soul, or as we would be more likely to say today, to a citizen-soldier's moral integrity or professional honor, is not disobedience to rightful authority but the killing of innocent men—or murder, to speak plainly—in unjust war. Jägerstätter (with his eighth-grade education in a one-room village schoolhouse) must have read Grotius!

Walters sums up the post-Aquinas classic just-war tradition on selective conscientious objection as threefold. *First*, "there was general agreement . . . that no citizen was obliged to participate in a war that was clearly unjust." *Second*, "Vitoria and Grotius . . . asserted unequivocally that the subject had a moral duty *not* to take part in a clearly unjust war," and *third*, that such an obligatory judgment was a matter of conscience, "a citizen's sincere conviction that a particular war was unjust."[27] Perhaps the most significant development was Grotius's reversal of what constituted the greater threat to a soldier's soul: not disobedience to lawful authority but the killing of innocent people in obedience to authority. Walters adds a final note: "the question of legal provision for SCO was largely ignored by the classic just-war tradition [of Vitoria and Suárez]. Grotius, however, recommended

---

23. Quoted in Walters, "Historical Perspective," 205.
24. Walters, "Historical Perspective," 206.
25. Walters, "Historical Perspective," 206.
26. Quoted in Walters, "Historical Perspective," 206; italics in original.
27. Walters, "Historical Perspective," 209.

the establishment of administrative machinery to accommodate the moral convictions of the selective objector."[28] This is essentially the position the United States Catholic Bishops have consistently and repeatedly articulated beginning in 1968, and as now appears in the *Compendium of the Social Doctrine of the Catholic Church*, as I will presently demonstrate. But this leads us to ask: how did the minority tradition become the official teaching of the Catholic Church? Let us remember that as late as 1956, Pope Pius XII stated that "a Catholic citizen cannot invoke his own conscience in order to refuse to serve and fulfill those [military] duties the law imposes."

This, of course, takes us to Pope John XXIII's *Pacem in Terris* and the Second Vatican Council's *Gaudium et Spes*. What do these famous documents say about conscience and war?

Pacem in Terris, Gaudium et Spes, the U.S. Bishops

In *Pacem in Terris* John XXIII did not address the question of war and conscience directly, but he did write forcefully of the general principles that would seem to govern the more particular question we are considering. According to the Pope, "since the right to command is required by the moral order and has its source in God, it follows that, if civil authorities pass laws or command anything opposed to the moral order and consequently contrary to the will of God, neither the laws made nor the authorizations granted can be binding on the consciences of citizens, since [quoting the Acts of the Apostles] 'God has more right to be obeyed than men.'"[29] In this encyclical of 1963, the same year as Dr. King's famous letter, John XXIII also cites Aquinas on the non-binding character of unjust laws which, in fact, are a "kind of violence."[30]

This prepares the way for the Second Vatican Council's well-known description of moral conscience in *Gaudium et Spes,* The Pastoral Constitution of the Church in the Modern World, as "the most secret core and sanctuary of a man [*sic*]. There he is alone with God, whose voice echoes in his depths." So sacred is a sincere conscience that even when it "errs from invincible ignorance" it does not lose its dignity.[31] Given this inviolable dignity of personal conscience, the Council fathers "cannot fail to praise those

28. Walters, "Historical Perspective," 210.

29. Pope John XXIII, *Pacem in Terris*, #51, 146.

30. O'Brien and Shannon, *Catholic Social Thought*, 146

31. Vatican Council II, *Gaudium et Spes* #16, 183.

who renounce the use of violence in the vindication of their rights and who resort to methods of defense which are otherwise available to weaker parties too, provided that this can be done without injury to the rights and duties of others or of the community itself."[32] This endorsement of the individual's right to embrace nonviolence and pacifism leads to a call for "laws that make humane provisions for the case of those who for reasons of conscience refuse to bear arms, provided, however, that they accept some other form of service to the human community."[33] A clearer repudiation of the position of Pope Pius XII less than a decade earlier could hardly be imagined.

While this discussion in *Gaudium et Spes* seems directed specifically at pacifists, the US Catholic Bishops[34] extend the argument for conscientious objection to those who refuse to participate not in all wars but in a particular war, and they do so, at least implicitly, for the first time in 1966, by referencing the Pastoral Constitution, promulgated one year earlier. As if responding to Augustine's influential dictum, in "Statement of the American Bishops on Peace November, 1966"[35] the US prelates write, "No one is free to evade his personal responsibility by leaving it entirely to others to make moral judgments. In this connection, the Vatican Council warns that men [*sic*] should heed not to entrust themselves only to the efforts of others, while remaining careless about their own attitudes. For government officials, who must simultaneously guarantee the good of their own people and promote the universal good, depend on public opinion and feeling to the greatest extent possible."[36] In matters of war and peace, citizens in a democracy have responsibilities not just of obedience but of independent moral judgment.[37]

In their 1968 statement, "Human Life in Our Day" (#144), issued at the height of the controversy over the Vietnam War, the bishops make their support for selective conscientious objection explicit. They observe that "for

32. Vatican Council II, *Gaudium et Spes* #78, 231.

33. Vatican Council II, *Gaudium et Spes* #79, 232.

34. All the US bishops' documents cited in this section can be accessed at www.usccb.org, and all but the first and last two cited can also be found in Benestad and Butler, *Quest for Justice.*

35. Drinan, *Vietnam*, 190–94.

36. Drinan, *Vietnam*, 191.

37. For a fine summary of the democratization of moral deliberation on war in post-Vatican II Catholic teaching up to the time of the first war in Iraq, see Duffey, "Just War Teaching."

many of our youthful protesters, the motives spring honestly from a principled opposition to a given war as pointless or immoral."[38] Furthermore, it cannot "be said that such conscientious objection to war . . . is . . . without reference to the message of the Gospel and the teaching of the Church: quite the contrary, frequently conscientious dissent reflects the influence of principles which inform modern papal teaching, the Pastoral Constitution, and a classical tradition of moral doctrine in the Church, including, in fact, the norms for the moral evaluation of a theoretically just war" (#145).[39] The US bishops then "seek to interpret and apply to our own situation the advice of the Vatican Council on the treatment of conscientious objectors" (#150),[40] which we have cited above. They observe that "the present laws of our country, however, provide only for those whose reasons of conscience are grounded in total objection to the use of military force. This form of conscientious objection [pacifism] deserves the legal provisions made for it, but we consider that the time has come to urge that similar consideration be given those whose reasons of conscience are more personal and specific" (#151).[41] The bishops "therefore recommend a modification of the Selective Service Act [conscription, the draft] making it possible, although not easy, for so-called selective conscientious objectors to refuse—without fear of imprisonment or loss of citizenship—to serve in wars which they consider unjust or in branches of service (e.g., the strategic nuclear forces) which would subject them to the performance of actions contrary to deeply held moral convictions about indiscriminate killing" (#152).[42]

The US bishops repeat this support for SCO in their 1969 "Statement on the Catholic Conscientious Objector": "In applying an evolving just war theory to the contemporary world, the person who is sincerely trying to form his [sic] conscience must judge whether or not the end achieved by a particular war or all-out war is proportionate, in any degree, to the devastation wrought by that war. On the basis of this judgment, he would justify either participation in or abstention from war."[43] In their 1971 "Declaration on Conscientious Objection and Selective Conscientious Objection," which Rev. Bryan Hehir called their "most expansive and explicit statement" on

---

38. In Benestad and Butler, *Quest for Justice*, 66.

39. In Benestad and Butler, *Quest for Justice*, 66–67.

40. In Benestad and Butler, *Quest for Justice*, 67.

41. In Benestad and Butler, *Quest for Justice*, 67.

42. In Benestad and Butler, *Quest for Justice*, 67.

43. USCC, "Statement on the Catholic Conscientious Objector," 1.

SCO,[44] the bishops affirm that "in the light of the Gospel and from an analysis of the Church's teaching on conscience, it is clear that a Catholic can be a conscientious objector to war in general or to a particular war 'because of religious training and belief'" [quoting a crucial phrase from a Supreme Court ruling in *U.S. v. Seeger* (1965) on qualifying for conscientious objector status].[45] In their 1980 "Statement on Registration and Conscription for Military Service," the bishops "affirm the Catholic teaching that the state's decision to use force should always be morally scrutinized by citizens asked to support the decision to participate in war," and once again they "support the right of selective conscientious objection (SCO) as a moral conclusion which can be validly derived from the classical teaching of Just-War Theory."[46] Hehir points out that this is the most explicit evocation by the bishops of the classical just-war tradition of Vitoria and Suárez and the first time that they use the language of *jus ad bellum* and *jus in bello* in their argument for SCO.[47] The bishops go on to observe that "the experience of the Vietnam War highlighted the moral and political significance of precisely this question. We are sure of the moral validity of SCO; we would welcome dialogue with legislators, lawyers, ethicists and other religious leaders about how to transpose this moral position into effective legal language."[48]

In this 1980 document the bishops also recognize that the formation of conscience in regard to war should not be left solely to the promptings of the Holy Spirit: "the issues of registration and conscription raise questions of the kind and quality of moral education that takes place in our educational system"; to that end, they "call upon schools and religious educators to include systematic formation of conscience on questions of war

44. Hehir, "U.S. Catholic Bishops," 73.

45. USCC, "Declaration on Conscientious Objection," 2.

46. USCC, "Statement on Registration and Conscription," 1, 2.

47. Hehir, "U.S. Catholic Bishops," 75.

48. USCC, "Statement on Registration and Conscription," 2. In one of his last writings before his death in 1967, Jesuit theologian John Courtney Murray, who had been a principal expert shaping the Second Vatican Council's document *Dignitatis Humanae: Declaration on Religious Freedom* (1965), and who had served on the President's Advisory Commission on Selective Service (1967), observed that "*Strictly on grounds of moral argument, the right conscientiously to object to participation in a particular war is incontestable.* I shall not argue the issue. The practical question before all of us is how to get the moral validity of this right understood and how to get the right itself legally recognized, declared in statutory law" ("War and Conscience," 25; emphasis added). It would seem that the bishops in their 1980 statement are in complete agreement with Fr. Murray, perhaps directly influenced by his writing.

and peace in their curricula and . . . pledge the assistance of appropriate diocesan agencies in counseling any of those who face questions of military service."[49] I would simply add that the draft may have been ended in 1973 in favor of an all-volunteer military, but the urgency of addressing questions of conscience regarding war and peace, and therefore of moral education, has not. As Hehir has noted, "To argue for SCO in the civil law is to call for a heightened capability for moral assessment in the body politic."[50] But as Fr. John Courtney Murray, SJ, remarked in his classic book, *We Hold These Truths: Catholic Reflections on the American Proposition*, "My impression is that this duty in social morality is being badly neglected in America at the moment."[51] Would Fr. Murray think our situation has improved more than fifty years later? Finally, the US bishops reiterated their support for SCO in their 1983 pastoral letter "The Challenge of Peace" and in its tenth anniversary document "The Harvest of Justice Is Sown in Peace." In this latter document, the bishops observe, "Given the particular problems that arise in the context of an all-volunteer military, individual objectors must exercise their rights in a responsible way, and there must be reliable procedures to verify the validity of their claims."[52] This is not elaborated.

More recently, in their November 13, 2002, "Statement on Iraq"—in which they state that they "find it difficult to justify the resort to war against Iraq, lacking clear and adequate evidence of an imminent attack of a grave nature"—the bishops acknowledge that "ultimately, our elected leaders are responsible for decisions about national security, but [the bishops] hope that [their] moral concerns and questions will be considered seriously by our leaders and all citizens."[53] While they "support those who risk their lives in the service of our nation," they "also support those who seek to exercise their right to conscientious objection and selective conscientious objection," as they have stated repeatedly in the past.[54]

49. USCC, "Statement on Registration and Conscription," 2.
50. Hehir, "U.S. Catholic Bishops," 77.
51. Murray, *We Hold These Truths*, 257.
52. NCCB, *Harvest of Justice*, 2.
53. USCCB, "Statement on Iraq," 1.
54. USCCB, "Statement on Iraq," 1.

Compendium of the Social Doctrine of the Church

But this is just one Catholic episcopal conference, albeit the one most readers of this book must attend to, in arguably the military superpower whose citizens by default are most in need of an indispensable moral formation regarding just and unjust wars. What, if anything, does the Vatican say? In 2004, the Pontifical Council for Justice and Peace[55] published the *Compendium of the Social Doctrine of the Church*. After acknowledging that "the requirements of legitimate defense justify the existence of armed forces" (#502), the *Compendium* states that "every member of the armed forces is morally obliged to resist orders that call for perpetrating crimes against the law of nations and the universal principles of this law" (#503).[56] In almost complete repudiation of Augustine's position, it goes on to state that "military personnel remain fully responsible for the acts they commit in violation of the rights of individuals and peoples, or of the norms of international humanitarian law. Such acts cannot be justified by claiming obedience to the orders of superiors" (#503), as if citing the famous Nuremburg Principle. Furthermore, "*Conscientious objectors who, out of principle, refuse military service in those cases where it is obligatory because their conscience rejects any kind of recourse to the use of force or **because they are opposed to the participation in a particular conflict**, must be open to accepting alternative forms of service*" (#503).[57] The *Compendium* then quotes *Gaudium et Spes* #79 as the source of this support of SCO: "It seems just that laws should make humane provision for the case of conscientious objectors who refuse to carry arms, provided they accept some other form of community service" (#503). Support for legal protection for COs, presumably the referent in the Vatican document, has now been extended to SCOs, in Catholic doctrine, if not in US public policy or opinion.[58]

---

55. Since renamed the Dicastery for Promoting Integral Human Development.

56. Pontifical Council, *Compendium*, 218–19.

57. Pontifical Council, *Compendium*, 219; italics in original; emphasis added.

58. For a discussion of a Catholic who cited *Gaudium et Spes* as the source of his claim to SCO in regard to the Vietnam war, see Capizzi, "Selective Conscientious Objection," 355. In *Negre v. Larson* (1970), the Supreme Court ruled 8–1 (Justice William O. Douglas dissenting) "that the government has legitimate reasons to violate an individual's religious concerns in times of war" (Capizzi, "Selective Conscientious Objection," 353). For an extended discussion of the fate of the Catholic argument for SCO at the Supreme Court, see Reid, "John T. Noonan."

SUMMARY

Given the long trajectory—sixteen centuries!—of this development in Catholic teaching on selective conscientious objection, it may be helpful to retrace briefly the major steps along the way from Augustine to the *Compendium.*

- Augustine asserted that "the iniquity of the one commanding makes the king guilty, but the order of serving makes the soldier innocent." Only if the soldier is certain that an order is unjust may he refuse it, and then only in battle, not as to the cause itself.

- Aquinas iterated the Augustinian position on obedience to lawful authority in his discussion not of warfare but of criminal justice. If an executioner knows that the condemned is innocent, he should refuse to perform his task. However, if there is no such certainty, the executioner should carry out his duty, but if the condemned is in fact innocent, it is not the executioner "who slays the innocent man, but the judge whose minister he is." Shakespeare's soldier in *Henry V, Part I* (4.1) sums up the Augustinian-Thomistic position nicely and suggests its reach into popular culture: "If his cause be wrong our obedience to the king wipes the crime of it out of us."

- Vitoria and Suárez break from this tradition by extending the soldier's moral responsibility from *jus in bello* to *jus ad bellum*, so that the two Spanish neo-scholastics may be said to have articulated a position that we would now call selective conscientious objection, or the right and duty to refuse to participate in manifestly unjust wars and not only to unjust orders within war. Grotius advanced the tradition beyond Vitoria and Suárez by shifting the benefit of the doubt regarding the justice of particular wars from the ruler to the soldier, arguing that causing the deaths of innocents was a greater threat to justice and personal salvation than disobeying the order of a lawful authority. He also proposed that administrative procedures be in place to address such situations.

- Pope Pius XII, in response to the notion that Catholics could be pacifists, invoked the classic position, asserting that "a Catholic citizen cannot invoke his own conscience in order to refuse to serve and fulfill those [military] duties the law imposes."

- Pope John XXIII, in *Pacem in Terris*, argued for the duty to refuse to obey unjust laws, but did not apply this argument to participation in warfare, despite his assertion that "it is contrary to reason to hold that war is now a suitable way to restore rights which have been violated" (*PT* #125).[59]

- Vatican Council II, in *Gaudium et Spes*, the Pastoral Constitution on the Church in the Modern World, extended John XXIII's teaching on conscience to warfare, and urged the establishment of laws recognizing the right to refuse participation in all wars, for pacifist conscientious objection, thus reversing Pius XII's teaching.

- The United States Catholic Bishops argued explicitly in statements published during and after the Vietnam War that legal protection should also be extended to those who conscientiously refuse to participate in a particular war they judged to be unjust.

- The *Compendium of the Social Doctrine of the Church*, published in 2004 during the reign of Pope John Paul II, in effect brought the US Bishops' endorsement of selective conscientious objection into the teaching of the global church. What was once a minority position, when it was an articulated position at all, has become the magisterial position of the Church. Whether it has been taught to and received by Catholics, within the US, much less around the world, is an entirely different question.

CONCLUSION

Of course, this does not mean the older majority position has disappeared entirely from episcopal teaching. Veteran Vatican journalist John Allen reports that even though Cardinal Renato Martino, then president of the Pontifical Council for Justice and Peace, observed that the opposition of the Vatican to the invasion of Iraq in 2003 was clear, he "stopped short of counseling Catholic men and women in the US armed forces to refuse to cooperate in the event of war. '*The responsibility is not theirs, it is of those who send them,*' he said."[60] Similarly, Allen writes, "The only possible

---

59. This is the passage cited in Vatican Council II, *Gaudium et Spes* (#80) when famously invoking the need "to undertake an evaluation of war with an entirely new attitude."

60. Allen, *All the Pope's Men*, 335; emphasis added.

reading of the record is that John Paul II was strongly opposed to the Iraq war." However, he continues, "This does not mean that in opposing the war the Pope intended to bind the consciences of Catholics."[61]

Perhaps Cardinal Francis Stafford's statement best summarizes the Church's current *practice* regarding selective conscientious objection: "Asked about whether Catholics in the Armed Forces should comply with orders to fight in the Iraq war, Stafford said: 'I can't make the decision for them. As mature, baptized Christians, each layperson has to decide if their being in Jesus Christ, whose peace extends to all persons, allows them to proceed to the destruction of some persons. Each person has to weigh what is being said by the country's leaders . . . and come to their own conclusion.' Stafford added that the Church has always supported a right to conscientious objection,[62] and he hoped that such a right would be available this time as well if it came to armed conflict."[63] To put it simply, a Christian's ultimate obedience should be neither to political nor military nor to ecclesial authority but rather to his or her own conscience, to what Blessed John Henry Newman called "the aboriginal Vicar of Christ" (as quoted in the *Catechism* #1778). Only that authority is ultimately binding.

What was once the minority theological tradition—soldiers have a moral responsibility to evaluate the justice of the wars they are asked to fight and to act accordingly—has gained official ecclesial acceptance. I like to think that the solitary witness of Blessed Franz Jägerstätter had something to do with this dramatic change in Catholic moral doctrine, so obviously relevant to the formation of Catholic consciences everywhere regarding participation in unjust wars.

But what *is* conscience in the Catholic theological tradition? The next chapter will answer that question from the perspective of Saint Thomas Aquinas, which has been foundational to the tradition from his time to the present, as is evident in the *Catechism of the Catholic Church*.

---

61. Allen, *All the Pope's Men*, 318.

62. As this chapter has made clear, this "always" needs qualification.

63. Allen, *All the Pope's Men*, 336.

3

Aquinas and Catholic Teaching on Conscience

The case for selective conscientious objection rests in large part on Aquinas's assertion . . . that a person should always obey his or her conscience, even if there is a possibility of being wrong. A soldier who cannot in good conscience fight in a given war would be acting immorally if he or she nevertheless chose to fight, whether it be due to fear of punishment or any other reason. Aquinas did, however, add an important proviso, which was that conscience needs to be informed.

—Ellner, Robinson, and Whetham[1]

INTRODUCTION

THIS CHAPTER IS CENTRAL to the overall argument of this book, that conscience is foundational to the Catholic understanding of the moral life, and that this holds doubly true for warriors in both the decision to go to war and how one conducts oneself in warfare, when irrevocable and ultimate matters of life and death, salvation and damnation,[2] are at hand. Chapter 1 narrated and theorized the example of selective conscientious objection in the case of Blessed Franz Jägerstätter, as presented by sociologist

1. Ellner, Robinson, and Whetham, Introduction to *When Soldiers Say No*, 4–5.
2. Pizan, "War and Chivalry," 218.

Gordon Zahn. Chapter 2 outlined how teaching on SCO has developed in the Catholic theological tradition, to the point that conscientious objection to unjust war is now the magisterial teaching of the Church, however unknown and unpracticed. Chapter 4 will explore the new concept (but ancient phenomenon) of combat-induced moral injury in relation to the personal conscience of the warrior, thus providing a decidedly dark portrait of conscience as dramatically vulnerable to traumatic betrayal by self or others in wartime. Chapter 5 argues that the Catholic just-war perspective and its teaching on selective conscientious objection will remain ineffective as a bulwark against unjust war unless the Church takes on the role of, at least for its own membership, a transnational court of *jus ad bello* deliberation, judgment, and guidance. Chapter 6 presents, first, a substantive analysis of reflective moral judgment derived from contemporary psychological research and theory, a secular counterpart of the Catholic concept of conscience, and second, how such reflective judgment might be taught in the postsecondary classroom—how personal conscience might be formed in a course on Christian Ethics of War and Peace.

That everything depends on how the Catholic Church understands conscience, and explicating that understanding, in particular its determinative origins in the ethics of Thomas Aquinas, is the burden of this chapter. I intend to provide the "deep background" to the teaching on conscience as presented in the *Catechism of the Catholic Church* and the *Compendium of the Social Doctrine of the Church*. Those two documents, especially the first,[3] are the pastoral bridges from the theology of Aquinas to the Church's instruction on the moral life, as in, for example, the quadrennial statement of the US bishops, *Forming Conscience for Faithful Citizenship*, which is intended to guide Catholics as they make prudential choices before entering the voting booth (and one hopes, in between elections as well).

I do not pretend to advance the scholarly understanding of the development of the tradition on conscience but to present one major expression

---

3. Whereas the *Catechism* devotes an entire article of three sections and nineteen paragraphs (#1776–94, plus eight "In Brief" summary statements) to "Moral Conscience," the *Compendium* devotes no one portion to conscience but rather disperses its teaching on conscience throughout; the Analytical Index lists forty-one places where conscience is related to other aspects of the Church's social doctrine, including "the right to conscientious objection" to unjust laws in general (#399), to conscientious objection to "participation in a particular conflict" (#503), and to the overarching right of the Church "to instruct and illuminate the consciences of the faithful, particularly those involved in political life, so that their actions may always serve the integral promotion of the human person and the common good" (#571).

of it as accurately and faithfully as possible. The entire point is that pastoral and personal appropriation of conscience in the context of war and peace depends on a basic understanding and practice of conscience available to the ordinary Catholic, including especially Catholics in the military and in public leadership. Franz Jägerstätter with his modest educational background—not even secondary schooling—is indeed the example *par excellence* of how conscience can become determinative in the lives of ordinary Catholics. As Franz demonstrates, one need not have taken a graduate seminar on Aquinas to take conscience seriously, even to the point of martyrdom.

Aquinas took up the question of conscience in three major works— the *Commentary on the Sentences of Peter Lombard, Disputed Questions on Truth*, and the *Summa Theologiae*—representing, respectively, early (1253–55), middle (1257–58), and late (1267–68) phases of his life (1225–74).[4] According to Luc-Thomas Somme, "From the *Commentario* to *De Veritate* to the *Summa*, St Thomas does not retract his own thought . . . but does, however, simplify its main argument."[5] Robert J. Smith observes, nonetheless, that "the latter two sources . . . reflect the maturity of his thought and evidence an internal consistency, and . . . are the most fully developed of his writings on conscience."[6] Because they are the most focused and straightforward texts for our purposes, I will refer chiefly to Question Sixteen, on Synderesis, and Question Seventeen, on Conscience, from *Truth*. The first question is what is synderesis and what does it have to do with conscience.

The term *synderesis* is described by scholarly specialists as probably an inadvertent corruption of *syneidesis*, the Latin transliteration for the Greek term for conscience, in the early biblical scholar St. Jerome's commentary on the book of Ezekiel. The details of what may have been a scribal typo but turned out to be a useful and important distinction for the medieval schoolmen, need not detain us.[7] Aquinas clearly addresses the two terms as distinct but related. In what follows, I summarize what the Angelic Doctor has to say about synderesis and conscience. That should give us an adequate overview of what the most influential Catholic theologian had to say about the central concept of this book. The final steps of this chapter will

4. Smith, *Conscience and Catholicism*, 4.

5. Somme, "Infallibility," 410.

6. Smith, *Conscience and Catholicism*, 4.

7. For the details, see Potts, *Conscience in Medieval Philosophy*, 9–11; Hogan, "*Synderesis, Suneidesis*"; Hoffman, "Conscience and Synderesis."

be to demonstrate how the Thomistic concept of conscience is embodied in the *Catechism,* and how that concept might be taught in a pastoral setting.

Aquinas organized his writing around questions or topics. Each question is followed by several "Difficulties" (or, in the *Summa,* "Objections"), drawn from the biblical, philosophical, and theological literatures, which all take one side of the question. Then, in a section introduced by "To the contrary," Aquinas addresses the question in summary fashion from his own perspective, before elaborating on that answer in his "Reply." Finally, he completes the circle with "Answers to Difficulties." For our purposes, his main statement of his position in the "Reply," in the middle of each article, is our principal focus. If a modern-day Thomas were to address the question, Is democracy the best form of government?, she would first rehearse several arguments in the negative. Then she would state her counter-thesis and explain fully her affirmative argument. Finally, she would rebut the opposing arguments with which she began. In other words, Aquinas argues dialectically, and it is crucial to know what part of his dialectical pattern one is reading; one should not quote a Difficulty as if that were Aquinas's considered judgment.[8]

SYNDERESIS

In *Truth* Q. 16, Aquinas asks, in the first article, "Is Synderesis a Power or a Habit?" Aquinas begins his main discussion with the biblical idea that human nature stands midway between the beasts and the angels. Insofar as human nature is like angelic nature, it "must both in speculative and practical matters know truth without investigation," as do the angels. "And this knowledge must be the principle of all knowledge which follows . . . since principles must be more stable and certain. Therefore, this knowledge must be in man naturally, since it is a kind of seed plot containing in germ all the knowledge which follows. . . . Furthermore, this knowledge must be habitual so that it will be ready for use." That leads to his main thesis: "there is in the soul a natural habit of first principles of action, which are the universal principles of the natural law. This habit pertains to synderesis." But Aquinas allows for some ambiguity in this definition: "the name *synderesis* designates a natural habit simply, one similar to the habit of principles, or it means some power of reason with such a habit." Either way, knowledge

8. Unless otherwise noted, all quotations of Aquinas in this chapter are from *Truth*, vol. 2.

of the first principles of the natural law belongs to reason, our highest capacity, because of a natural habit, called synderesis. There is no English translation, due to its peculiar origins.

If the reader stumbles over the idea of a *natural* habit, it is because we normally think of habit as acquired through repetition, through practice. Aquinas's point is that synderesis is not acquired by effort but a given of human nature. It can be described as a habit because it is "ready for use." Readiness for use is the point of habits. Acting out of habit means we don't have to think about how to perform the action. We might say in the digital age that we are hard-wired for moral knowledge. Ultimately the source of this capacity is our creation by God in God's own image. We cannot know the eternal law as God knows it, but we can know its reflection in the natural law, as built into Creation and as creatures ourselves. Another contemporary metaphor may be helpful (if we set aside any unwanted baggage it may carry): all humans are possessed with a moral compass, which always points true north—toward moral truth. Synderesis, "by reason of a natural habit, always inclines to good," and so may be compared to a moral compass. It points us in the right direction. Whether we move in that direction is another question entirely. As Aquinas notes, "it does not follow from this [understanding of synderesis] that a man with purely natural gifts can perform a meritorious act." Synderesis is the natural habit of moral orientation. Does that mean that the compass always points north and never south or east or west? Is synderesis infallible?

The second article asks, "Can Synderesis Err?" Aquinas states his thesis: "What is naturally present is always present. But it is natural for synderesis to warn against evil. Therefore, it never consents to evil, and so never sins." If indeed we do sin, we cannot blame it on synderesis! If I get lost, I cannot blame it on the compass. The argument is from necessity: "for probity to be possible in human actions, there must be some permanent principle which has unwavering integrity, in reference to which all human works are examined, so that permanent principle will resist all evil and assent to all good. This is synderesis . . . there can be no error in it." The upshot of this is that "the act of synderesis is not strictly an act of virtue, but a kind of prelude to the act of virtue." A compass orients, points to true north infallibly, but that doesn't mean we can't get lost through our misuse of the information it gives us. I may also need to know how to read a map. But a compass can be broken and no longer serve its purpose. What about synderesis?

The third article ponders, "Are There Some in Whom Synderesis Is Extinguished?" Aquinas takes us back to Jerome, "Who says of synderesis: 'Not even in Cain was it suppressed . . . [for] it is clear that he despaired, for he said: "My iniquity is greater than that I may deserve pardon.""" Aquinas observes that "remorse of conscience is caused by synderesis protesting against evil. Therefore, synderesis is not destroyed" even in an arch-sinner, a murderer such as Cain. However, "extinguished can be understood in two ways. In one, it is considered in so far as it is an habitual light, and in this sense it is impossible for synderesis to be extinguished." On the other hand, "the act of synderesis is said to be extinguished inasmuch as it is completely interfered with." This possibility will be crucial in the next chapter on moral injury. Here Aquinas observes that such interference "happens in those who do not have the use of free choice or of reason because of an impediment due to an injury to the bodily organs from which our reason needs help." Traumatic brain injury (TBI), often associated with combat, would seem to be such an interference that might extinguish synderesis, depending on its severity. Short of TBI, we can act *as if* synderesis were destroyed in us, by ignoring its guidance, when we choose to sin, but "absolutely speaking, we concede synderesis is never destroyed." Aquinas's final word on this matter is emphatic: "as long as the nature [the natural habit of synderesis] remains, the inclination to good cannot be taken even from the damned," not even from a fratricidal Cain. As Luc-Thomas Somme sums it up in his title, Aquinas argues for "The Infallibility, Impeccability and Indestructibility of Synderesis." So the problem of human sinfulness must lie elsewhere. That takes us from Aquinas's discussion of synderesis to his discussion of conscience.

CONSCIENCE

Truth Q. 17 considers "Is Conscience a Power, a Habit, or an Act?" Aquinas's considered opinion is that "conscience seems to be an act, for it is said to accuse and excuse. But one is not accused or excused unless he is actually considering something. Therefore, conscience is an act." He buttresses this line of argument with a brief lesson in etymology: "Knowledge which consists in comparison is actual knowledge. But conscience denotes knowledge with comparison. For one is said to be conscious (*conscire*), that is, to know together (*simul scire*). Therefore, conscience is actual knowledge, by which

I believe he means knowledge of acts. One might even say that conscience is a knowledgeable act.

However, Aquinas acknowledges that conscience can have several meanings: [1] "at times it is taken for the thing itself of which one is conscious, just as faith is taken for the thing believed." [2] "Sometimes it is taken for the power by which we are conscious, and [3] sometimes for the habit. And some say [4] "that it is also taken for the act." A similar pattern of multiple meanings can be found with regard to "*understanding* [which] sometimes . . . signifies the intellective power itself; sometimes a habit, and, sometimes, an act." Aquinas resolves this issue by simply observing that "with names such as these, the commonly accepted meaning should be followed." That is, common usage, presumably among his fellow theologians and philosophers, and his own best arguments converge: "the name *conscience* means the application of knowledge to something," and that application is an act.

Aquinas then returns again to Jerome, who "calls conscience *synderesis* in so far as conscience acts by reason of its power. This answer is especially apt because he wanted to show how synderesis can fail. For it does not err in regard to universal principles, but only in regard to the application to individual acts. Thus, synderesis does not err in itself, but, in a sense, errs in conscience." Aquinas's most succinct definition is that "Conscience . . . is a judgment of reason derived from the natural law." Or, "conscience is an act proceeding from the natural habit of synderesis." Synderesis, he reminds us, is "imprinted" in us by God, who thus "endows our nature with the knowledge of first principles." It seems then that while synderesis is infallible, conscience is not. How does Aquinas address this question more fully?

Article 2 asks "Can Conscience Be Mistaken?" In an almost arithmetic formulation, Aquinas reiterates his basic definition: "reason joined to synderesis constitutes conscience." While "error has no place in the general judgment of synderesis . . . a mistake can occur in the judgment of higher reason, as happens when one judges something to be licit or not illicit which is not, as heretics who believe that oaths are forbidden by God. . . . Similarly, error can occur in conscience because of error which exists in the lower part of reason, as happens when one is mistaken about civil norms of what is just or unjust, good or bad." But "error also occurs because conscience does not make a correct application to acts." One can incorrectly argue to a false conclusion. But when the distance from the universal principles known by synderesis to "the particular act to which conscience is applied" is negligible, "conscience can never make a mistake." In such cases, conscience simply assents to the infallible judgement of synderesis and its immediate application. Synderesis binds—and binds absolutely. But what about fallible conscience? To what extent, if any, does it also bind? Must one always obey conscience?

Article 3 of *Truth* Q. 17 takes up the question, "Does Conscience Bind?" In a word, "certainly." To bind means to impose necessity, but there are two kinds of necessity, one of which is coercion by an outside agent." But "coercion . . . has no place in movements of the will, but only in physical things, because by its nature the will is free from coercion." But another kind of necessity "can be imposed on the will, so that one must, for example, choose this means if he is to acquire this good, or avoid this evil." If I want to interpret Aquinas correctly and not misrepresent him, I must read him carefully, perhaps with the help of authorities. In what seems a bit of a leap, or at least an analogy, Aquinas observes that "the action by which the will is moved is the command of the one ruling or governing." But "no one is bound by the command of a king or lord unless the command reaches him who is commanded; and it reaches him through knowledge of it." Similarly, "no one is bound by a precept except through his knowledge of the precept." But if one knows the precept, as the argument seems to go, one is bound to act accordingly. "Consequently, since conscience is nothing else but the application of knowledge to an act, it is obvious that conscience is said to bind by the power of a divine precept." Since what conscience applies is infallible knowledge about good and evil as provided by synderesis, conscience must act on that knowledge as if commanded by God, the source of synderesis. But Aquinas has already acknowledged that such application can be mistaken. Does conscience *still* bind?

Article 4 pursues "Does a False Conscience Bind?" It would seem that "when conscience gives orders contrary to the commands of God, the command of a mistaken conscience seems to impose no obligation whatever." Thomas thus begins with a dramatic confrontation between conscience and God, and there would seem to be no question that God is the higher authority and must be obeyed. This is, I believe, what most Catholics would say, and they would add that the Church is the infallible interpreter of the infallible commands of God. Therefore, the Church must always be obeyed. In Thomas's more technical language: "a false conscience, especially about things which are intrinsically evil [always and everywhere wrong], has no probability at all. Therefore, such a conscience does not bind." There would seem to be no rebuttal to that argument (which Thomas states as a "Difficulty").

To the contrary! Aquinas takes an example from the early Christians' relationship with the prescriptions of Mosaic law, specifically male circumcision. Observance of the prescription "in the new dispensation of grace" was said to be "not indifferent but intrinsically evil." Thomas cites Gal 5:2: "'If you be circumcised, Christ shall profit you nothing.' Nevertheless, conscience prescribing the observance of circumcision was binding." The following verse from Galatians attests that "every man circumcising himself . . . is a debtor to do the whole law." Thomas concludes from this that "a false conscience binds [even] in things intrinsically evil." If a Gentile man *truly believed* that he must be circumscribed to faithfully follow Christ, even though this belief was taught by the community to be wrong, he must follow his conscience, and the community must support him in this decision, however erroneous.

Aquinas might well have cited another Pauline discussion of this dilemma, the famous passage in 1 Corinthians 8 regarding the eating of idol meat. In brief, since idols are not real, idol meat is just meat, and may be eaten by Christians. But if a Christian in good conscience cannot eat meat from animals that have been sacrificed to idols, he must abjure, and most importantly, more knowledgeable Christians must respect his weak conscience. To encourage a fellow Christian to act against his conscience is to bring him to destruction. In a summary statement that makes the point as emphatically as Aquinas himself does, Paul teaches that "when you sin in this way against your brothers and wound their consciences, weak as they are, you are sinning against Christ. Therefore, if food causes my brother to sin [by acting against his conscience], I will never eat meat again, so that I may not cause my brother to sin" (1 Cor 8:12–13 NAB). Note that the sin Aquinas says is decisive is committed by the knowledgeable conscience acting against the weak conscience, not the weak conscience acting on false belief.

Aquinas's own summary statement could hardly be clearer: "one who has a false conscience, whether in things intrinsically evil or in anything at all, believes that what is opposed to his conscience is contrary to the law of God. Therefore, if he decides to do that, he decides to act contrary to the law of God, and so, he sins. Consequently, conscience, no matter how false it is, obliges under pain of sin." That does not mean that the person's subjective judgment makes his action objectively right. And it does not mean that the false conscience cannot or should not be changed. Nor does it mean that a false conscience, when acted upon, excuses one from actions that are transgressions against civil law.

To take an extreme and hypothetical example from military ethics, if as a warrior sworn to defend my country I truly believe that I should kill a tyrant in another country who I believe threatens my homeland's security, should I act on this belief, in effect becoming a *selective conscientious assassin*, even though it is clearly a vigilante act and against the law? Remember that Aquinas has said that "conscience, no matter how false it is, obliges under pain of sin." If I am a fellow warrior who knows of this intention and cannot convince my brother otherwise, should I try to impede him from acting on his conscience? Would I become an accomplice to his crime if I did not try to stop him? How do I simultaneously honor my conscience (not to mention the chain of command) and his, when they are in profound disagreement? Unfortunately, as far as I am aware, Aquinas does not take up such examples. Circumcision, after all, is not the same kind of intrinsic evil as is murder.[9] He does address another thorny example, however.

The fifth and final article of Q. 17 in *Truth* asks, "Does Conscience in Indifferent Matters Bind More Than the Command of a Superior, or Less?" At first glance, conscience seems to bind less, "But conscience is an intrinsic spiritual bond, whereas the office of the superior is physical and extrinsic, as it seems, because all his authority is based on a dispensation which is limited to time. Hence, when we reach eternity, it will cease. . . . Therefore, it seems that one should obey his conscience rather than a superior." It is no surprise that Aquinas argues that "a correct conscience binds absolutely and perfectly against the command of a superior." But what about a false conscience? It "binds against the command of a superior even in indifferent matters with some qualification, because it does not bind in every event, but on condition that it endures. One can and should change such a conscience." But "as long as that conscience remains . . . he sins more if he does not do what his consciences dictates . . . since it binds more than the precept of the superior." But what about the vow of obedience? There are in the member of a religious community "two opposite obligations. One of these, conscience, is greater, because more intense, and less, because more easily removed; the other is just the opposite."[10] Finally, Aquinas appeals

---

9. On why the term is problematic, see Kaveny, "Intrinsic Evil."

10. I cannot help wondering if the remark about a change in conscience being more easily removed than a precept of a religious superior is a bit of a joke by Thomas, of the Order of Preachers.

to higher authority: "Although a superior is higher than a subject, God, in virtue of whose command conscience binds, is greater than the superior." One may never transgress against a command of God *as one understands it,* and not as anyone else does.

One of the "Ten Reasons Why Thomas Aquinas Is Important for Ethics Today," according to James F. Keenan, SJ, is that *"Thomas upholds the primacy of conscience. . . .* In his first major work, the *Commentary on the Sentences*[,] Thomas entertains Peter Lombard's (1095–1160) position on the possible conflict between what the Church teaches and what our conscience dictates. Lombard writes that in such a situation, we should follow the Church. Thomas writes 'here the Master is wrong' . . . and argues that it is better to die excommunicated [barred from the Sacraments] than to violate our conscience."[11] In one of the most famous *bon mots* in Catholic theology, (now) Saint John Henry Cardinal Newman concluded his "Letter Addressed to His Grace the Duke of Norfolk" by remarking that "certainly, if I am obliged to bring religion into after-dinner toasts (which indeed does not seem quite the thing), I shall drink—to the Pope, if you please,—still, to Conscience first, and to the Pope afterwards."[12] The Pope may be the Vicar of Christ, but "conscience is the aboriginal Vicar of Christ."[13] That last statement is cited in the *Catechism of the Catholic Church.*[14] It neatly sums up the essential teaching of Aquinas, which has become the teaching of the Church, as we will now demonstrate.[15]

CATECHISM OF THE CATHOLIC CHURCH

The article on Moral Conscience begins by quoting the famous description in *Gaudium et Spes: The Pastoral Constitution of the Church in the Modern World* (#16):

11. Keenan, "Ten Reasons," 357–58.

12. Newman, "Letter," 457.

13. Newman, "Letter," 449.

14. *Catechism,* Part III, Article 6, #1778.

15. Neither the *Catechism* itself nor the definition from *Gaudium et Spes* that opens the article on conscience quotes Aquinas directly nor even cites him as an indirect influence. I am not making the claim that no other theologian had similar perspectives on conscience or that Aquinas is the only source for magisterial teaching. Both Aquinas and the *Catechism,* of course, are grounded in scripture. Rather, I am contending is that the *Catechism* and Aquinas on conscience are convergent.

Deep within his conscience man discovers a law which he has not laid upon himself but which he must obey. Its voice, ever calling him to love and to do what is good and to avoid evil, sounds in his heart at the right moment. . . . For man has in his heart a law inscribed by God. . . . His conscience is man's most secret core and his sanctuary. There he is alone with God whose voice echoes in his depths.[16]

We have seen that Aquinas's most succinct definitions are that "Conscience . . . is a judgment of reason derived from the natural law," or that "conscience is an act proceeding from the natural habit of synderesis," which is "imprinted" in us by God, and that synderesis inclines us infallibly toward good and away from evil. As a consequence of its origin, conscience must always be obeyed.

The *Catechism* (#1778) goes on to say, "Conscience is a judgment of reason whereby the human person recognizes the moral quality of a concrete act that he is going to perform, is in the process of performing, or has already performed." We have just quoted Aquinas on conscience as a judgment of reason, and we have seen him describe conscience as the application of the universal moral knowledge provided by synderesis to a specific act. He does not use the metaphor of voice as does the *Catechism*, but he likens the dictates of conscience to the command of God. The *Catechism* (#1780) explicitly refers to synderesis in terms consonant with those of Aquinas: "Conscience includes the perception of the principles of morality (synderesis); their application in the given circumstances by practical discernment of reasons and goods; and finally judgment about concrete acts yet to be performed or already performed." Although Aquinas generally treats conscience as applied to acts yet to be performed rather than already performed, his citing of Jerome on Cain's despair after the murder of his brother indicates Aquinas was aware of this dimension of synderesis/conscience as well.

The *Catechism* (#1782) quotes *Dignitatis Humanae: Declaration on Religious Freedom* of Vatican II: the human person "must not be forced to act contrary to his conscience. Nor must he be prevented from acting according to his conscience, especially in religious matters." While the historical and cultural contexts are obviously different, Aquinas did address the question of obedience to a religious superior. This is a religious matter internal to the Church, not external to the Church in its relationship with

16. Vatican Council II, *Gaudium et Spes*, 438.

secular society, but Aquinas's affirmation of the higher authority of conscience suggests how he would deal with issues of personal conscience and external authority other than a religious superior.[17]

Aquinas spoke little of the formation of conscience, the subject of three paragraphs in the *Catechism*, but he did acknowledge that we are responsible not only *to* but *for* our consciences. False conscience can and should be changed, but he says little about how this is to come about, but presumably in response to acknowledged conflict with a civil judge or religious superior regarding personal judgment of action.

Perhaps nowhere in the *Catechism* is a Thomistic perspective seen more clearly than in its treatment of Erroneous Judgment (#1790–94). "A human being must always obey the certain judgment of his conscience. If he were deliberately to act against it, he would condemn himself." As Aquinas repeatedly wrote, to act against a certain conscience is always to sin. "Yet," according to the *Catechism*, "it can happen that moral conscience remains in ignorance and makes erroneous judgments about acts to be performed or already performed." If this ignorance can and should have been corrected, "the person is culpable for the evil he commits." Aquinas would have no argument with this, but he seems to be more concerned with the ignorance that is "invincible," to use the *Catechism*'s term, or as Aquinas would have put it, when a false judgment endures. Although he doesn't spell it out, "endures" suggests that there is awareness of external conflict with one's judgment or opposition to it, and that one attends to it, but may remain convinced of his decision. In this case, according to the *Catechism*, "the evil committed by the person cannot be imputed to him." As *Gaudius et Spes* (#16) puts it, "Conscience frequently errs from invincible ignorance without losing its dignity," or as Aquinas might say, without losing its absolute authority.

I have argued that the teachings of Aquinas and the *Catechism* converge on essential points, are consonant or in harmony. But it is also apparent that the Angelic Doctor pushes the boundaries in a way that the *Catechism* does not, just as it quotes Newman on conscience as the Aboriginal Vicar of Christ but makes no reference to the context of that phrase in a letter that jokes about toasting the pope but only after toasting conscience first. It does not explicitly draw the inference that conscience speaks with an authority greater even than that of the Pope. It does not

17. But see the discussion of Aquinas on obedience to secular authority in the matter of war, in chapter 2.

invoke the infallibility of synderesis as does Aquinas, but reserves that attribute to the Church, both "the People of God, under the guidance of the Church's living Magisterium," and especially the Pope when "he proclaims by a definitive act a doctrine pertaining to faith or morals."[18] But Aquinas's more daring portrait of conscience remains in the deep background of the Church's teaching. There is no contradiction but keeping Thomas in mind when reading the *Catechism* or invoking Church teaching on conscience gives that teaching a sharper resonance.

Dare a Catholic warrior make Aquinas his or her *vade mecum*, a necessary companion when consulting personal conscience about going to war, especially in tandem with the *Compendium of the Social Doctrine of the Church*, with its endorsement of conscientious objection to unjust war? "The case for selective conscientious objection rests in large part on Aquinas's assertion . . . that a person should always obey his or her conscience, even if there is a possibility of being wrong. A soldier who cannot in good conscience fight in a given war would be acting immorally if he or she nevertheless chose to fight, whether it be due to fear of punishment or any other reason. Aquinas did, however, add an important proviso, which was that conscience needs to be informed."[19]

TEACHING CONSCIENCE IN PASTORAL SETTINGS

A notice in the parish bulletin that Father Goodpastor will offer a lecture on Saint Thomas Aquinas on "The Infallibility, Impeccability, and Indestructability of Synderesis" is not likely to draw a huge crowd. A follow-up presentation on what the *Catechism* and the *Compendium* teach about conscience might not do any better. "Please bring your well-read copies with you!" How, then, can Thomistic theology and Church doctrine on conscience be taught so that the intimidation factor of big words and heady authorities might be overcome? Pastoral theologian Timothy E. Connell offers one approach that may be helpful. O'Connell devotes a chapter in his well-known textbook, *Principles for a Catholic Morality*, to conscience. That his presentation passes scholarly muster is indicated by that chapter's inclusion, in slightly abbreviated form, in a book referred to in chapter 1, Charles E. Curran's edited volume *Conscience*, under the title "An Understanding of Conscience." O'Connell offers language that may be more parish-friendly

18. *Catechism*, #890–91.

19. Ellner, Robinson, and Whetham, *When Soldiers Say No*, 4–5.

than either the technical, dialectical argument of Aquinas or the stilted verbiage of the *Catechism*. This is indeed the purpose of his chapter: "in this writer's experience, [such terms as *synderesis*, moral science, and *syneidesis*] are never particularly helpful and, indeed, often distract from the matter at hand. We will substitute for them, therefore, some terms of our own."[20]

Perhaps not only for the sake of simplicity but also to suggest the organic unity of the three dimensions of personal moral experience, O'Connell speaks of conscience/1, conscience/2, and conscience/3. With conscience/1 "we are referring to conscience as an abiding human *characteristic*, to a general sense of value, an awareness of personal responsibility, that is utterly emblematic of the human person."[21] What Aquinas calls synderesis, which the *Catechism* describes as "the perception of the principles of morality," O'Connell refers to as the "human capacity for self-direction, [and] . . . a sense of the goodness and badness of their deeds and of their accountability for these deeds."[22] Only sociopaths and psychopaths lack this characteristic and capacity. The very name we give such people indicates a judgment that they are morally lacking in a way that seems to deny their full humanity.

Synderesis empowers persons to make moral choices by applying fundamental knowledge of good and evil to circumstances. As O'Connell says, "conscience/1 forces individual human persons to search out the objective moral values of their situation. . . . This search, this exercise of moral reasoning, can be termed conscience/2. . .For if conscience/1 is a characteristic, conscience/2 is the *process* which that characteristic demands . . . the ongoing process of reflection, discernment, discussion, and analysis in which human beings have always engaged."[23] But this process is liable to error. O'Connell cites the notorious example of (nominally Christian) Germany in the 1930s, when "the people of Germany were guilty of a moral blind spot, of an inability to see and appreciate the evil of their situation."[24] He might well have offered the counter-example of Franz Jägerstätter, a Catholic whose attention to his conscience, in light of the saints and martyrs of the early church, enabled him to see through or past this nationalistic, racist, and militaristic blind spot and forge his resistance to the evil of

20. O'Connell, "Understanding Conscience," 25.
21. O'Connell, "Understanding Conscience," 26.
22. O'Connell, "Understanding Conscience," 26.
23. O'Connell, "Understanding Conscience," 27.
24. O'Connell, "Understanding Conscience," 28.

Hitler's unjust wars. Somehow, this minimally educated farmer processed the moral values and disvalues of his situation and formed his conscience in solitary witness against Nazism. His story also illuminates O'Connell's (and Aquinas's) point that "conscience/2 is not directly accountable to the Church. No, it is accountable to the truth and nothing else." Franz consulted his pastor and his bishop but acted against their counsel. It cost him his life but made him a future saint.

Finally, "If conscience/1 is a characteristic and conscience/2 is a process, conscience/3 is an *event* . . . the concrete judgment of a specific person pertaining to her or his own immediate action."[25] But one must choose whether to accept the decision of conscience/3, whereby "the moral agent engages either in an act of sanctity or in actual sin."[26] At this point, "because the non-negotiable [infallible!] obligation of conscience/1 permeates and fertilizes [recall Aquinas's metaphor of the "seed plot"] the fallible judgment of conscience/2, we find ourselves in the moment of action with a tentative but absolute guide for our actions."[27] In what could be a plainspoken version of a central Thomistic theme, O'Connell writes, "It is the quintessence of human morality that we should do what we *believe* to be right, and avoid what we *believe* to be wrong."[28] The fallibility of conscience/2 "in no way obviates that fundamental moral obligation. Therefore, if it was accurate to say that conscience/2 kneels before the altar of truth, it is equally accurate to say that we kneel before the altar of conscience."[29]

Father Goodpastor might be well advised to title his talk something like, "You *Are* a Conscience: Catholic Teaching for Beginners and Other Adults," and then introduce the three dimensions of conscience as a *characteristic*, a *process*, and an *event*. He might mention an influential origin in Saint Thomas Aquinas, Doctor of the Church, for this portrait of human morality, and he might refer to how those three dimensions are articulated in the *Catechism*. But he wouldn't let those authorities stand in the way of an accessible presentation. That's no guarantee of an SRO turnout, but it might give Father G a fighting chance.

If there were any veterans or families or friends of veterans in Fr. Goodpastor's audience, they might very well be wondering about the

25. O'Connell, "Understanding Conscience," 29.

26. O'Connell, "Understanding Conscience," 29.

27. O'Connell, "Understanding Conscience," 29.

28. O'Connell, "Understanding Conscience," 30.

29. O'Connell, "Understanding Conscience," 30.

relationship of conscience to one of the most troubling consequences of combat experience, the phenomenon now called "moral injury." The conscience can be wounded in war as grievously as the body. That is the topic of the following chapter.

4

Moral Injury and Unjust War

If the quarrel is unjust, he that exposes himself in it condemns his soul.

—CHRISTINE DE PIZAN (CA. 1364–CA. 1431), *THE BOOK OF DEEDS OF ARMS AND OF CHIVALRY*[1]

There is a line that a man dare not cross, deeds he dare not commit, regardless of orders and the hopelessness of the situation, for such deeds would destroy something in him that he values more than life itself.

—J. GLENN GRAY[2]

INTRODUCTION

"MORAL INJURY" IS A recently invented term for the millennia-old phenomenon[3] of conscience-wounding or character-altering trauma experienced

1. Pizan, "War and Chivalry," 218.
2. Gray, *Warriors*, 222.
3. Shay's *Achilles in Vietnam* makes exactly this point by interpreting the moral experience of Achilles in *The Iliad* in light of the moral trauma Shay encountered in the Vietnam vets he worked with over many years for the Veterans Administration. Achilles,

by warriors in combat that, while sharing symptoms with post-traumatic stress disorder (PTSD, another recent coinage), and sometimes occurring simultaneously with PTSD, has its own distinct source in the conscience of the warrior. That makes moral injury especially pertinent to this book and its focus on conscientious objection to unjust war. Because we believe veterans themselves should "define" moral injury, we will begin with their accounts and leave formal definitions for later in the chapter. For immediate purposes we will use the working definition employed by Schorr and colleagues in their research with US veterans of World War II and the wars in Korea, Vietnam, Afghanistan, and Iraq: moral injury is "a violation of deeply held moral beliefs and expectations."[4]

Our first task is to provide credible evidence that moral injury, by whatever name or scientific definition, is indeed distinct from PTSD. Then follows a psychiatric interpretation of Shakespeare's symptomatic portrait of the post-combat behavior of Harry Hotspur in *Henry IV, Part I*. Again, moral injury may be a new term but the human experience of post-combat personal suffering is not. The heart of the chapter comprises brief portraits of four warriors suffering from diverse moral injuries, based on their own memoirs or an intimate journalistic account. The drone warrior with whom we begin the chapter expands the diversity even further. Given this sampling of sources or types of moral injury as a kind of baseline, the chapter then proposes a definition of moral injury adequate to the diversity of even these five warriors. We close by addressing the challenge moral injury puts to just war ethics.

EYAL PRESS, "THE WOUNDS OF THE DRONE WARRIOR"

Award-winning journalist Eyal Press, author of *Beautiful Souls: The Courage and Conscience of Ordinary People in Extraordinary Times*, provides in a *New York Times Magazine* cover article[5] a compelling narrative of what can

---

of course, is a fictional character in an ancient epic poem, but his portrayal by "Homer" has endured for centuries of readers as a credible account of a warrior's experience in combat.

4. Schorr et al., "Sources of Moral Injury," 3.

5. Press, "Wounds."

be thought of as a natural experiment[6] that addresses the questions, What is moral injury[7] and how is it distinct from post-traumatic stress disorder?

After the 9/11 attacks in 2001, Christopher Aaron had been inspired by the memory of his grandfather, a WWII veteran, to go to work for the National Geospatial-Intelligence Agency as an imagery analyst, although his work had no direct relation to the military responses to 9/11. Later, work at the Counterterrorism Airborne Analysis Center in Langley, Virginia, made that connection. He spent several months in a noncombatant role in Afghanistan before doing similar work for a private military contractor. When an offer from another contractor was made to him, "something strange happened: He began to fall apart physically. The distress began with headaches, night chills, joint pain. Soon, more debilitating symptoms emerged—waves of nausea, eruptions of skin welts, chronic digestive problems." Continuing such work was "out of the question. 'I could not sign the paperwork,' he said. Every time he sat down to try, 'my hands stopped working—I was feverish, sick, nauseous.'"[8]

Press continues the story: "He was 29 and in the throes of a breakdown. . . . He consulted several doctors, none of whom could specify a diagnosis. In desperation, he experimented with fasting, yoga, Chinese herbal medicine. Eventually his health improved, but his mood continued to spiral. Aaron couldn't muster any motivation. He spent his days in a fog of gloom. At night, he dreamed that he could see—up close, in real time—innocent people being maimed and killed, their bodies dismembered, their faces contorted in agony. In one recurring dream, he was forced to sit in a chair and watch the violence. If he tried to avert his gaze, his head would be jerked back into place, so that he had to continue looking. 'It was as though my brain was telling me: Here are the details you missed out on,' he said. 'Now watch them when you're dreaming.'"

6. According to Lynne C. Messer, writing in *Encyclopedia Britannica*, a natural experiment is an "observational study in which an event or a situation that allows for the random or seemingly random assignment of study subjects to different groups is exploited to answer a particular question. Natural experiments are often used to study situations in which controlled experimentation is not possible, such as when an exposure of interest cannot be practically or ethically assigned to research subjects. Situations that may create appropriate circumstances for a natural experiment include policy changes, weather events, and natural disasters. Natural experiments are used most commonly in the fields of epidemiology, political science, psychology, and social science."

7. While moral injury can occur in non-combat experiences (e.g., rape), our focus is on moral injury as induced by combat.

8. Press, "Wounds," 32.

Press describes Aaron's work situation at Langley as facing a wall of monitors feeding "classified videos from drones in distant war zones." Sometimes "what unspooled before Aaron's eyes was jarringly intimate: coffins being carried through the streets after drone strikes; a man squatting in a field to defecate . . . ; an imam speaking to a group of 15 young boys in the courtyard of his madrasa. If a Hellfire missile killed the target, it occurred to Aaron as he stared at the screen, everything the imam might have told his pupils about America's war with their faith would be confirmed." The vexing challenge was that "identifying who was in the cross hairs of a potential drone strike wasn't always straightforward. . . . 'On good days . . . we had a strong sense that who we were looking at was the person we were looking for,' Aaron said. 'On bad days, we were literally guessing.'"[9]

Aaron's dreams mirrored his waking experience peering at video monitors depicting events happening thousands of miles away. He was a virtual but not an actual warrior. He exposed himself to no physical danger, no threat of being shot at or blasted by a roadside bomb. He was working in an air-conditioned office and going home to a typical American middle-class lifestyle. Nonetheless, he suffered the symptoms described above. They represent not PTSD, which requires exposure to physical threat, but rather moral injury: "a violation of deeply held moral beliefs and expectations."

Press reports that according to "the Bureau for Investigative Journalism, a London-based organization that has been tracking drone killings since 2010, US drone strikes have killed between 7,584 and 10,918 people, including 751 to 1,555 civilians, in Pakistan, Afghanistan, Yemen, and Somalia. The US government figures are far lower," but as a report by the Columbia Law School Human Rights Clinic and the Sana'a Center for Strategic Studies pointed out, "In Pakistan, Somalia, and Yemen . . . the government officially acknowledged just 20 percent of more than 700 reported strikes since 2002."[10] Using the lowest numbers in the BIJ report (751 civilian deaths out of 7,584 of all deaths), and assuming that those numbers apply at least roughly to the results of Aaron's work, he had a one in ten chance of unintentionally killing a civilian. Call it drone-roulette. But one individual does not a phenomenon make.[11]

Press moves from the single case of Christopher Aaron to a much larger sample of individuals with similar professional roles. In research

9. Press, "Wounds," 32.

10. Press, "Wounds," 33.

11. For a well-informed and insightful analysis, see Himes, *Drones*.

conducted at the School of Aerospace Medicine at Wright-Patterson Air Force Base, in interviews with "141 intelligence analysts and officers involved in remote combat operations to assess their emotional reactions to killing . . . three-fourths reported feeling grief, remorse, and sadness. Many experienced these 'negative, disruptive emotions' for a month or more." In fact, according to another Air Force study, "drone analysts in the 'kill chain' are exposed to more graphic violence—seeing 'destroyed homes and villages,' witnessing 'dead bodies or human remains'—than most Special Forces on the ground."[12] Press points out that while some researchers treat moral injury as "intentionally doing something that you felt was against what you thought was right," others observe that "moral injury is sustained by soldiers in the course of doing exactly what their commanders, and society, ask of them."[13] Either way, or both ways, that would seem to describe the experience of Christopher Aaron.

Another former drone operator "described a scenario in which an operator executed a strike that killed a 'terrorist facilitator' while sparing his son. Afterward, 'the child walked back to the pieces of his father and began to place the pieces back into human shape,' to the horror of the operator." No talk of the justifiability of "collateral damage" is likely to erase that horrific image from the mind of the operator who made that decision and witnessed the results. No talk of patriotic duty or national security is likely to prevent enduring moral injury—even at thousands of miles of remove from the actual dismemberment of a father and his "remembering" by his child, who will no doubt suffer grievously from that horror the rest of his life, and who might be susceptible to anti-American recruitment. Moral injury happens at both ends of the drone strike.

Aaron told Press that "the hardest thing to come to terms with was that a part of him had enjoyed wielding this awesome power—that he'd found it, on some level, exciting.[14] In the years that followed, as his mood darkened, he withdrew, sinking into a prolonged period of shame and grief. . . . He struggled with 'quasi-suicidal' thoughts." Eventually, with the support of other veterans facing similar breakdowns, Aaron began to recover. "He still

12. Press, "Wounds," 34.

13. Press, "Wounds," 35.

14. This may exemplify what Augustine famously called *libido dominandi*, the lust to dominate. See the *Excursus* immediately following this chapter for a discussion of something very like moral injury in Augustine's dark parable of a wise judge who presides over a courtroom dependent on the sometimes lethal torture of both accused prisoners and witnesses.

has his share of violent dreams. . . . But he appears to have recaptured what for many years he had lost—his sense of moral purpose." Part of that recovery of moral purpose is telling his story in public. On one such occasion, he began by asking for a moment of silence "for all of the individuals that I killed or helped to kill."[15]

SHAKESPEARE, *HENRY IV*, AND JONATHAN SHAY, *ACHILLES IN VIETNAM*

Before recounting the morally injurious combat experiences of other veterans, allow me to quote at length from Jonathan Shay, in *Achilles in Vietnam*, who quotes from Shakespeare's depiction in *Henry IV, Part I*,[16] in the voice of his wife, of Harry Hotspur's post-combat behavioral state. Running parallel with Lady Percy's monologue is Shay's psychiatric interpretation:[17]

O, my good lord, what are you thus alone?	Social withdrawal and isolation
For what offense have I this fortnight been A banish'd woman from my Harry's bed?	Random, unwarranted rage at family, sexual dysfunction, no capacity for intimacy
Tell me, sweet lord, what is't that takes from thee Thy stomach, pleasure,	Somatic disturbances, loss of ability to experience pleasure
and thy golden sleep?	Insomnia
Why dost thou bend thine eyes upon the earth,	Depression
And start so often when thou sit'st alone?	Hyperactive startle reaction
Why hast thou lost the fresh blood in thy cheeks,	Peripheral vasoconstrictive, autonomic hyperactivity
And given my treasures and my rights of thee To thick-eyed musing and cursed melancholy?	Sense of the dead being more real than the living, depression
In thy faint slumbers I by thee have watch'd	Fragmented, vigilant sleep

15. Press, "Wounds," 49.

16. Act 2, Scene 3, lines 40–62.

17. Shay, *Achilles*, 165–66.

And heard thee murmur tales of iron wars,	Traumatic dreams, reliving episodes of combat, fragmented sleep
Speak terms of manage to thy bounding steed,	
Cry "Courage! to the field!" And thou hast talk'd	
Of sallies and retires, of trenches, tents,	
Of palisades, frontiers, parapets,	
Of prisoner's ransom, and of soldiers slain,	
And all the currents of a heady fight.	
Thy spirit within thee hath been so at war	
And thus hath so bestirr'd thee in thy sleep.	
That beads of sweat have stood upon thy brow,	Night sweats, autonomic hyperactivity
Like bubbles in a late-disturbed stream;	

It is not clear from this speech whether Hotspur suffers from what today we would call PTSD or moral injury, or both. He certainly has been exposed to dangerous threats (source of PTSD), but he has also had the awesome moral responsibility of command and has seen some of his soldiers die (source of moral injury). The key line refers to war in two senses: Hotspur's *spirit* has experienced actual combat as traumatic and since then Hotspur's spirit has been at war *with itself*. He is broken, not the person his wife knew before the war. Harry carries the trauma of combat with him in a way that severely hampers his taking up civilian life again. He has been, to borrow further from Shay, and thus from Homer, *Achilles* enraged on the battle-field and *Odysseus* struggling to come home. But however keen an observer of human life, Shakespeare is imaging what a historical figure might have experienced. Perhaps Shakespeare had observed the troubled behavior of returned warriors, or perhaps in his genius he simply intuited what would have been the effects of combat. At any rate, we must turn from imaginative literature to memoir, the recollected experiences of actual combat veterans.

MORAL INJURY IN MEMOIRS AND INTIMATE PORTRAITS OF VETERANS

J. Glenn Gray, *The Warriors*

J. Glenn Gray's celebrated memoir, *The Warriors: Reflections on Men in Battle,* first published in 1959, was written to heal "the intellectual wounds of World War II" that he experienced as a soldier, which were reopened a decade later (when he wrote a new foreword) by observing as a civilian "the peculiar horrors of the Vietnam war and the violence, chaos, and emotional perplexity these horrors have occasioned—or reflected—in our own land."[18] In the penultimate and longest chapter, "The Ache of Guilt," Gray reflects on these "intellectual wounds." He observes that "in World War II the number of civilians who lost their lives exceeded the number of soldiers killed in combat. At all events, the possibilities of the individual involving himself in guilt are immeasurably wider than specific deeds that he might commit against the armed foe. In the thousand chances of warfare, nearly every combat soldier failed to support his comrades at a critical moment; through sins of omission or commission, he has been responsible for the death of those he did not intend to kill. Through folly or fear, nearly every officer [such as Hotspur?] has exposed his own men to needless destruction at one time or another. Add to this the unnumbered acts of injustice so omnipresent in war, which may not result in death but inevitably bring pain and grief, and the impartial observer may wonder how the participants in such deeds could ever smile again and be free of care."[19]

Gray quotes his own wartime diary on the inescapability of conscience (he might have said *synderesis*): "I was directly or indirectly the cause of their death. . . . I hope it will not rest too hard on my conscience, and yet if it does not I shall be disturbed also."[20] He gives a particularly poignant rendering of the primacy of conscience: "there is a line that a man dare not cross, deeds he dare not commit, regardless of orders and the hopelessness of the situation, for such deeds would destroy something in him that he values more than life itself."[21] Physical death is not always, not everywhere, not for everybody the ultimate sacrifice (see chapter 1.) And conscience is inescapable in a second way: "I am ashamed not only of my own deeds, not

18. Gray, *Warriors*, xix.

19. Gray, *Warriors*, 204–5.

20. Gray, *Warriors*, 209.

21. Gray, *Warriors*, 222.

only of my nation's deeds, but of human deeds as well. I am ashamed to be a man."[22] Yet conscience is not only a burden but also a source of hope that war in the modern world can be tamed: "If guilt is not experienced deeply enough to cut into us, our future may well be lost."[23]

Daniel Lang, *Casualties of War*

Published a decade after *The Warriors*, Daniel Lang's *Casualties of War* evokes a similar tribute to the conscience of the soldier, or at least one particular soldier, private Sven Eriksson (a pseudonym given to PFC Robert Storeby). The story Lang tells is based on an actual event, known as Incident on Hill 192, which became infamous when four of Eriksson's fellow soldiers were court-martialed, pronounced guilty, and sentenced to lengthy prison terms for the abduction, gang rape, and murder of a young Vietnamese woman (pseudonym Mao); all four were dishonorably discharged.[24] Eriksson resisted and then reported the atrocity. For this soldier, "Conscience was one thing that crossed over from civilian life to war. . . . It was as much a part of us as our legs and arms."[25] He distinguished himself from his squad members in his response to the existential challenge of combat: "We all figured we might be dead in the next minute, so what difference did it make what we did? But the longer I was over there, the more I became convinced that it was the other way around that counted—that *because* we might not be around much longer, we had to take extra care how we behaved. Anyway, that's what made me believe I was interested in religion. Another man might have called it something else, but the idea was simply that we had to answer for what we did. We had to answer to something, to someone—*maybe just to ourselves*."[26] Sergeant Tony Meserve (also a pseudonym), on the other hand, "apparently undergoing changes" as a result of his combat experience, "had exhibited a mean streak toward the Vietnamese."[27] Eriksson told Lang that it "sounded as though he had become a kind of war casualty." Meserve instigated the rape gang.

22. Gray, *Warriors*, 247.
23. Gray, *Warriors*, 254.
24. One sentence was reversed on a procedural error; the others were shortened.
25. Lang, *Casualties of War*, 73.
26. Lang, *Casualties of War*, 110 (emphasis added).
27. Lang, *Casualties of War*, 27.

Despite Eriksson's moral heroism, at least as diametrically compared to his four squad mates, a year-and-a-half after returning to civilian life back home in Minnesota, "He has yet to come to terms with the incident on Hill 192. . . . He still has a tendency to fight off its memory . . . and he thinks the reason for this is that although the experience he had may have revealed certain strengths in himself, he is far more concerned with the limitations it exposed. The thought of them . . . makes him feel discouraged at times about his future."[28] "He had yet to exonerate himself from the self-imposed charge of having failed to save Mao's life."[29] Although Lang reports no PTSD-like symptoms beyond persistent discouragement and self-condemnation, can it be doubted that Sven Eriksson, despite being on the right side of the existential divide between atrocity and conscience, is a victim of moral injury? Precisely because he is a man of conscience, he, too, is a casualty of war.

As Philip Caputo writes in *A Rumor of War*, "Some of our friends had been killed, others maimed. We had survived, but in war, a man does not have to be killed or wounded to become a casualty. His life, his sight, or limbs are not the only things he stands to lose."[30]

Philip Caputo, *A Rumor of War*

After his three-year enlistment was up in 1967, Philip Caputo, age twenty-four, came home from Vietnam "almost completely ignorant about the stuff of ordinary life. . . . But I had acquired some expertise in the art of killing."[31] He had seen "all manner of violence and horrors so grotesque that they evoked more fascination than disgust. Once I had seen pigs eating napalm-charred corpses—a memorable sight, pigs eating roast people." Such gruesome experiences left him with "all the symptoms of *combat veteranitis*: an inability to concentrate, a childlike fear of darkness, a tendency to tire easily, chronic nightmares, an intolerance of loud noises—especially doors slamming and cars backfiring—and alternating moods of depression and rage that came over me for no apparent reason." After a decade of civilian life, he writes that "recovery has been less than total."[32]

28. Lang, *Casualties of War*, 116.
29. Lang, *Casualties of War*, 120.
30. Caputo, *Rumor of War*, 207.
31. Caputo, *Rumor of War*, 3.
32. Caputo, *Rumor of War*, 4.

One incident in Vietnam "amounted to a degrading manhunt; pulling bodies out of the mud had left us feeling ashamed of ourselves, more like ghouls than soldiers. And the mutilation caused by modern weapons came as a shock. . . . The sight of mutilation did more than cause me physical revulsion; it burst the religious myth of my Catholic childhood. I could not look at those men and still believe their souls had 'passed on' to another existence, or that they had had souls in the first place. I could not believe those bloody messes would be capable of a resurrection on the Last Day."[33] At one point Lieutenant Caputo was ordered to take care of the day's work, four slain Vietcong, and in particular to make it possible for his superior officer to "show them to the general." He made a cardboard sign for his desk: "OFFICER IN CHARGE OF THE DEAD."[34] At this stage of his deployment he "still believed in the cause for which we were supposed to be fighting, but what kind of men were we, and what kind of army was it that made exhibitions of the human beings it had butchered?"[35] Later in his narrative, a dream embodies OFFICER IN CHARGE OF THE DEAD with a vengeance: he "was given command of a new platoon. . . . They marched along, my platoon of crippled corpses, hopping along on the stumps of their legs, swinging the stumps of their arms, keeping perfect time while I counted cadence. I was proud of them, disciplined soldiers to and beyond the end. They stayed in step even in death."[36] In subsequent days he began to see his living comrades "prefigured in death. . . . Asleep and dreaming, I saw dead men living, awake I saw living men dead."[37]

In a textbook case of the berserk state,[38] in the village of Ha Na, Caputo's "platoon exploded. It was the collective emotional detonation of men who had been pushed to the extremity of endurance. I lost control of them and even of myself. Desperate to get to the hill, we rampaged through the rest of the village, whooping like savages, torching thatch huts, tossing grenades into the cement houses we could not burn."[39] Caputo comes to understand that the rampage "had been a catharsis, a purging of months of fear, frustration, and tension. We had relieved our own pain by inflicting

33. Caputo, *Rumor of War*, 128.

34. Caputo, *Rumor of War*, 175.

35. Caputo, *Rumor of War*, 179.

36. Caputo, *Rumor of War*, 199.

37. Caputo, *Rumor of War*, 201.

38. See Shay, *Achilles*, chapter 5, "Berserk."

39. Caputo, *Rumor of War*, 304.

it on others. But the sense of relief was inextricably mingled with guilt and shame."[40] The platoon "had needlessly destroyed the homes of perhaps two hundred people."[41] In war, "a man does not have to be killed or wounded to become a casualty. His life, his sight, or limbs are not the only things he stands to lose."[42]

Writing before the term became commonplace, Caputo does not speak of "moral injury." But by our working definition—"a violation of deeply held moral beliefs and expectations"[43]—he certainly embodies that phenomenon as a casualty of war. Twenty-four years later, Tyler Boudreau, writing in 2011 as a veteran of the war in Iraq, makes the term the title of a long essay on his combat experience, and provides some personal background in a brief reflection on the conscience of a commander.

Tyler Boudreau, "The Morally Injured"

Former Marine Corps infantry captain Tyler Boudreau is aware of "the dangers of introspection," the title given to his brief personal statement for the 100 Faces exhibition, which offers formal painted portraits and statements of one hundred veterans of the wars in Afghanistan and Iraq.[44] He has come to realize that "a commander must be cautious not to look too closely into his own heart." Boudreau describes what he calls "a mission to troop ratio. A commander must believe in both; he must love them both; but ultimately he must love the mission a little more. He must be prepared to sacrifice the lives of his men for the success of the mission. But what if a commander looks into his heart and finds that that ratio has somehow reversed itself?" This is what happened to Captain Boudreau. "From the disparity I witnessed between the policies in Washington and our actions in Iraq, an ambivalence formed inside me. It began to grow geometrically, doubling and re-doubling itself until I was utterly consumed by it. Suddenly I looked at the faces of my marines and I realized my reverence for them had overwhelmed my reverence for the mission. By definition, then, I was unable to command. I resigned my commission. After twelve years

---

40. Caputo, *Rumor of War*, 305.

41. Caputo, *Rumor of War*, 306.

42. Caputo, *Rumor of War*, 207.

43. Schorr et al., "Sources of Moral Injury," 3.

44. http://100facesofwarexperience.org/.

of service, I left the Marine Corps."[45] Cognitive dissonance, yes, but dissonance of conscience even more.

This penchant for introspection and demonstration of professional integrity suggests Boudreau's reflections on "The Morally Injured" might be particularly worthy of attention. He begins his essay by describing a nonviolent but surprisingly provocative incident: the search of a farmhouse in a small town in Iraq. "There was no shouting or pushing. The Marines wore friendly smiles. They stepped gently through the house and were careful to replace anything they moved. Outside, other marines chatted playfully with the kids and gave them pieces of candy. When the search was complete and nothing was found, we thanked the man and apologized for the inconvenience. . . . Not a shot was fired, not a drop of blood or a tear was shed, and yet, as we withdrew from that farmhouse and roared off into the night, I felt something inside me begin to hurt. . . . What can I call that hurt?"[46]

Years later, no longer a Marine, Boudreau viewed "a short video clip . . . of two soldiers searching an Iraqi home," as seemingly benign as his own experience had been. But "one of the soldiers, clad in body armor, sunglasses, and an automatic rifle . . . leaned toward a young Iraqi man . . . and gave him a hug. The Iraqi submitted with limp arms and an unenthusiastic smile. The soldier laughed. . . . And that was it." Despite the harmlessness of the encounter in the video, Boudreau writes that he "felt my face get hot with rage. I blurted something out in anger, something profane, to match the profanity of what had just been presented in this documentary." Outrage because of a hug? "I was angry at how this type of atrocity could be shrouded in a guise of bonhomie." But how could a good-humored hug be seen as an atrocity? "The trouble is that no matter how that Iraqi man felt about the hug, there's nothing he could have done to stop it. . . . Nobody at all could stop that American soldier from hugging that Iraqi man—and you could see in their faces, they both knew it. That's what an occupation looks like. And that's the harm in a hug."[47]

As a result of this trivial event, Boudreau "began to grasp the grave reality of American foreign policy and the extent of what it means to be a superpower. . . . It means nothing can stop us from going anywhere and doing anything we want, whether bombing, or building, shooting, or hugging—anything. . . . When that Iraqi was hugged by the soldier, he felt, in

45. http://100facesofwarexperience.org/portrait-gallery/100-faces/14696889.
46. Boudreau, "Morally Injured," 746.
47. Boudreau, "Morally Injured," 752.

that instant, the embrace of total American power. . . . That was the atrocity that I could only convey through exaggerated emotion." He comes to this conclusion about the American warriors' experience in Iraq: "Our moral fibers have been torn by what we were asked to do and by what we agreed to do."[48] And yet that is not how Boudreau wants us to understand moral injury. After coming home from the war, he was diagnosed as having PTSD by the VA. He'd been exposed to enough combat to make that diagnosis authentic, "but inwardly I knew that the greatest pain I felt was not linked to those moments when violence was being directed at me but when I was inflicting it on others."[49]

Boudreau reminds us "that the US presence in Iraq has been far more perilous for Iraqis than it has for Americans. . . . However, mentioning the several hundred thousand Iraqi people killed since the US invasion in 2003, or the two and a half million displaced, or the millions more without money or medical care, appears to be taboo in the American media, the government, and in social circles. Nobody wants to talk about the Iraqis. It's always about the troops."[50] Here Boudreau makes a salutary intervention in present discussions of combat-induced moral injury: "'moral injury' by definition includes the memories of those who have been harmed. Without the Iraqi people, the troops can have no moral injuries to speak of. And the only way Americans can fathom the meaning of this term, 'moral injury,' is to acknowledge the humanity of the Iraqis."[51] A hug would seem to do just that. But in the context of a superpower's occupation of a long-beleaguered, impoverished country, a hug can be an atrocity, a moral injury for both the hugger (or his witness) and the hugged.

48. Boudreau, "Morally Injured," 752.

49. Boudreau, "Morally Injured," 748.

50. In the Author's Note, the first words we hear from him in *What Have We Done*, David Wood makes a similar point: "Even as our wars were getting under way in 2002, most Afghans and Iraqis were enduring high levels of anxiety, depression, fear, grief, bitterness, and hopelessness from past conflicts and repression. The years that followed must have deepened their physical and psychological trauma to levels of pain we can scarcely imagine." A poster in my son's home captures this perspective poignantly: "Why, for example, don't they ever take a moment of silence for all the Iraqi kids who died?"

51 Boudreau, "Morally Injured," 751.

FROM MEMOIRS TO DEFINITIONS

This chapter has demonstrated, by investigating "The Wounds of the Drone Warrior," that combat-induced moral injury is distinct from post-traumatic stress disorder, even though it may present similar symptoms. It has also offered a prescient litany of those symptoms as observed by William Shakespeare centuries before the terms PTSD or "moral injury" came into use; psychiatrist Jonathan Shay, with many years of experience working with Vietnam veterans, interpreted those symptoms in modern medical terminology. We then offered a small but diverse sampling of how veterans themselves have reflected on their own morally injurious combat experience, from World War II to Vietnam to Afghanistan and Iraq.[52] J. Glenn Gray reflected on the inescapability and primacy of conscience in wartime: "there is a line that a man dare not cross, deeds he dare not commit, regardless of orders and the hopelessness of the situation, for such deeds would destroy something in him that he values more than life itself."[53] Daniel Lang told the story of Sven Eriksson whose conscience led him to try to resist and then report a gang rape and murder by his comrades of a young Vietnamese woman; he cannot escape self-condemnation for having failed to save her life; although physically uninjured, he, too, became a casualty of war. Philip Caputo wrote of the gruesome sights and horrific events he witnessed and participated in as a Marine officer in Vietnam, including his berserk platoon's wanton destruction of a peasant village in an explosive catharsis that left him feeling deeply ashamed, and led to enduring PTSD-like suffering. Tyler Boudreau's post-combat suffering resulted not from his exposure to enemy fire but from the realization that he was participating in a superpower's occupation of a struggling people whose humanity could not thereby be respected; like Christopher Aaron, the drone warrior, Boudreau was morally injured by what he saw on a video screen, but in his case as a reminder of what he had witnessed in person.

Our working definition of moral injury, "a violation of deeply held moral beliefs and expectations,"[54] seems to apply to all these veterans, no matter the war they fought in, the "good war" of Gray or the morally

---

52. Perhaps any wartime memoir could be combed for similar experiences. A few that have come to my attention that I have not referred to but can recommend for their particular relevance include Morris, *Evil Hours*; Marlantes, *What It Is Like*; and Brennan and O'Reilly, *Shooting Ghosts*.

53. Gray, *Warriors*, 222.

54. Schorr et al., "Sources of Moral Injury," 3.

compromised American wars in Vietnam (Eriksson, Caputo) or in Iraq (Aaron, Boudreau), and no matter their rank or role or degree of exposure to extreme combat situations. In the final section of this chapter it remains to discuss two of the many definitions offered for moral injury, and then to propose our own synthesis. Finally, I discuss the obvious point that the phenomena of moral injuries would seem to be more likely in unjust war, which is all the more reason to prevent them (and therefore eliminate or at least reduce the need for just wars) by encouraging warriors to refuse to participate.

Defining Moral Injury

Portraits of post-combat trauma in Homer and Shakespeare make the point that the phenomenon now called moral injury is hardly new. Contemporary moral-injury researcher Rachel MacNair offers this brief history of the progenitors of our current term:

> In the US Civil War, it was called "soldier's heart," and could lead to being executed. In World War I, the term "shell shock" was used to describe the phenomenon, and it was essentially thought to be a physical problem. The Germans regarded it as something that should be discouraged and, to avoid coddling those who got it, sent them immediately back to the front lines. . . . In World War II, it was called "battle fatigue" or "combat fatigue," and it was finally admitted to be psychological in origin.[55]

Of course, it is only recently that PTSD and moral injury have been distinguished, so as with our discussion of Harry Hotspur, the symptoms alone don't tell us which kind of trauma we might be dealing with.

Although Jonathan Shay is often credited with coining the term or of popularizing it, in fact his two masterful books, *Achilles in Vietnam* and *Odysseus in America*, use "moral injury" so little that neither book includes the term in its index. Both indices do, however, have extensive entries for post-traumatic stress disorder—despite Shay's dissatisfaction with *that* term.[56] Nevertheless, building on his two books, in 2014 he published an article that did provide an influential definition. "Moral injury is: [1] A betrayal of what's right [2] by someone who holds legitimate authority (e.g., in the

---

55. MacNair, "Perpetration-Induced Traumatic Stress," 264.
56. Shay, *Odysseus*, 4.

military—a leader) [3] in a high stakes situation."[57] He goes on to explain that "the nature and importance of moral injury first crystallized for me from [reading] Homer's *Iliad*. . . . The narrative of Achilles in this poem *is* a story of moral injury"[58]—at the hands of his general Agamemnon. Thus his definition, which emphasizes betrayal of what's right *by an authority*. Shay does, however, in the same paper acknowledge that clinician-researchers such as "Brett Litz, Shira Maguen, and William Nash, have done an excellent job of describing an equally devastating second form of moral injury that arises when a service member does something in war that violates *their own* ideals, ethics, or attachments."[59] Although Shay does not do so himself, his own definition might be revised accordingly: Moral injury is: [1] A betrayal of what's right [2] by someone who holds legitimate authority *or by oneself* [3] in a high stakes situation.

Those same three clinician-researchers and colleagues have provided the other most frequently cited definition of moral injury: "*Perpetrating, failing to prevent, bearing witness to, or learning about acts that transgress deeply held moral beliefs and expectations.* This may entail participating in or witnessing inhumane or cruel actions, failing to prevent the immoral acts of others, as well as engaging in subtle acts or experiencing reactions that, upon reflection, transgress a moral code. We also consider bearing witness to the aftermath of violence and human carnage to be potentially morally injurious."[60] This definition (and its elaboration) has the advantage of specifying four different ways moral injury may take place: [1] a warrior may perpetrate an immoral act, [2] fail to prevent an immoral act, [3] witness an immoral act, or [4] learn later about an immoral act, including its human wreckage. The disadvantage, however, may be that it makes no explicit mention of what Shay identified as primary: betrayal by legitimate authority. What does all this add to our working definition: "a violation of deeply held moral beliefs and expectations"?[61] I propose the following synthesis: *Moral injury is caused by a betrayal of what's right by legitimate authority or an individual's perpetrating, failing to prevent, witnessing, or learning about an incident or its aftermath that violates deeply held moral*

57. Shay, "Moral Injury," 4.
58. Shay, "Moral Injury," 4.
59. Shay, "Moral Injury," 5.
60. Litz et al., "Moral Injury," 700.
61. Schorr et al., "Sources of Moral Injury," 3.

beliefs and expectations. Let's test this definition by returning to our five examples of moral injury.

J. Glenn Gray, rather than focusing on one or more specific incidents, reflects on the way war by its very nature inevitably compromises a normal sense of human decency and responsibility for others. So profound is this recognition that its full expression is species-shame: "I am ashamed not only of my own deeds, not only of my nation's deeds, but of human deeds as well. I am ashamed to be a man."[62] And this was in the so-called "Good War." Our understanding of "legitimate authority" might have to be expanded to include not only military and political leaders, not only one's unit and one's nation, but all of humanity—on whose behalf, supposedly, a just war is fought.

Sven Eriksson mainly did, or tried to do, what's right, but condemns himself for not having done enough to prevent a legitimate authority, his sergeant, from betraying what's right. As a consequence, he witnessed an event that violated not only an innocent young woman but also his own moral identity. She lost her life and he lost peace with himself. Our definition seems adequate to his simultaneously inspiring and regrettable case.

Philip Caputo witnessed the mutilation and degradation of human beings who had been the enemy, in the aftermath of a successful combat mission—so successful that his superior officer ordered him to prepare the bodies for exhibition—for Caputo a profound betrayal of what's right. But he also participated in the wanton, wholesale, and even gleeful—but ultimately shameful—destruction of a village of some two hundred homes. Our definition addresses both dimensions of Caputo's moral injury, that perpetrated by others and that perpetrated by himself.

Tyler Boudreau is certain that beneath his PTSD symptoms is a moral injury that ultimately stems from realization that he has been complicit in a superpower's arrogant occupation of a poor country and oppression of a beleaguered people, who don't have the simple option to refuse a hug as an uninvited invasion of personal privacy and respect. Too late he learns that his own sense of mission as a Marine officer has been betrayed by his nation's leaders and their policies. Especially thanks to Jonathan Shay's influence, our definition seems to encompass the case of the nobly sensitive conscience of Tyler Boudreau, but with the addition that betrayal by an authority can implicate those who carry out authoritative orders.

62. Gray, *Warriors*, 247.

83

Christopher Aaron appeared first in our sampling of troubled vets because his case demonstrates that moral injury can occur absent actual combat experience. But he and other drone operators may witness more violence and human carnage than warriors on the ground. Unlike bomber or artillery crews, drone warriors see the results of their decisions and targeting in an immediate if geographically removed way. With the touch of a button, he has perpetrated and then witnessed the aftermath of actions that leave him morally injured. Like Boudreau, he cannot continue the mission; his body and his soul rebel at the thought of more of the same. His high-tech role does not shield him from moral injury.[63]

In all these examples of moral injury and in the definitions we have explored and proposed, what seems to go without saying but that needs to be said (as especially Boudreau reminds us) is that *the fundamental moral belief* put to the test in warfare is the dignity of the human person and all that implies. I would expand our synthetic definition by giving content to "what's right" and "deeply held moral beliefs and expectations": Moral injury in warfare is caused by a betrayal of what's right by legitimate authority or an individual's perpetrating, failing to prevent, witnessing, or learning about an incident or its aftermath that violates deeply held moral beliefs and expectations, *especially the right to life and respect for human dignity.*[64]

This emphasis on killing as trespassing against the right to life, even when it is not murder, corresponds to the lessons drawn by journalist David Wood from a study of Afghanistan and Iraq veterans by Shira Maguen. Of those veterans

> who had killed in combat, just over half had killed only enemy combatants; the rest had killed both enemy combatants and at least one noncombatant, a male civilian, a woman or child, or an elder. All those who had killed were twice as likely to develop severe psychological symptoms as those who had not. Those who

63. For analysis of the history of attempts to define moral injury, see Hodgson and Carey, "Moral Injury," which provides a table that lists seventeen authors and definitions, including Shay and Litz.

64. The right to life of noncombatants has long been recognized in the just-war tradition. For a classic defense of the principle, see Ford, "Morality of Obliteration Bombing." Respectful treatment of prisoners of war is fundamental to the Geneva Conventions and other international instruments of the law of war. Wood, *What Have We Done*, 191, points out that one of George Washington's Five Rules for Honorable War was "don't abuse prisoners."

had killed a noncombatant, she found, were most likely to carry home the depression, anger, shame, and guilt of moral injury.[65]

Later in his account of "The Moral Injury of Our Longest War," Wood observes that "even the most hardened of our military killers . . . are haunted in the end by the taking of life, justifiable though it may be. Our newest generation of veterans may have experienced grief and loss, remorse and regret, even anger at having felt betrayed. But it is killing that lies at the heart of their 'moral injury.'"[66] No one has written so bluntly about the job of the warrior as has researcher Rachel MacNair: "Killing is not merely something that is not in our nature, as the field of psychology has ascertained for some time. . . . Killing as a stressor that can cause PTSD symptoms shows that killing can be understood as being against our nature; it tends to make us sick."[67]

Thou shalt not kill.

Anger, Guilt, Shame

But there is another and more straightforward way to demarcate moral injury from PTSD. What particularly identifies moral injury, but not PTSD, are the emotions of anger (when a person in authority betrays shared moral beliefs), guilt (when you have violated your own moral norms), and shame (when you have undermined your own moral identity). In moral injury, anger, guilt, and shame may be better thought of as enduring states of mind or soul rather than emotions, which suggest transience. As many memoirs and portraits of warriors demonstrate, moral injury does not come and go, and recovery is arduous and prolonged. No one is ever returned to their pre-combat condition, but many do slowly discover new purpose and initiative. Anger, guilt, and shame as profound as that produced by moral injury in combat leave a permanent mark on the soul.[68]

65. Wood, *What Have We Done*, 14.

66. Wood, *What Have We Done*, 143.

67. MacNair, "Perpetration-Induced Traumatic Stress," 269.

68. There is a burgeoning literature on therapies and strategies for recovery, for example, in chronological order: Lifton, *Home from the War*; Verkamp, *Moral Treatment*; Shay, *Achilles in Vietnam*; Shay, *Odysseus in America*; Tick, *War and the Soul*; Brock and Lettini, *Soul Repair*; Morris, *Evil Hours*; Sherman, *Afterwar*; and Brennan and O'Reilly, *Shooting Ghosts*. Articles in the scientific and popular press are too numerous to list here. David Wood regards grief as a "combat injury," alongside anger, guilt, and shame, but

The seminal article by Litz et al. describes "guilt [as] a painful and mo-tivating cognitive and emotional experience tied to specific acts of trans-gression of a personal or shared moral code or expectation. Shame [on the other hand] involves global evaluations of the self . . . along with behavioral tendencies to avoid and withdraw. . . . Generally, research has shown that shame is more damaging to emotional and mental health than guilt. . . . Consequently, shame may be a more integral part of moral injury."[69] But, as if they had read their Aquinas, Litz et al. observe that "inherent in our working definition of moral injury is the supposition that **anguish, guilt, and shame are signs of an intact conscience** and self- and other-expec-tations about goodness, humanity, and justice."[70] A person incapable of shame, and therefore without a working conscience, may be a sociopath and might suffer from PTSD but not from moral injury.[71]

At the risk of overloading our definition, I would revise it one last time: Moral injury in warfare is caused by a betrayal of what's right by legitimate authority or an individual's perpetrating, failing to prevent, witnessing, or learning about an incident or its aftermath that violates deeply held moral beliefs and expectations, especially the right to life and respect for human dignity. **It presents as enduring and debilitating anger, guilt, and shame.** Or, to return to our working definition: moral injury is "a violation of deep-ly held moral beliefs and expectations,"[72] producing anger, guilt, and shame.

MORAL INJURY AND THE JUST-WAR TRADITION

In the late medieval period, French author Christine de Pizan (1364–1431), in *The Book of Deeds of Arms and of Chivalry*, advised,

> Every man who quite properly wishes to expose himself to war should, before he becomes involved, be well informed of the nature of the quarrel in order to know whether the challenge is just or not. If you ask me how he shall be able to know this, as all

---

he stops short of calling it a moral injury (see his chapter "Grief Is a Combat Injury," in *What Have We Done*).

69. Litz et al., "Moral Injury," 699; emphasis added.

70. Litz et al., "Moral Injury," 701; emphasis added.

71. For analysis, see Nazarov et al., "Role of Morality," 4–19. For the distinction not only of shame from guilt but also of the many forms of shame, see Bergman, "Journey Into Shame."

72. Schorr et al., "Sources of Moral Injury," 3.

parties that wage war insist that their cause is just, let him inquire if this war has first been judged by competent jurists or lawyers,[73] or whether it may be for the cause of defense, for all wars are just in case of defense, which is to say, defending one's country when it is attacked. In this matter the warrior should be well informed before he engages in it. You should know that if the quarrel is unjust, he that exposes himself in it condemns his soul; and if he dies in such a state, he will go the way of perdition without great repentance through divine grace at the last.[74]

Pizan obviously was embedded in a quite different religious worldview than we are in the twenty-first century, when self-condemnation for unjust acts in combat is understood to disrupt the "soul" in *this* life, in the form of moral injury, with little reference to the next. But as recently as WWII, Franz Jägerstätter would have agreed wholeheartedly with Pizan, and he acted accordingly, though it cost him his life. And Sven Eriksson expected to be judged in some ultimate way.

Despite the distance of six centuries, however, Pizan's advice remains sound. It is no accident that the very concept of moral injury became current through the experiences of US veterans of the wars in Vietnam and Iraq. Understanding Achilles's behavior as moral injury would not have been possible had not Jonathan Shay counseled so many Vietnam vets suffering in similar ways from betrayal by military and political authorities of moral beliefs and expectations. Robert J. Lifton believed that protesting the Vietnam War was both effective therapy for the troubled vets he worked with but also a moral responsibility that came to him in solidarity with them and as their advocate. *Home from the War* is saturated with the perspective that the immorality of the war was the ultimate source of the suffering he encountered in his patients.

David Wood gives powerful voice to the similar perspective of veterans of the war in Iraq. He writes of the fundamental importance of trust to the warrior:

> Beyond that immediate moral covenant [with one another], the men and women we send to war trust that the physical preparation and other training they've been given will enable them to survive and prevail in combat; that their weapons and equipment work and are better than those of the enemy; and that their

73. In this, Pizan seems to have anticipated, in germ, the argument of chapter 5 of this book.

74. Excerpted in Reichberg, Syse, and Begby, *Ethics of War*, 218.

superiors, up to the commander in chief, are competent and act in their best interests. They have to trust that their friends and allies won't shoot them in error or in anger; that they won't be left behind; that medics will save them if wounded; that their lives will not be squandered by politicians back home. That the war they are fighting is moral and just, and that their service will be seen as honorable. In war, betrayal of that trust is inevitable. . . . In the wars of Iraq and Afghanistan, betrayal seemed to come from all directions.[75]

Wood quotes Brandon Friedman's book, ironically titled *The War I Always Wanted*, on his outrage toward the legitimate authorities who sent him and his fellow soldiers to Iraq:

> I had always wanted to fight. But I never wanted any part of something like this. I was a professional soldier. I wanted to believe in my work. Instead I was watching as politicians with no military experience hijacked the army. . . . I hated the president for his ignorance. I hated [then Defense Secretary] Donald Rumsfeld for his appalling arrogance and lack of judgment. . . . I hated Colin Powell for abandoning the army—for not taking care of his soldiers—when he could have done something to stop these people. . . . I hated them because now, it meant that my guys could be next [to become casualties]. . . . I felt like I was being taken advantage of. We were professionals sent on a wild goose chase using a half-baked plan for political reasons.[76]

Wood observes, "This betrayal of trust is the most basic violation of our sense of right and wrong and can carve a jagged moral wound deep in the soul. Betrayal sours into cold fury and a bitterness that veterans know civilians find hard to understand. Betrayal corrodes their ability to trust again, extending the moral injury through families and colleagues and impairing participation in civic life."[77] The stakes could not be higher.

Not only young lieutenants like Brandon Friedman express a sense of betrayal regarding deployment to Iraq. Lieutenant General James M. Dubik, PhD, US Army (retired), now a senior fellow at the Institute for the Study of War, confesses,

75. Wood, *What Have We Done*, 175.
76. Wood, *What Have We Done*, 177.
77. Wood, *What Have We Done*, 176.

War sometimes involves sacrifices made in vain. Losing a battle or engagement, fighting a battle that is unconnected to a larger purpose, [risking] being killed or maimed in an unjust, or imprudent, or unnecessary battle or war—any of these can give rise to a sense of betrayal. From any one can emerge a sense of having one's life used for no good purpose. Any one of these can give birth to a sense of being suckered into losing or risking the most precious thing a human being has—his or her life—*or worse*: being suckered into ending someone else's life for no good reason. This kind of smoldering resentment illuminates a deep moral truth: each of us—even our enemies—is a human being, not an object. As human beings, each of us has moral worth beyond our instrumental utility to a task or to society. Demanding that a soldier risks his or her life for no good reason is to treat that soldier as an object, not a human being. This is, perhaps, *the ultimate moral injury.*[78]

We will address the question of legitimate authority in the last chapter. Here it is enough to acknowledge that warriors themselves have told us that sending them to fight in an unjust war gives rise to a profound sense of betrayal, perhaps even the ultimate moral injury.

The summary word in this chapter on moral injury and unjust war goes to Jeff McMahan:

> The alternative to granting rights of selective conscientious objection is to force soldiers to bear an unfair share of the burden of national security. They are already asked to bear the physical risks of combat. And they bear the moral risk of inadvertently engaging in gravely immoral action, which in turn increases the risk of profound psychological damage if they survive the war.[79]

What we do to our warriors and their consciences by sending them into "an unjust, or imprudent, or unnecessary" war should be on the conscience of every citizen. It certainly was on the mind of Saint Augustine, whose "wise judge" suffers something very like moral injury. That's the focus of the Excursus to follow.

78. Dubik, "Foreword," xv; emphasis added.
79. McMahon, "Foreword," xvi.

Excursus

"Lord, Deliver Me from My Necessities!"

Augustine's "Dark Parable" on judicial torture and Lt. Col. Bill Edmonds, *God Is Not Here: Torture, Trauma, and the Moral Injuries of War* (2015)

FORCED TO USE FORCE

In *The Early Fathers on War and Military Service*, Louis J. Swift[80] observes that "In all of Augustine's comments on war and peace these words are, perhaps, his most succinct statement of the problem":[81]

> They tell us, however, that the wise man will wage just wars. As if the wise man, when he recalls his own human limitation, will not all the more decry the fact that he was forced to do so. For, unless the wars were just, he would not have to wage them, and in such circumstances he would not be involved in war at all. It is the other side's wrongdoing that compels the wise man to wage just wars, and even if that wrongdoing gave rise to no unavoidable conflicts, it should cause man sorrow because man is responsible for it. . .

The wise man is forced to wage just war in response to another's injustice, and this causes the painful emotion of sorrow.

Swift almost immediately goes on to say that "It is along these same lines that Augustine justifies a Christian's serving as a judge in the criminal courts even though such a position entails acts of violence that are objectively wrong."[82] Then follows what can be thought of as Augustine's "dark parable" of the wise judge:[83]

---

80. Swift, *Early Fathers*, 116.
81. *City of God*, 19.7, in Swift, *Early Fathers*, 116; my emphases.
82. Swift, *Early Fathers*, 117.
83. *City of God* 19.6, in Swift, *Early Fathers*, 117–118; my emphases.

Amidst all these dark corners of public life in society will the wise man sit as judge or not? Undoubtedly he will. For society, which he considers it truly immoral to cut himself off from, constrains him and forces him to fulfill this obligation. He does not consider it a sin, that innocent witnesses are subjected to torture in someone else's trial, or that the accused who are tortured despite their innocence frequently give in to the pain and, after making false confessions, are punished in spite of their innocence; or that they often expire under torture or as a result of it even without even being condemned to death; or that the accusers themselves are condemned by a judge who does not know the facts when the charges they bring—perhaps from a desire to serve society and punish crime—are true but cannot be substantiated in the face of false witnesses and a defendant who fiercely resists torture and makes no confession. All these horrible things the wise judge does not consider sins inasmuch as he does them not out of desire to do harm but because of unavoidable ignorance and a judgment that he cannot shirk because society requires it of him. This is the kind of misery in the human condition that I am talking about even though no evil intent is involved. If the wise man's inescapable ignorance and the necessity of passing judgment forces him to torture and punish innocent men, is it not enough that he be considered guiltless without needing to be happy as well? On the contrary, how much more sensitive and more in tune with his humanity is it for him to recognize the misery involved in that necessity, to loathe it in himself, and, if he is reverent and wise, to cry to God, 'Deliver me from my necessities' (*Psalm* 25:17).

As the eminent Augustine scholar R. A. Markus points out, "the parable of the conscientious judge. . .immediately precedes the longest discussion of war in the *City of God*." He observes that "no political thinker, not even excepting Hobbes, has ever given a more powerful or more disturbing description of the contradictions inherent in human society."[84] Markus sums up Augustine's general perspective thusly: "The quest for justice and order is doomed; but dedication to the impossible task is demanded by the very precariousness of civilized order in the world."[85] Or, as Swift puts it, "it is hard to overemphasize the importance of Original Sin in the bishop's

---

84. Markus, "Saint Augustine's Views," 10.
85. Markus, "Saint Augustine's Views," 10.

thinking."[86] That is the conflicted worldview in which Augustine takes up the question of war.[87]

DISTRESS OR NECESSITIES?

This dark parable presents two issues to be addressed before considering its relevance to this book and its focus on war and conscience and thereby on combat-induced moral injury. One issue is textual: Augustine's translation of Psalm 25:17; and one contextual: the function and nature of the torture used in Roman courts at the time of Augustine's writing in the early fifth century.

Both the New Revised Standard Version and the New American Bible render Psalm 25:17 as "Relieve the troubles of my heart, and bring me out of my distress." Nothing in the Psalm as a whole or in verses 16–20, the immediate context of verse 17, suggests the particular kind of troubles and distress that Augustine captures with "necessities," as embodied in the parable with its litany of unavoidable conflicts, judgment that cannot be shirked, tasks required by society, inescapable ignorance—all of which force the judge, as a matter of conscience, to preside over horrible acts. But this only suggests what is to be found in the original Hebrew, to which Augustine would have had only indirect access through whatever ancient Latin translation he was using. As to the Hebrew, my former colleague at Creighton University, Dr. Nicolae Roddy, a specialist in the Hebrew Bible, informed me that "The word in question is *tsaroth*, plural of *tsarah*, which according to the leading Hebrew lexicon, Brown-Driver-Briggs (p. 865), means trouble, distress, straits (as in dire straits). Other psalms in which the word (or some form of it) appears include Psalms 9:10; 10:1; 20:2; 22:12; 25:22; 31:8; 34:7; 34:18; 37:39; 46:2; 50:15; 54:9; 71:20; 77:3; 78:49; 81:8; 86:7; 91:15; 116:3; 120:1; 138:7; 142:3; and 143:11."[88] In all but two

---

86. Swift, *Early Fathers*, 111.

87. For a recent comprehensive analysis, see Wynn, *Augustine On War*. Wynn makes his own the quoted statement of Peter Haggenmacher: "We do not doubt that the work of St. Augustine includes many reflections on war, or that the work demonstrates its familiarity with the Roman notion of just war, nor finally that his work will be decisive for the creation of the [Christian] doctrine of just war. Rather, we only dispute that his work actually contained this doctrine" (31.) Still, it seems to the present author that one can legitimately, if carefully, refer to Augustine, as is often done, as the "father" of the Christian just-war tradition—if one remembers that fathers do not on their own produce progeny.

88. Nicolae Roddy, personal correspondence, February 18, 2019. Dr. Roddy added,

of these twenty-three instances, the NAB renders *tsaroth* as "distress" and never as "necessities."

What about the Latin translations at Augustine's disposal? "He mostly used what is termed the *Vetus Latina*, . . . old Latin translations from the Greek text, which were used in the Western world before—very slowly—what would be called the Vulgate translation by St. Jerome took precedence. Only very gradually did Augustine start to make greater use of Jerome's translations from the Hebrew found in the Vulgate."[89] Assuming Augustine might have referred to it in this case, how does Jerome's translation render Psalm 25:17? Again, I defer to Professor Roddy: "I am sure Augustine would have used an old Latin version based on the Greek (likely the LXX [Septuagint] by that time) and not the Greek directly. The Vulgate translation is: "tribulationes cordis mei multiplicatae sunt de necessitatibus meis erue me" (24:17, which follows the LXX number; 25:17 in the Masoretic Text). I am aware that Jerome had the Greek and Hebrew texts at his disposal and used whichever text suited him in the moment. For example, in Genesis 3:16, he translates the Hebrew "conceptions" in place of the traditional "childbearing"; yet opts for the LXX's "submission" (to the husband) instead of the Hebrew term *teshuqa* (amorous desire), which would probably be a scary thought for him."[90]

I conclude that Augustine was most likely quoting Jerome's Latin (or some other Latin version) which was based on the Hebrew (*tsaroth*), but more tellingly on the LXX Greek (*necessitatibus*), and that his use of "necessities" (as in Swift's English translation) is therefore perfectly legitimate, even if that is not the most obvious translation of the Hebrew *tsaroth as* "distress," as in modern English translations. The crucial point is that "necessities" fits Augustine's argument and perspective precisely, in a way that "distress" does not.

---

charmingly, "Keep in mind that a wide range of English synonyms can be derived from a single Hebrew word. Case in point, the word *issabon*, (Gen 3:16), in the famous pain in childbirth passage, can also mean trouble, toil, and distress, as well as physical pain. On that basis, the Blessed Augustine could probably justify necessities, but I would go with troubles."

89. "Augustine's Bible." Another Creighton colleague, Dr. John O'Keefe, a patristics scholar, affirmed the essential correctness of this short unsigned article; personal correspondence, February 18, 2019.

90. Personal correspondence, February 20, 2019.

THE RACK, ETCETERA

What about the specific necessity of the torture of innocent persons forced upon the wise judge that is not sinful but yet a horrible thing? According to Edward Peters in his landmark book, *Torture*,[91]

> Although they had some misgivings about the legitimacy of torture, the Romans also had few misgivings about its effect upon human beings. Between the second and fifth centuries, they expanded and developed a method of investigation about whose reliability they had few illusions. Instead of questioning the method, they surrounded it with a jurisprudence that was designed to give greater assurance to its reliability, a jurisprudence that is admirable in its skepticism and unsettling in its logic.

Apparently, Augustine's wise judge was a typical figure of his time, when skepticism about the legitimacy of torture did not necessarily undermine reliance on its assumed public utility.[92]

Peters goes on the describe the actual methods of Roman judicial torture:

> The standard means of torture . . . was the rack, a wooden frame set on trestles in which the victim was placed with hands and feet fastened in such a way that the joints could be distended by the operation of a complex system of weights and ropes. Such distension of the joints and muscles was the aim of related tortures such as the *lignum*, two pieces of wood that pulled the legs apart. A torture that seems to have been derived from capital punishment was that of the *ungulae*, hooks that lacerated the flesh. Torture with red-hot metal, flogging, close constriction of the body in confinement (the *mala mansio*, or 'evil house') . . . constituted additional forms of torture . . . The jurist Callistratus . . . lists 'castigation with rods, scourging, and blows with chains' . . . The Romans prohibited poisoning and strangling, and they reserved crucifixion for slaves and particularly despicable criminals.

Augustine gives no hint of what method or methods of torture his wise judge, presumably a Christian, might be contemplating, but it is ironic that "the historians and the Christian apologists offer . . . detailed accounts of Roman penal practices, including torture [as used against Christians

91. Peters, *Torture*, 35.
92. Peters, *Torture*, 35.

pre-Constantine and thus presumably known to Augustine]. Lactantius' *On the Deaths of the Persecutors* and Eusebius' *History of the Church* offer amazing detail of both formal and informal torments inflicted upon Christians, including all of those mentioned above."[93] Peters concludes by observing that "skepticism about the reliability of evidence gained from torture pales as a moderating element in a society which knew of no way procedurally to avoid torture and therefore was inevitably committed to its excesses."[94] This sums up the "necessities" of Augustine's wise judge precisely.

MAN COME OF AGE

John Langan has pointed out that two elements of Augustine's just-war theory, "a search for authorization for the use of violence" and a "passive attitude to authority and social change,"[95] "both involve a denial of the active role of the responsible citizen in shaping defense policy and in making decisions about the use of force."[96] In assessing the value of Augustine's position for contemporary appropriation, Langan argues that such a position may lack contemporary resonance because it "attempts to export responsibility for the violence to higher powers (human or divine) and . . . does this in a way that does not conform to an awareness of 'man come of age' and . . . is at odds with conceptions of human agency and moral responsibility that are found in contemporary western cultures and in various liberation movements."[97] He concludes with rhetorical flourish: "This is one issue where one could line up Jefferson, Kant, Freud, and Marx along with Bonhoeffer, the Niebuhrs, Vatican II, and Gutierrez in united opposition to Augustine."[98] A modern wise judge may find herself making Augustine's pleading lament her own, "Lord, deliver me from Augustine's necessities."

93. Peters, *Torture*, 36.

94. Peters, *Torture*, 36.

95. Langan, "The Elements," 19.

96. Langan, "The Elements," 34. The final chapter of this book takes up the question of legitimate authority in more depth.

97. Langan, "The Elements," 34.

98. Langan, "The Elements," 34.

FROM ANCIENT ROME TO MODERN IRAQ

That indeed may be the disposition of Lieutenant Colonel Bill Edmonds, whose book *God Is Not Here: A Soldier's Struggle with Torture, Trauma, and the Moral Injuries of War* (2015) can be read as a contemporary dark parable not unlike that of Augustine's wise judge. The difference is not only fifteen centuries, rather that this book-length memoir is not hypothetical but all too real, and the protagonist is not a judge presiding over orderly public proceedings in which others do the actual work of torture, but an "enhanced interrogator" himself, serving in the chaos of the war in faraway Iraq. In either case, it is not clear that the overall enterprise can be credibly described as just. Another significant difference is that Augustine's referent is sin, while Lt. Col. Edmonds' referent is moral injury.[99] While for Augustine such socially responsible action as carried out by the wise judge may not be sinful, it may nonetheless, for Edmonds, cause moral injury, not just a painful emotion but a long-term disability (disintegration of character or moral integrity) with symptoms similar to post traumatic stress disorder.

It will be instructive to explore how "*Torture, Trauma, and the Moral Injuries of War*" challenge the sinlessness Augustine imputes to his parabolic figure of the judge. As Peters remarks, in reference to the reappearance of torture in post-Enlightenment times at the hands of French military forces in response to the Algerian independence uprising of the mid-1950s, "I have received enough confidences in Algeria and in France, to know into what injuries, perhaps irreparable, torture can lead the human conscience. Many young men have 'taken up the game' and have thereby passed from mental health and stability into terrifying states of decay, from which some will probably never recover."[100] Or, as Peters admirably sums it up, "if the victim is conceived to be without human dignity and therefore vulnerable to torture, the torturer also divests himself of human dignity."[101]

As described by Bill Nash, former director of Combat and Operational Stress Control programs for the U.S. Marines, in his Introduction to *God Is Not Here*, Lt. Col. Edmonds is "a special operations officer: an elite warrior in the mold of an ancient champion or medieval chivalric knight, to whom the word 'hero' must retain some of its original Greek meaning of

---

99. For an insightful analysis of how Augustine's conception of sin enhances contemporary understandings of combat-induced moral injury, see Powers, "Moral injury and original sin."

100. Edmonds, *God Is Not Here*, 179.

101. Edmonds, *God Is Not Here*, 187.

'protector.' The author was an apple that didn't fall far from the tree planted by his Peace Corps parents. He volunteered to go to Iraq because *he wanted to do good* . . . the job he was assigned was [putatively] to prevent torture in a Kurdish/Iraqi jail and interrogation center in Mosul."[102] But as pointed out by Thomas Ricks, Pulitzer Prize-winning author of two books about the Iraq war, in his foreword to *God Is Not Here*, "If the Army in some perverse experiment had consciously wanted to try to traumatize one of its officers, it could not have done a more effective job than it did on Edmonds."[103] As a result, according to Nash, "the author's trust in his own moral values—and his belief in the rightness of what his nation had sent him to the other side of the world to do—was slowly eroded, day by amazing day, by moral dilemmas that he was poorly prepared to meet."[104] Decisions about whether to use torture "to do good" lead to trauma, and thus to moral injury.

HORRIBLE CHOICES

In his preface, Edmonds writes that "Memories from war never fade. If left alone, they come alive to seep and reach through time with searching and grasping claws. Ignored, they consume, just as they consume me now. So how do I make this right? By rethinking every thought, every word, every choice, and then finally accepting that **I'm a good person forced to make many horrible choices**."[105] Here Edmonds nearly replicates the language and perspective of Augustine's wise judge. Sometimes it seems clear that the subject of Edmonds's interrogation has indeed committed horrible crimes (as was no doubt true of some defendants brought before an actual Roman court), as when a prisoner named Shoeib makes this confession:[106]

> "I have done ten operations . . . . Cutting off heads, or killing them by a bullet to the head . . . Six times I was told to do the killing myself." . . .
> "But who were these people you killed?"
> "I don't know. I am not told the names of the people."
> "So why then did you do this?"
> "I was paid fifty dollars."

102. Edmonds, *God Is Not Here*, 15.

103. Edmonds, *God Is Not Here*, 2.

104. Edmonds, *God Is Not Here*, 16.

105. Edmonds, *God Is Not Here*, 19; my emphasis.

106. Edmonds, *God Is Not Here*, 27.

Edmonds reports that "Shoeib starts to cry and then he raises his hands above his head and wails, 'Wa-Allah, Wa-Allah!' and from only a few feet away I feel the shimmers of evil come off this man, this same man who dares to sit here and plead for God's help. Well, **God is not here.**"[107] To this confession and prayer Edmonds replies (in his memory of the event years later), "Tonight, for the first time in my life, I passionately, fervently want to kill another human being . . . God, I want to hurt, to kill this man who takes innocent life and then pleads for our mercy. God, I desperately want to give in, to forget about such things as wrong and right . . . I become a man I no longer recognize. I've lost myself."[108] However much Edmonds's basic intentions are good, here he confesses to what Augustine argues "rightly deserves censure in war . . . the desire to do harm, cruel vengeance, a disposition that remains unappeased and implacable, a savage spirit of rebellion, a lust for domination [the famous *libido dominandi*] and other such things."[109]

As damaging to his self-image as such an incident is for Edmonds, equally troubling is the following realization, echoing the situation of the wise judge who knows he is presiding over the torture and killing of the innocent:[110]

> I give advice on the rule of law in a lawless society. I try to instill morality in a place devoid of human decency. I struggle with this role as I sit in these small cells and feel these evil men consume me. I want to hurt them, and that makes me afraid. I understand that there is a possibility that some of them are actually innocent. . . .In

107. Edmonds, *God Is Not Here*, 27–28; my emphasis.

108. Edmonds, *God Is Not Here*, 29.

109. *Against Faustus* 22.74, in Swift, *Early Fathers*, 120. Augustine's *libido dominandi* seems to align closely with many of the characteristics of the berserk state as described in Shay, *Achilles in Vietnam*, 82 (and with Edmonds's description of his reaction to Shoeib's brutality): "Beastlike / Godlike / Socially disconnected / Crazy, mad, insane / Enraged / Cruel, without restraint or discrimination / Insatiable / Devoid of fear / Inattentive to own safety / Distractible / Indiscriminate / Reckless, feeling invulnerable / Exalted, intoxicated, frenzied / Cold, indifferent / Insensible to pain / Suspicious of friends." Shay's comments are instructive: "After Pátroklos's death, Achilles—to use the words of our veterans—'lost it.' When a veteran says he 'lost it,' what did he lose? What did Achilles lose? I believe that the veterans and Homer shared similar views of this subject. In the veterans' own words, they lost their humanity. Beast-god and god-beast replaced human identity." Edmonds writes that in his reaction to Shoeib "I've lost myself." Augustine suggests something similar when he observes that a man who does not feel sorrow at his "necessities" is not in tune with his humanity.

110. Edmonds, *God Is Not Here*, 126, my emphasis.

a counterinsurgency the innocent always become entangled in the net made for sharks. . .I don't want this power over life: it is real and forever. I'm conflicted; but I still have a duty, and my weakness doesn't absolve me of a horrible responsibility."

Five years later, in a counselor's office in Germany, Edmonds reports on the previously latent effects of his experience in Iraq now made manifest: *"There are too many things happening to me, too many things going wrong, and I'm scared . . . I no longer have an appetite. I've lost over fifteen pounds and I'm not trying. I barely eat anything at all, yet I still feel filled with energy. I'm not sleeping . . . And when I do wake up I don't feel tired. I feel full of energy and excited until suddenly, sometime later in the day, I slump down exhausted . . . Then there are the headaches, intense headaches that come on so suddenly and from nowhere."*[111] Also, as reported by many warriors suffering from moral injury, "There are flashbacks: the constant flood of memories when I'm both asleep and awake."[112]

Edmonds finally confesses to the counselor, "I've started to imagine doing something really, really stupid, like jumping off a cliff or driving the car off the side of the road . . . It's a satisfying feeling and it reminds me of how I felt in Iraq, how it felt to stand up in the turret, with my head exposed, with death all around. Does he [the counselor] realize that dying is addictive?"[113] Edmonds doesn't "have the words to describe that inner fight, how my many selves struggled to navigate a year-long moral mine-field. How every day I was forced to make a choice—do I torture another human being or not—and how every day, over and over again, no matter the decision, I made a soul-crushing wrong choice."[114] He concludes his recollection of this first counseling session with these words: *"for the last thirty days . . . I've been in a fight to the life. And I'm losing. I have a family I desperately love. Can you help?"*[115]

Edmonds discovers his best help is his own writing. Toward the end of his book he reflects yet again on the situation he faced daily in Iraq: "I am overwhelmed by the atrocity and the inhumanity of these killers and here, in these cells, I have the power to stop them. And I'm morally wrong when I do, and when I don't. I now realize that I am just trying to use logic

111. Edmonds, *God Is Not Here*, 30.

112. Edmonds, *God Is Not Here*, 31.

113. Edmonds, *God Is Not Here*, 32.

114. Edmonds, *God Is Not Here*, 32, my emphasis.

115. Edmonds, *God Is Not Here*, 32–33.

to convince myself that wrong is right, that black is white, and that torture is justified . . . But God damn it! I know that this is bullshit, because I've *seen* and I *know* how torture is always the immoral choice."[116] Yet, despite this seemingly certain moral clarity, he must ask, "If I am right, if I am a good person, why do I constantly feel such guilt and shame for the things I don't do? Why do I feel weak for all of my choices? I have the power to make a difference. So why don't I? Every day another killer is let loose, and then the day becomes just another day where I've taken innocent life."[117] Or he comes at his dilemma not as omission but as commission: "I tell myself I saved lives. But at what cost? Do the ends justify becoming a monster?"[118] "But I have faith, I always have faith that things will get better . . . So I will write my way through this. And even now I can sense a faint and distant light up ahead. An exit? I hope so. It's been a long and lonely journey— tangled, rough, and savage. God, I want to arrive."[119] *Lord, deliver me from my necessities.*

THE EVILS OF WAR

With Lt. Col. Edmonds's testimony of moral injury in mind, we should revisit Augustine and his wise judge. Our guide will be Kevin Carnahan in his article "Perturbations of the Soul and Pains of the Body: Augustine on Evil Suffered and Done in War." Carnahan builds on R. A. Markus's influential work on Augustine's political thought, *Saeculum: History and Society in St. Augustine's Theology*, and especially his article on "Saint Augustine's Views on the 'Just War,'" by emphasizing that while Markus is correct to argue that Augustine's normative approach to war was consistent over his lifetime, his understanding of the evils of war changed significantly. Central to Carnahan's analysis is seeing Augustine's thought in three stages, with *De libero arbitrio, Contra Faustum, and De civitate Dei* representing early, middle, and late stages, respectively. As our interest is in the parable of the wise judge, which appears in *City of God*, we will focus on Carnahan's commentary on it, setting the baseline, as it were, with summaries of the two earlier stages: [120]

116. Edmonds, *God Is Not Here*, 252.

117. Edmonds, *God Is Not Here*, 267.

118. Edmonds, *God Is Not Here*, 270.

119. Edmonds, *God Is Not Here*, 280.

120. Carnahan, "Perturbations," 272. Carnahan observes that "in the last years of

In the first stage, Augustine's perspective is heavily influenced by the Stoic and Neoplatonic arguments that have allowed him to break from his earlier Manichaeism. These sources underwrite an overly detached view of evil suffered in war, a view that would ultimately be rejected in Augustine's mature thought. In the second stage of Augustine's thought, he develops a richer sense of the ways in which evil suffered in history intrudes upon the self, but the context of his argument prevents him from bringing this sense of human fragility to full force in his treatment of war. The final stage of Augustine's work is developed as a direct rejection of the Stoic detachment that marked his earlier work on the subject. Here Augustine shows that he has come to experience and appreciate the full horror of war, and this experience finds expression in the emphasis he now places on the need to avoid the suffering of war if possible.

The movement to Augustine's final stage is provoked particularly by "the major political event that shakes the ground of the ancient world in CE 410: the sacking of Christian Rome."[121] At the same time, Augustine is "fashioning new ways of talking about worldly goods that avoids raising them to the level of spiritual goods but recognize their worth in the world . . . He even suggests at this point that these worldly goods are so valuable as to be worthy of defense."[122] Even as Augustine's political world is falling apart, he is developing new appreciation for the values to be found in this contingent and fallen human condition. Carnahan points out that "Much of book three of *De civitate Dei* recounts the wars of the Roman Empire. Again and again, Augustine laments the horrible loss of life that has occurred in these wars."[123] In *Contra Faustum* of his middle period, Augustine had famously dismissed killing as the main problem in war:[124]

> What is it about war, after all, that is blameworthy? Is it that people who will someday die anyway are killed in order that the victors might live in peace? That kind of objection is appropriate to a

his life, Augustine formulates his own statement of the requirement of last resort in recourse to war. As Augustine would write to Darius . . . , 'Great glory is due to warriors' who pacify the provinces. 'However, greater glory still is merited by killing no men with swords, but war with words, and by acquiring or achieving peace not through war but through peace itself'" (290).

121. Carnahan, "Perturbations," 284.

122. Carnahan, "Perturbations," 285

123. Carnahan, "Perturbations," 287.

124. *Against Faustus* 22.74, in Swift, *Early Fathers*, 120.

timid man, not a religious one. What rightly deserves censure in war is the desire to do harm, cruel vengeance, a disposition that remains unappeased and implacable, a savage spirit of rebellion, a lust for domination [*libido dominandi*] and other such things.

As Carnahan observes, "For the mature Augustine, the evils suffered in war are real evils. The loss of life and community that wars entail are real harms."[125] I doubt that the saint would think himself any less religious for coming to such a conclusion. And perhaps not timid either, but less confident of understanding the place of evil in God's world.

BURDENED VIRTUE

With this general background set, Carnahan makes several points about the parable of the wise judge. "First, the torture and death of the innocent are 'serious evils' in Augustine's view here, even if they have not been brought about by ill intent on the part of the judge . . . The judge is freed from wickedness in this case, but he is not cut off from **the suffering that attaches itself to the person** by virtue of the very situation where he must choose whether the other lives or dies without full knowledge of the full justice of his act."[126] The judge is not wicked in intent, the interrogator volunteered to deploy to Iraq to do good, but both suffer from doing their duty with its inherently flawed reliance on torture. The suffering of the victims of torture attaches itself to them.

As contemporary philosopher Lisa Tessman puts it in her book *Burdened Virtues*: "some of the virtues that conditions of oppression intensify the need for—including the disposition to be sensitive and attentive to others' suffering—have a structure that is atypical for an Aristotelian virtue, that is, they are intrinsically painful . . ."[127] Perhaps Tessman was not thinking of an ancient Roman courtroom or a modern wartime interrogation center when speaking of oppression, but surely the term applies to the experience of the judge and of the interrogator. As wise and intending only good, no doubt both have a "disposition to be sensitive and attentive to others' suffering," and obviously they find their experience "intrinsically painful." As Augustine said at the end of his dark parable, "how much more

---

125. Carnahan, "Perturbations," 287–288.
126. Carnahan, "Perturbations," 289, my emphasis.
127. Tessman, *Burdened Virtues*, 95.

sensitive and more in tune with his humanity is it for him to recognize the misery involved in that necessity, to loathe it in himself, and, if he is reverent and wise, to cry to God."

In Augustine's final years, in Carnahan's incisive commentary, "Evil suffered penetrates the person who is forced to make decisions under the conditions of sin. This evil erodes the extent to which we can speak of any person who must make such decisions as living a good life . . . there is no secure refuge even in the intent of the participant."[128] Lt. Col. Edmonds struggles to believe himself a good person and not a monster, but "It's been a long and lonely journey—tangled, rough, and savage. God, I want to arrive."[129]

The wise man wages only just wars, for fighting in unjust wars causes moral injury to the warriors themselves. But even in a necessary war (or courtroom), even for a warrior (or judge) who would be just, there is no certain refuge from evil. *Lord, deliver me from my necessities*, from the horrible choices imposed on my conscience at the rough edges of social order. Lord, from this loathsome misery, from this moral injury, *deliver me!*[130]

---

128. Carnahan, "Perturbations," 290–291.

129. Edmonds, *God Is Not Here*, 280.

130. For a survey of how four major figures in the just-war tradition have addressed the "uneasy conscience" of warriors even in a just war, see chapter 6, "The Modern Rationale," in Bernard J. Verkamp, *The Moral Treatment of Returning Warriors in Early Medieval and Modern Times*, Scranton: University of Scranton Press, 2006 (originally published 1993), 77–92. The authors treated are Reinhold Niebuhr, James F. Childress, Paul Ramsey, and Michael Walzer. Should a just warrior feel regret or remorse for the necessary killing he has caused in a justifiable war? Should he feel sorrow or guilt? It seems to me that Augustine points to a third alternative, one that Verkamp himself addresses in a previous chapter when he distinguishes between guilt and shame: "Whereas guilt is aroused by the transgression of boundaries set by the conscience . . . , shame occurs when an idealized goal is not reached . . ." (23). Augustine does not use the term, but perhaps shame comes closer to categorizing the loathsome misery his wise judge experiences than does regret for misfortune or remorse for wrongdoing. The human condition itself, as symbolized in Augustine's dark parable with its dreadful necessities, fallen from grace and struggling toward redemption, suggests an idealized goal not reached. Especially as observed by a loving God, a religious person can only feel ashamed. Verkamp himself gathers the following names for this experience in a later chapter: "'metaphysical guilt' [J. Glen Gray], 'the wound in the order of being' [Martin Buber], 'the world's pain' [Peter Marin], 'surd evil' [Robert J. Lifton],' or in more traditional religious terms, 'the original sin of the world' [William P. Mahedy]" (page 98). For an analysis of the many forms of shame, see Bergman, "Journey into Shame"

5

Preventing Unjust War
The Role of the Catholic Church[1]

The application of the [just-war] criteria is not serious if the discerning of limits is left to the integrity of individual impulse and heroic conscientiousness. Resistance to unjust orders or selective objection will fall apart under divide-and-conquer pressures of the authorities if the discernment and the refusal to serve are not concerted. That demands agencies of shared decision.

—John Howard Yoder[2]

THIS CHAPTER REHEARSES PHILOSOPHER Jeff McMahan's proposal for preventing unjust war by the establishment of an *ad bellum* world court, composed of a diversity of experts united by a commitment to the just-war tradition as McMahan and others have recently begun to revise it. Central to this argument is a critique of Michael Walzer's "moral equivalence" of soldiers on the just and unjust sides of a war, or what McMahan calls the doctrine of "Permissibility of Participation." Finally, the chapter proposes how the Catholic Church, its doctrine of the primacy of conscience placed squarely within its just-war teaching, might contribute to a global ethic of

1. This chapter first appeared in the forum "Ethics in Focus: Special Issue on The Future of Just War Theory in Catholic Social Thought" in the journal *Expositions: Interdisciplinary Studies in the Humanities*.

2. Yoder, *When War Is Unjust*, 126.

selective conscientious objection, the right—even duty—of solders to refuse to participate in unjust wars.

POSING THE QUESTION

How might the just-war tradition be made more robust and stringent in its
implementation so that last resort becomes ever more remote? According
to the statement of the Rome conference referred to in the Introduction,
"there is no 'just war.' Too often the 'just war theory' has been used to endorse rather than prevent or limit war. Suggesting that a 'just war' is possible
also undermines the moral imperative to develop tools and capacities for
nonviolent transformation of conflict."[3] I take a different perspective. The
first part of my thesis is that the problem is not the just-war tradition; *the
problem is the unjust-war tradition*, the propensity of nations to engage in
aggression, oftentimes rationalizing it by specious use of just-war language,
which may justify a war by other nations to defend human life and human
rights against such aggression. Every war is unjust on at least one side. But
not all sides are always unjust. How might the just-war tradition contribute
meaningfully to preventing, and not only responding militarily to, unjust
war once it has begun? I confess, I do not know that it ever has. But perhaps
this is a new moment.

My argument proceeds in two stages. First, I present in summary
fashion the argument of philosopher Jeff McMahan of Oxford University,
who in his book *Killing in War*, published in 2009, has provided the most
substantial alternative to Michael Walzer's famous and seminal book on
the just-war convention, as he calls it, first published in 1977. According to
the editors of a book of essays titled *Reading Walzer*, McMahan is "unques-
tionably the most influential critic of the tradition represented in Walzer's
Just and Unjust Wars."[4] McMahan's essay "The Prevention of Unjust Wars"
of 2014 is my principal source. Second, I apply McMahan's ideas to the
Catholic Church, an application that McMahan himself does not envision,
as he writes as a secular philosopher. But I do not propose that the Catholic
Church could or should be *solely* responsible for implementing McMahan's
proposal, but rather that it can play a significant role in developing a practical global ethic against unjust war, and in so doing, provide much-needed
guidance especially to Catholics in the military, and even to Catholics in

3. Pax Christi, "Appeal."

4. Benbaji and Sussman, *Reading Walzer*, 229.

government, faced with making decisions about going to war (*jus ad bellum*). And of course to ordinary citizens, Catholics especially, but others of good will as well.

THE DOCTRINE OF PERMISSIBILITY OF PARTICIPATION

McMahan's argument itself proceeds in three major steps. First, he outlines and critiques "the doctrine of permissibility of participation," his name for the traditional view that combatants have no personal responsibility for judging the morality of the war in which they are ordered to fight, but only to refuse to disobey illegal or immoral orders within whatever war they are participants. This, of course, leads to the curious situation in which combatants on both sides of a war, only one of which can be just, have moral equivalency, so long as they abide by the rules of war, which mainly means not targeting civilians. Combatants on both sides have the same moral right to kill combatants on the other side. McMahan puts this provocatively: "Those who accept the Permissibility of Participation . . . accept that while political leaders cannot themselves permissibly kill or order the killing of soldiers in another state who have not attacked them . . . it nevertheless becomes permissible for their solders to kill other soldiers when their leaders impermissibly order them to."[5] Simply put, an impermissible act becomes permissible when it is carried out under orders. It is possible for combatants, but not for leaders, to fight an unjust war justly. It is because he rejects this paradoxical core doctrine of the war convention, as canonically expressed by Walzer, that McMahan has become the focus for debate on this issue.[6]

I will not rehearse fully McMahan's rebuttal to critics who argue for the impracticality of his position. In brief, however, he argues that we can reject the moral doctrine of Permissibility of Participation and the moral equivalency of combatants (1) without rejecting the legal protections that all combatants should enjoy, (2) without undermining the capacity

5. McMahan, "Prevention."

6. In his classic WWII memoir *The Warriors*, first published in 1959, philosopher J. Glenn Gray anticipated McMahan's position: "To what extent is a German soldier in the last war guilty who kept himself free of personal crimes but was forced to experience, more or less directly, atrocities committed by his fellow soldiers and who was not blind to Hitler's mad ambitions? Is he not in an utterly different position from the soldier of a nation like ours who fought the war defensively to repel aggression?" (240)

of nations to field the necessary military resistance to aggression against their territory or people, and (3) without giving undue advantage to those states that do not allow for conscientious objection to particular wars by individual soldiers. At least, as McMahan says, the "risk of reduced military efficiency in just wars must be weighed against the potential benefits of a widespread rejection of the Permissibility of Participation. . . . As long as we continue to accept [this doctrine], we will deprive ourselves of *an important resource for the prevention of unjust wars: namely, the moral conscience of individuals.*"[7] That sentence succinctly articulates a second part of the thesis of this chapter, and indeed, the basic argument of this book. Crucially, unsuccessful attempts to prevent *unjust* wars by encouraging acts of personal conscientious refusal need not threaten the capacity to wage just wars in response. Conscience goes both ways.

But how is this resource to be tapped effectively, given the understandable reluctance of individuals under authority to break ranks when national survival is proclaimed to be at stake, however speciously? This brings us to the second stage of McMahan's argument, to his "practical proposal."

MCMAHAN'S PRACTICAL PROPOSAL

McMahan acknowledges that the just-war tradition needs greater clarity in its definition of what constitutes "just cause" if it is to "provide soldiers, political leaders, and the global public generally with authoritative guidance in matters of *jus ad bellum*"—the justice of going to war—or not. It is not surprising that he sees this as "a task for moral philosophers." I would add moral theologians, scholars of the Catholic just-war tradition, and will say more about this in the last chapter. "The next step," in this practical proposal, according to McMahan, "should be to codify our improved understanding of *jus ad bellum* in a body of deontic principles stating prohibitions, permissions, and perhaps requirements concerning the resort to war and the continuation of war." He believes it is possible for such principles "to lack the authority of law while nevertheless being more than merely hortatory." The third takes us to the heart of the matter: "to establish a court or court-like institution that would interpret and apply the principles to particular cases."[8]

7. McMahan, "Prevention," 238, emphasis added.
8. McMahan, "Prevention," 242.

Again, even if this court lacked legally-binding authority, its moral authority could inform public debate and influence governmental decision-making, perhaps making it harder for a government to begin or continue what the court judged an unjust war. Such a court would not have the responsibility to enforce its findings against individual combatants in a war the court judged unjust. The aim of an *ad bellum* court, rather, would be to achieve and maintain a reliable degree of independent epistemic authority and therefore of trans-national moral authority.[9]

McMahan addresses how such a court could be implemented. First, it would have to be "a congress of eminent and respected authorities [of diverse national and religious (including nonreligious) backgrounds][10] on international law and just war theory,"[11] and second, it "would have to be procedurally constrained to ensure that its judgments would be epistemically justified." It would "invite submissions from belligerents and welcome briefs from *amici curiae* [friends of the court]."[12] Judges "should be required to recuse themselves from cases involving any state to which they had close ties, such as citizenship."[13] But returning to an earlier theme, McMahan acknowledges that such a court might be unlikely to exert much direct influence on "the deliberations of government . . . but that it is possible that many soldiers could be persuaded to refuse to fight by the judgment of an *ad bellum* court that their war was unjust, particularly if the doctrine of Permissibility of Participation had been discredited in their culture."[14]

In short, "the central practical effect of the court would thus be on the consciences of individuals, including soldiers, civilians, and perhaps even a few government officials." Furthermore, McMahan speculates that "if states could anticipate that a ruling against them by the court might provoke resistance to their unjust war from their citizens and soldiers, thereby threatening their domestic legitimacy, the court could have a significant deterrent effect."[15] McMahan addresses several problems this court would face, which I mention only in brief. If asked to rule on a war in progress, or a war imminently to begin, the judges might be forced to "compromise

9. McMahan, "Prevention," 245.
10. McMahan, "Prevention," 247.
11. McMahan, "Prevention," 246.
12. McMahan, "Prevention," 247.
13. McMahan, "Prevention," 248.
14. McMahan, "Prevention," 248.
15. McMahan, "Prevention," 248.

between the values of rapidity and soundness of judgment. . . . Another problem the court would face is that it might lack access to empirical information that would be critical to its ability to evaluate a war."[16] Here's my own understatement: states have been known to misrepresent facts on the ground to justify putting boots on the ground, from the Gulf of Tonkin incident during the Vietnam War to the question of weapons of mass destruction before the 2003 invasion of Iraq.

And then there is the issue of classified information, sometimes claimed to justify entry into war on behalf of a citizenry asked to trust their political leaders in a time of alleged national crisis.[17] McMahan strikes the right note in all this, it seems to me: despite these epistemic challenges, "the important question is not whether an *ad bellum* court would be infallible, but whether its judgments could be reasonably believed to be more reliable than those of any state or individual." To buttress its epistemic authority, the court could have "its own research staff, each of whom would be a recognized specialist in the history, politics, or culture of a particular state or region," who would be "on call" to assist the court in its information gathering and analysis.[18]

McMahan also addresses some procedural matters. The court "might not issue a judgment that a war was just but only judgments of unjust or not unjust," so that the court was not perceived to become a party to any war, even one manifestly, to most informed observers, just. The court's responsibility would be to help resist unjust wars, not to promote just wars. Judgments could be issued on the strength of a simple majority vote, but a unanimous or near-unanimous vote would produce "a high degree of credence" with conscientious soldiers faced with making an extremely difficult decision. A strongly divided court would have, of course, the opposite effect.[19] With all these procedural challenges to be faced, McMahan argues, nonetheless, that "an international, impartial, and disinterested *ad bellum* court . . . would at least offer a reasonable prospect that a war satisfy not just the letter but also the substance of this traditional just war requirement."[20] However preliminary and speculative this proposal, McMahan concludes

16. McMahan, "Prevention," 249.

17. I would add that going to war is so grave a decision that its justification must be obvious and certain.

18. McMahan, "Prevention," 250.

19. McMahan, "Prevention," 252.

20. McMahan, "Prevention," 253.

that "we should agree that young people who are commanded by their rulers to risk their lives in order to kill others deserve moral guidance that we know they will not receive from those who seek to use them in this way."[21]

Retired Army Lieutenant General James M. Dubik, PhD, who was also quoted in the previous chapter, articulates compellingly what is at stake for soldiers in such a context:

> *War sometimes involves sacrifices made in vain.* Losing a battle or engagement, fighting a battle that is unconnected to a larger purpose, being killed or maimed in an unjust, or imprudent, or unnecessary battle or war—any of these can give rise to a sense of betrayal. From any one can emerge a sense of having one's life used for no good purpose. Any one of these can give birth to a sense of being suckered into losing or risking the most precious thing a human being has—his or her life—or worse: being suckered into ending someone else's life for no good reason. This kind of smoldering resentment illuminates a deep moral truth: each of us—even our enemies—is a human being, not an object. As human beings, each of us has moral worth beyond our instrumental utility to a task or to society. Demanding that a soldier risks his or her life for no good reason is to treat that soldier as an object, not a human being. This is, perhaps, the ultimate moral injury, another manifestation of war's hellishness[22]

In effect, it is to avert such "ultimate moral injury" that McMahan's proposal, and my response to it, is addressed.

THE ROLE OF THE CATHOLIC CHURCH

In this final section it remains to sketch out what contribution the Catholic Church might make in bringing to reality this proposal by Jeff McMahan for preventing unjust war—and therefore war itself. I do so in nine observations. **First,** it should be remembered that since the time of Bishop Ambrose of Milan in the late fourth century and Bishop Augustine of Hippo in the early fifth century, the Church has been the primary carrier and developer of the just-war tradition that informs McMahan's proposal, even as that tradition has been secularized in international law and in moral philosophy such as that of Walzer and McMahan. **Second,** I believe it is fair

---

21. McMahan, "Prevention," 253.
22. Dubik, "Foreword," xv; italics in original.

to say that no ethical tradition gives higher value and authority to personal conscience than does Catholicism, at least in theory. There is a straight line from the primacy of conscience as articulated by Thomas Aquinas[23] to the *Catechism of the Catholic Church*, which quotes Cardinal Newman's assertion that conscience is "the aboriginal Vicar of Christ."[24] According to Aquinas, in James Keenan's paraphrase, "it is better to die excommunicated than to violate our conscience."[25]

Third, the Church has in recent years begun the no doubt long struggle to discredit within its own culture what McMahan calls "the doctrine of Permissibility of Participation" by officially endorsing the right of selective conscientious objection, as evident in many documents of the US Bishops during and after the Vietnam War, and in the *Compendium of the Social Doctrine of the Catholic Church*, published in 2004 during the reign of John Paul II, as recounted in chapter 2. In brief, the Church's teaching on the primacy of conscience in all matters and the Church's teaching on the ethics of war have now been joined. In that chapter I did not, however, claim that this new position is being taught in Catholic parishes, schools, seminaries, or universities. I understand that such would mark a sea change in Church practice, but such a change is clearly the logical inference of the teaching itself, if that teaching is to be taken seriously.

Fourth, the Catholic Church has become truly global and is the largest religious affiliation in the world, with over a billion adherents, many of whom serve in governments and militaries on six continents. In terms of demographics and centralized authoritative teaching, the Church is positioned like no other human entity to influence world affairs around issues of war and conscience. **Fifth**, the Church has within its ranks untold numbers of experts and scholars in the various disciplines McMahan argues should comprise an *ad bellum* court of international, impartial, disinterested judges. Imagine the congress of such persons that could be assembled just from the hundreds of Catholic universities in the United States alone.

Sixth, I am not arguing, however, that a Catholic version of the world court McMahan proposes would itself instantiate fully what he has in mind. He explicitly calls for a court made up of diverse perspectives, religious

23. See chapter 3.

24. *The Catechism of the Catholic Church* may be found online at http://www.vatican.va/archive/ENG0015/__P5Y.HTM. The article on moral conscience is Part Three, Section One, Chapter One, Article 6.

25. Keenan, "Ten Reasons," 358.

and non-religious. Such a court would have the advantage of speaking at least potentially to all peoples, of all religions and none. If the Catholic Church were to establish its own *jus ad bellum* court, its priority would be to provide guidance to Catholics, especially those serving in the military or in governments. I see it as a matter of institutional integrity that the Church would provide such guidance especially to its young, as McMahan rightly advises cannot be expected from governments. A transnational and trans-religious court could and should still be established, along the lines of McMahan's proposal. Two courts might indeed be better than one, although the potential for disagreement and competition cannot be denied. Catholics would then have to decide which authority and which argument were most persuasive. What McMahan says about disagreement within a court would itself be edifying, if only to demonstrate the difficulty of making judgments about the justifiability of a pending or current war.

Seventh, the Church is clearly in a moment of ferment regarding the future of the just-war tradition and the practice of nonviolent peacebuilding, as suggested not only by the 2016 conference in Rome but also by the Second Vatican Council's call more than fifty years earlier "to undertake an evaluation of war with an entirely new attitude."[26] That new attitude has remained unspecified, unless it can be identified with the recent popes' increasingly skeptical perspective on the practice of war in the modern world. There has never been an encyclical on just war, nonviolence, peacebuilding, and the role of conscience, but perhaps now is the time.

Eighth, in the Dicastery for Promoting Integral Human Development (formerly the Pontifical Council on Justice and Peace), the Church has in germ the kind of *ad bellum* court McMahan calls for. Perhaps the Council does not itself take on the role of the court, but rather takes responsibility for establishing, staffing, and supervising such a court, whose judges would be drawn from all the relevant disciplines, from many countries and cultures, representing diverse political perspectives—but all united by a critical loyalty to the Catholic just-war tradition and its continuing development and real-world application.

My **final** observation is that when Franz Jägerstätter of Austria became the first officially recognized martyr of the Catholic just-war tradition, beatified by Pope Benedict XVI in 2007 as a conscientious objector to the wars of Nazi Germany, his "reference group," over against the politically compliant churches of Germany and Austria, was the church of the martyrs

26. Vatican Council II, *Gaudium et Spes*, #80.

of the early Christian centuries. His witness was indeed solitary, if not unique.[27] Perhaps the second miracle needed for his canonization could be that the Catholic Church of the twenty-first century takes the just-war tradition in relation to personal conscience as seriously as he did. To Blessed Franz's ancient church of the martyrs could be added a modern court of Catholic moral authority. To paraphrase McMahan in this new context: "we should agree that [Catholic] young people who are commanded by their rulers to risk their lives in order to kill others deserve moral guidance [from their Church] that we know they will not receive from those who seek to use them in this way."[28] This would be precisely the type of moral guidance young Germans and Austrians did not receive from their bishops and pastors in the 1930s and 1940s.

A CONCLUDING COUNTERFACTUAL NARRATIVE

To conclude, let me pose this counterfactual scenario, as a way of concretizing how a Catholic *jus ad bellum* court might play out. Shortly after the close of the Second Vatican Council (let us imagine retroactively), Pope Paul VI established a Catholic Court of War and Peace, made up of widely respected jurists and legal scholars, international affairs experts, and moral theologians, with responsibility to evaluate imminent and current wars according to the Catholic just-war tradition, which it articulated in newly robust and precise terms. Suppose that by the turn of the millennium, this Court had achieved a substantial degree of credibility in its epistemic and moral authority, as it weighed in on various wars across the globe, whether or not it had definitively prevented or halted any of them.

Suppose that in the run-up to the invasion of Iraq in March 2003 this court was empowered by the pope to publish a deeply informed judgment about the justifiability of the proposed US-led war against Saddam Hussein. Suppose further that the court issued a near-unanimous decision that such an invasion would be unjust, for all the reasons that were in fact advanced by Catholic and other just war ethicists at the time, but with the kind of credibility and global influence that not even the pope on his own, in *ad hoc* commentary, could muster. Suppose, perhaps even more boldly, that selective conscientious objection had been taught in Catholic high schools and colleges throughout the United States, as has been called for by the US

27. See chapter 1.
28. McMahan, "Prevention," 253.

bishops: "the issues of registration and conscription raise questions of the kind and quality of moral education that takes place in our [Catholic] educational system." To that end, the bishops "call upon schools and religious educators to include systematic formation of conscience on questions of war and peace in their curricula and . . . pledge the assistance of appropriate diocesan agencies in counseling any of those who face questions of military service."[29] Suppose that teachers, pastors, and parents urged Catholic men and women in uniform *not* to assume that they had no choice but to deploy as ordered, if such orders did in fact come. Suppose that public surveys revealed that a not insignificant number of Catholics, and others as well, were planning to refuse, and that they had the support of many citizens, pastors, and bishops. Would President Bush have proceeded anyway? Suppose that Catholics in the military understood that serving in an unjust war risked not only their lives and limbs, but also their moral integrity, over against "the ultimate moral injury."[30]

Theologian William T. Cavanaugh has speculated similarly:

> Let us imagine that significant numbers of Catholics in the military—not everyone, perhaps, even just 10 percent—agreed with the pope and the U.S. Conference of Catholic Bishops that this particular war is unjustifiable, and decided to sit it out. Let us imagine that significant numbers of Catholic citizens—again, not necessarily everyone—did not agree that the president's judgment was final, and found ways to protest and refuse to support the war effort. Would we be witnessing the church overstepping the boundaries of its authority, or the dangerous mixing of politics and religion? No. We would be witnessing Catholics recovering their primary loyalty to Christ from the idolatry of the nation-state. And we would be witnessing, for once, the just-war theory being used to limit violence rather than justify it.[31]

But the point, of course, is not to imagine stopping a disastrous war that has already happened. It is to stop the next unjust war. Does anyone seriously doubt that the occasion will arise? Inspired by its own newly robust moral engagement with the problem of war, the Catholic Church could make a significant contribution to world peace—by being true to its own tradition.

29. USCC, "Statement on Registration and Conscription," 2.

30. This chapter does not address the question of making selective conscientious objection a legal right but see Appendix 5.

31. Cavanaugh, "At Odds With the Pope," last paragraph.

If the Catholic Church were to implement this proposal, that would put a new focus on the consciences of millions of young people around the world, those likely to be called by their governments to fill the ranks of the military services and to fight their wars. Are they capable of exercising their moral responsibility to judge the justice of particular wars? Can an eighteen-year-old recruit or conscript be expected to weigh such complex questions intelligently and as a mature adult? In the US an eighteen-year-old can vote for the president, but can they be expected to think critically and responsibly about such world-shaking decisions as the president is entrusted to make? The next chapter responds comprehensively to that question from the perspective of psychological science.

But first, five appendices support the argument of this chapter from a variety of contexts. The thoughtful reader will have asked herself questions such as these: 1. Has any state ever brought normative values and procedures into the war-making decision, especially on the authority of religious leaders? 2. Is there any realistic chance that the Catholic Church would embrace such a proposal as described in this chapter? 3. Can a group of diverse experts be expected to come to any shared judgment on such controverted questions as the justice of particular wars? 4. Has any nation granted not only exemption from military service on grounds of conscience, usually as determined by religious affiliation to a pacifist religious tradition, but also exemption from military service in a particular war on ethical grounds? In a word, is SCO legal anywhere? 5. Could a nation permit SCO without endangering its security, and why would it essentially make civil disobedience legally possible? Each of these questions is addressed in the following appendices.

Appendices to Chapter 5

APPENDIX 1: THE *JUS FETIALES* OF ANCIENT ROME

IN AN ARTICLE PUBLISHED in *Classical Philology* in 1912, Tenney Frank observed, "Every general handbook on international law begins with a chapter describing the remarkable institution of the Roman fetial college, a semireligious, semipolitical board which from time immemorial supervised the rites peculiar to the swearing of treaties and declaration of war, and which formed as it were a court of first instance in such questions of international disputes as the proper treatment of envoys and the execution of extradition. . . . Hugo Grotius, the father of modern international law, pointed it out as a worthy example for his degenerate day."[1] Frank goes on to say, "The most noteworthy point in the practices of the fetial board is doubtless the assumption, which underlay every treaty as well as every declaration of war, that peace was the normal international status, and that war was justified only on the score of an unjust act, as, for instance, the breach of a treaty, a direct invasion, or the aiding of one's enemy."[2] Frank insists that there was nothing cynical in this "naïve assumption that tribes and states, being collections of individuals, must conduct themselves with justice and good faith, even as individuals [would do]";[3] "so far as we know, there is no act in Roman history before the opening of the first Punic war [264 BCE] which can prove that the fetial law was not honestly interpreted

1. Frank, "Import of the Fetial Institution," 335.
2. Frank, "Import of the Fetial Institution," 335.
3. Frank, "Import of the Fetial Institution," 336.

and sincerely adhered to."[4] But what was this law and how did the fetial college function?

Alan Watson, writing ninety-one years later than Frank, argues that "in the stages leading up to a Roman declaration of war, which were cast in the form of a trial process, the gods were not called upon to be witnesses, as is always claimed, but to be judges";[5] "for the Romans the gods were the International Court of Justice."[6] The *fetiales* were "one of the oldest Roman priestly sodalities . . . responsible for the proper, religious conduct of international relations," dating from "the regal period (which traditionally runs from 753 to 509 B.C.)."[7] Watson quotes at length Dionysius of Halicarnassus (flourished c. 20 BC) on "'the multitude of duties' . . . that fall within the province of these *fetiales*":

> It is their duty to take care that the Romans do not enter upon an unjust war against any city in alliance with them, and if others begin the violation of treaties against them, to go as ambassadors and first make formal demand for justice, and then, if the others refuse to comply with their demands, to sanction war. . . . Afterwards, [the chief of the *fetiales*] . . . appeared before the senate and declared that they had done everything that was ordained by the holy laws, and that, if the senators wished to vote for war, there could be no obstacle on the part of the gods. But if any of these things was omitted, neither the senate nor the people had the power to vote for war.[8]

Like Frank, Watson argues for the integrity of the *fetiale* process: "There is no asking here for the gods to favor or intercede for the Romans. There is no promise to do something in return for a favor from the gods. Rather, the call is simply to the gods to judge whose claim is just."[9]

The Romans' idea of just war had two requirements: "a formal declaration of war made in the proper way," and "a just cause of war, and the other people must have refused to make redress."[10] That is, "not only are the fetials to ensure that the war is just, the declaration itself is represented as a *last*

4. Frank, "Import of the Fetial Institution," 341.

5. Watson, *International Law*, xi.

6. Watson, *International Law*, xii.

7. Watson, *International Law*, 1.

8. Watson, *International Law*, 2.

9. Watson, *International Law*, 13.

10. Watson, *International Law*, 28.

resort."[11] Furthermore, "No individual, not even the most senior, could wage a just war without the consent of the people."[12] That democratic principle speaks to the role of the conscience of the citizen referred to in the preceding chapter and indeed throughout this book.

Watson himself comments on the contemporary relevance of such an institution and practice: "The insistence that the gods first judge a war to be just before the Romans declare it brings sharply to mind President Bush seeking United Nations' approval before the Gulf War."[13] Whatever one thinks about the justice of that war, especially its *in bello* conduct,[14] one must applaud the president for pleading his case before a world body. One can only speculate what response he might have received had he had the opportunity to make his case before a Catholic court of international experts in the just-war tradition, along the lines proposed in the previous chapter. Ancient Rome, which has contributed so much to the legal traditions of the Western world, provides a precedent, although hardly an exact model, for the international *ad bellum* court recently proposed by Jeff McMahan and adapted to the Catholic tradition in this chapter.

APPENDIX 2: AN INTERVENTION AT VATICAN COUNCIL I

John Howard Yoder calls David Urquhart (1805–77), a Scot of aristocratic background and of diplomatic experience in Turkey in the 1830s, a "Knight Errant for the Just War Tradition in the Age of Empire."[15] Although an Anglican and preferring to call it "the law of nations," Urquhart believed the just-war tradition as developed by the Catholic Church was the best hope for preventing unjust wars in his time. He was a tireless advocate for that tradition both to the public at large, especially through pamphlets, and to the Catholic hierarchy. He believed that all the traditional *ad bellum* criteria must be met before a war could be considered just and was especially concerned that the requirement of a formal declaration of war was increasingly ignored. Yoder makes a compelling case, on Urquhart's behalf, for the cogency of this position. In Yoder's summation, "An undeclared war is therefore prima facie an unjust war, a war crime, and anyone participating

11. Watson, *International Law*, 53 (my emphasis).

12. Watson, *International Law*, 29.

13. Watson, *International Law*, xii.

14. See Hersh, "Overwhelming Force"; and Palmer-Fernandez, "White Flags."

15. Yoder, *David Urquhart*, 1.

in it is committing murder."[16] Surprisingly, Urquhart's commitment to the just-war tradition and its demands on personal conscience arose from an encounter with "a Turkish soldier whose unit had refused to fight, and had surrendered their fortress to the Russians, on the moral grounds that the war in which they were engaged had not been legitimately declared according to Islamic law."[17] This encounter and commitment eventually led Urquhart to found "a lay education movement" in the form of "Committees for the Study of Foreign Affairs," which were "linked island-wide in an 'Association for the Study of Diplomatic Documents,'" which no less a public intellectual than John Stuart Mill extolled as developing "mind among the working classes."[18]

Yet more impressively, "The work of the committees reached even beyond Britain . . . [as] they asked France for help in establishing international law," specifically in the form of a "*Tribunal without whose sanction no war shall be declared*" and therefore "*involving no wound to conscience, no desecration of faith or morals.*"[19] Yoder the pacifist points out that for Urquhart this was "in no sense a gradual approximation to a principled pacifism. A people and an army assured that they will not be asked to fight unjustly will fight with undivided courage and therefore more successfully."[20] Urquhart also founded, edited, and wrote for a periodical published both in English in London and in French in Paris. Having moved for reasons of health to Catholic Savoi, not yet annexed to France,

> he began to perceive that the Roman Church might be a fitting vehicle for his concerns, for several reasons: a) . . . the Roman communion is in principle worldwide, not formally subject to the government of any one state, and should therefore offer more potential than the national churches for recovering the kind of moral objectivity that could or should transcend the interests of a particular nation. b) . . . the corpus of canon law . . . specifies that all killing is murder unless justified by civil justice or international due process. . . . c) . . . the living practice of confession and absolution . . . [o]ver the centuries . . . had been a most effective instrument of moral education. Why should that same strength

16. Yoder, *David Urquhart*, 4.
17. Yoder, *David Urquhart*, 4.
18. Yoder, *David Urquhart*, 9–10.
19. Yoder, *David Urquhart*, 10–11, emphasis added.
20. Yoder, *David Urquhart*, 11.

not now be drawn upon to retrieve the awareness of the immorality of unjust wars?[21]

Urquhart came to believe that the most effective way to regenerate "awareness of the sinfulness of unjust war . . . would be that there should exist on the world level a counterpart to his 'Foreign Affairs Committees,' namely a 'diplomatic college,' authorized by Rome in the name of world Christianity, qualified to rule on whether a given war meets the JW [just war] requirements." This, the Protestant Urquhart reasoned, "would have to issue in the refusal of absolution for all killing in unjust wars, and then in a generalized refusal of unjust orders by all communicant soldiers."[22] Apart from the disciplinary instrument of the confessional, Urquhart's proposal provides a model for what we are proposing, especially since he argued that a Catholic tribunal would prevent the wounding of conscience likely to be suffered if fighting in an unjust war.

As Yoder explains, the first Vatican Council "was for Urquhart an obvious instrument to implement his vision. . . . Pius IX . . . assured him of his support for the project . . . [and] named Monsignor (later Cardinal) Franchi as his liaison to Urquhart."[23] The proposal "enjoyed the support of the bulk of the bishops of France and Britain. The original version of the monitum [admonition or advice] was submitted in Latin, French, and English over the signatures of forty bishops, with England's Cardinal Manning at their head. It was accepted for the Council agenda. There was no significant opposition."[24] Yoder observes, "There is little reason to doubt that if the Council had not been broken off by the outbreak of the Franco-Prussian war [one more war of the kind he had hoped the church could seize the power to forbid] . . . the Council would have taken affirmative action on Urquhart's project."[25] The irony of this unhappy ending is obvious. Nonetheless, Urquhart's project lived on in his disciple Robert Monteith's book, *Discourse on the Shedding of Blood and the Laws of War*, "a fuller and still more broadly documented statement of the case for the church's pastoral obligation to condemn killing in unjust wars."[26] That book was submitted

21. Yoder, *David Urquhart*, 12–14.

22. Yoder, *David Urquhart*, 15. For a more cautious perspective on the role of the confessional in the context of unjust warfare, see Ford, "Morality," 268–69.

23. Yoder, *David Urquhart*, 15–16.

24. Yoder, *David Urquhart*, 16–17.

25. Yoder, *David Urquhart*, 18.

26. Yoder, *David Urquhart*, 19.

to and received by the Vatican in 1885, but apparently nothing came of it, although it is still in print and deserves renewed attention.[27]

The present book can be seen as an attempt to resurrect in the early twenty-first century a bold idea from the late nineteenth century, originated by a Scottish Protestant "knight errant for the just war tradition in the age of empire" who believed in the power for good of the Catholic Church regarding war and peace far more than many Catholics did then or do now. Nonetheless, it had a welcome hearing at the highest level of Church leadership.

APPENDIX 3: HOW JUST WERE AMERICA'S WARS?

A very different kind of precedent for a Catholic *jus ad bellum* court is offered by three Canadian researchers in their recent publication, "How Just Were America's War? A Survey of Experts Using a Just War Index." Dorn, Mandel, and Cross surveyed 109 "doctorate holders, university professors, chosen primarily from the membership list of the International Studies Association,"[28] asking them to rank eighteen uses of military force by the United States from 1900 forward, based on the seven criteria of the just-war tradition, as derived from the writings of two major scholars of the tradition, James Turner Johnson and Michael Walzer. A table presents the "Just War Criteria and Definitions Used in the Study."[29]

---

27. Monteith, *Discourse*. Monteith's argument is that warriors who fight on the unjust side of a war sin against the Fifth Commandment and are murderers, and cites, for example, the Catechism of the Council of Trent and Pius IX in support. He seems to be unaware of the history of the question of SCO (as outlined in chapter 2) up through Grotius, whom he otherwise cites, and yet anticipates the current debate on the moral equivalency of warriors (Walzer) or the doctrine of permissibility of participation (McMahan). As appendix 1 does, he sees the Fecial [Fetial] College of ancient Rome as a model for bringing the natural law and the Law of Nations into deliberations about war. His proposal is for a revival of the English Privy Council as a deliberative body, a "Board of Public Faith."

28. Dorn, Mandel, and Cross, "How Just," 273. Approximately 1,000 surveys were distributed; 132 were returned but 23 disqualified for various reasons. It is not indicated if these experts had previous experience with the just-war criteria.

29. Dorn, Mandel, and Cross, "How Just," 271, Table 1. Notably missing is the traditional criterion of *reasonable hope of success*, which the authors argue is "inherent in the need for a *net benefit*: a conflict waged unsuccessfully would not have a substantial *net benefit*." It is not suggested by the authors that Johnson and Walzer were asked to approve the list of criteria said to be derived from their writings.

Criterion	Meaning
Just cause	A right, fair, ethical, honorable, righteous, moral, etc., purpose or reason to apply armed force.
Right intent	The degree to which the actual motivation behind the use of force is the same as declared motivation.
Net benefit	The benefit to the intervening country, the conflict region, and the local population outweighs the costs and negative effects.
Legitimate authority	One which is legally and socially recognized under national and international law as able to authorize the use of armed force.
Last resort	Armed force is used only after all peaceful means have been exhausted.
Proportionality of means	The level of armed force is necessary and appropriate to achieve the aim and is not excessive.
Right conduct	Armed force is applied humanely in accordance with the laws of armed conflict, including the exercise of noncombatant immunity.

Although this list is not identical to the *ad bellum* and *in bello* criteria as defined in *The Challenge of Peace*, it is clearly recognizable as a generic version of the same criteria and was suitable for the purposes of the survey.

The survey asked the respondents to rank each of eighteen US conflicts, here listed chronologically from 1900 to 2009: World War I, World War II, Korean War, Vietnam War, Grenada Invasion, Lebanon Intervention, Libya Bombing, Panama Invasion, Gulf War, Iraqi No-Fly Zone, Haiti Intervention, NATO Bombing in Bosnia, Kosovo Bombing, Global War on Terror (GWOT), Operation Enduring Freedom (Afghanistan), International Security Assistance Force in Afghanistan, Iraq Invasion, and Anti-Piracy Mission near Somalia.[30] Each respondent was asked to rank each of these conflicts on a seven-point Likert Scale *overall* and on *each of the seven criteria*.[31] A Justness Score (J) and a Just War Index (JWI), respectively, were tabulated from the survey responses. A graph of these two

30. Dorn, Mandel, and Cross, "How Just," 273, Table 2. Not all 109 respondents ranked all eighteen conflicts on all seven criteria; the average number of responses ranged from 89.4 (Anti-Piracy) to 105.6 (GWOT).

31. "For example . . . they were asked, 'To what extent do you agree or disagree that the United States had *just cause* to use armed force in the following conflicts.' The possible responses ranged from -3 (strongly disagree) through 0 (neutral) to +3 (strongly agree), with intermediate levels anchored with the terms *moderately* for values of +/-2 and *slightly* for values of +/-1." Dorn, Mandel, and Cross, "How Just," 274.

measures indicates a "high degree of correspondence"[32] between the two ways of evaluating the conflicts, which one would hope for if the normative criteria were integral to the overall ranking. That suggests validity of the ranking methodology.

The authors provide fascinating analysis of the results, the specifics of which are less relevant to this book than is the process itself of asking experts to use the just-war criteria to rank various military conflicts accordingly. Would there be any agreement or even consensus among these experts on the overall scores or on any of the individual criteria for any of the conflicts? Would any of the criteria get consistently high or low rankings across the range of conflicts? Of course, we are most likely to want to know which wars scored highest and lowest (World War II and World War I, and Vietnam and Iraq 2003, respectively—no surprises there).[33] Readers can review various tables to see how each conflict was ranked on each criterion. Of particular interest in the context of this book, as explored in chapter 7, is what we learn about legitimate authority in these experts' rankings. The authors note that "conflicts ranked in the lower half lacked a UN mandate from a Security Council resolution, while those with scores in the top half almost all had such authorization, excluding wars fought before the United Nations was created [i.e., World Wars I and II]."[34] Specifically, "the 2003 Iraq Invasion was congressionally authorized but it ranked at the bottom of the list in legitimate authority. Taken together, these findings suggest that to be perceived as legitimate, entry into conflict requires authorization from a body independent of the conflict participant."[35]

A transnational court—a body independent of *all* conflict participants—as proposed by McMahan, and as adapted to the Catholic Church in chapter 5, would not judge a pending war as just, as if granting an endorsement, but would issue judgments that a pending war did not clearly pass muster according to the just war ethic. In the latter context, such a judgement would be similar to a *nihil obstat* [nothing hinders], but in the contrary [perhaps a *nonnihil obstat*, something hinders]. The point is a *nihil obstat* is not an endorsement of the book reviewed by the Catholic censor appointed by a bishop. If a war were *not* judged to be clearly unjust, it would be entirely up to individual consciences whether to support or participate

32. Dorn, Mandel, and Cross, "How Just," 274.

33. Dorn, Mandel, and Cross, "How Just," 275, Figure 1, and 276, Table 4.

34. Dorn, Mandel, and Cross, "How Just," 277.

35. Dorn, Mandel, and Cross, "How Just," 277–78.

in the war. But if a war were reviewed and found to be wanting when viewed through the lens of Catholic ethical tradition, the Catholic public (and the public at large) would at least know where the experts within the tradition stand.

The most salient difference between this "precedent" and the previous two is that the experts participating in the survey had the advantage of hindsight. They were not being asked to evaluate a pending war, the results of which (*net benefit?*) would be a matter of speculation, however well-informed and judicious, to point out only the most obvious challenge—a challenge the legitimate authorities themselves cannot avoid. But I daresay that if the experts who are members of the International Studies Association *were* to publish a judgement against a pending war, perhaps in a major newspaper, it would draw attention and provoke debate, at least among those who take expert opinion seriously. And the ISA does not have more than a billion members on all continents, nor an authoritative structure and a two-millennium tradition of ethical reflection, not to mention a comprehensive vision of human life. Especially since Pope John XXIII called the Second Vatican Council, the pope has been one of the most well-known figures around the globe, and not just among Catholics. Presumably a Catholic *ad bellum* court, however expert and independent, would not publish a judgment without the *nihil obstat* and *imprimi potest* [it may be printed] of the pope. Can anyone doubt such a statement would get enormous attention?

The survey of ISA members and similar experts does importantly suggest that ethical deliberation on various wars does not result in random patterns. The experts in this case generally agreed on their rankings (although they did not actually deliberate in person), the most salient difference being between those self-identified as on the left and the right of the political spectrum. But even then, the *relative* rankings among the conflicts remained nearly identical, although those on the right tended to rank almost all the US conflicts higher on the justice scale than did those on the left.[36] The authors insightfully observe that "the difference between left and right is more a question of where the *threshold* for justness is placed."[37] Needless to say, *The Challenge of Peace* and the recent popes have placed the threshold very high. A Catholic *ad bellum* court would presumably reflect a similar spectrum of views, even though deep loyalty to and knowledge of

36. Dorn, Mandel, and Cross, "How Just," 280–81.
37. Dorn, Mandel, and Cross, "How Just," 284.

the Catholic tradition would be a *sine qua non* of appointment to the court. It could not and should not be otherwise.

APPENDIX 4: *INNERE FÜHRUNG*

Many nations, including the United States, have permitted pacifists, those who refuse to kill under any circumstances, to claim conscientious objection to *all* wars. In the US that possibility arose early on in our history from respect for the so-called "peace churches," especially the Mennonites, Brethren, and Society of Friends (Quakers), which were and are pacifist by creed and conviction. Supreme Court decisions during the Vietnam era, however, most notably *U.S. v. Seeger* (1965) and *U.S. v. Sisson* (1969), have changed that requirement. "The *Seeger* case accomplished the removal of a belief in a God or gods as a requirement of the exemption. The *Sisson* case determined that the claims of an objector need not be based upon conventional religious belief at all."[38] Proof of sincerity became paramount, and "the test of sincerity of one's conscience becomes whether one absolutely renounces all forms of force or not."[39] In 1971, in "the two most significant SCO cases: *Gillette v. the United States*, and its companion piece, *Negre v. Larsen*, . . . the Supreme Court conclusively slammed the door on any selective conscientious claims."[40] As Ralph Potter provocatively observed three years earlier, "Under existing law, unless one would be unwilling to fight *against* a new Hitler, one may be compelled to fight *for* a new Hitler."[41] Pacifism, *si*, just war, *no*.

As far as I have been able to determine, only one nation in the world, and only recently, has permitted its warriors to refuse to serve in particular wars, to claim selective conscientious objection. On reflection, it is not

38. Capizzi, "Selective Conscientious Objection," 348.

39. Capizzi, "Selective Conscientious Objection," 349.

40. Capizzi, "Selective Conscientious Objection," 349. For an in-depth investigation of the Negre case as promoting governmental religious discrimination against Catholics and other traditions that embrace the just-war tradition, see Reid, "John T. Noonan, Jr." That recent court decisions might offer new perspectives, see Prusak, "Right Not to Fight." The question of SCO had also been considered by the "Marshall Commission," formally the National Advisory Commission on Selective Service, whose 1967 report, *In Pursuit of Equity: Who Serves When Not All Serve?*, outlined the arguments pro and con. A majority of the Commission rejected SCO but supported CO. John Courtney Murray, SJ, was a vocal member of the minority. See his "War and Conscience."

41. Potter, "Conscientious Objection," 60; emphasis added.

surprising that that one nation is Germany. "After World War II and the fall of the Third Reich, the new West German constitution, the so-called 'Basic Law for the Federal Republic of German,' was adopted and proclaimed in May 1949. In it every citizen was guaranteed the fundamental human right to freedom of faith and conscience as well as right to refuse to perform military service involving the use of arms against their conscience."[42] In support of this provision of the new constitution, one leader "argued that 'we have gone through a "mass slumber of conscience" . . . [in which] millions of Germans said: orders are orders, and killed in view of that. . . . [N]ow we want to break with this notion that orders are orders.'"[43]

But "it was only in 2005 that the Federal Administrative Court provided explicit clarification on this matter with its judgement in a lawsuit against a Major in the German Army who had refused to obey several orders during the war against Iraq on moral grounds."[44] This court, "subordinate only to the highest German court, the Federal Constitutional Court, accepted such a courageous stance for the first time in the history of post-war Germany."[45] I believe that statement is too cautious and that we might say "for the first time in history." German military law now makes it clear that "the strong commitment to law and order" and "the strong commitment of individual soldiers to their conscience" deserve equal respect.[46] These commitments "constitute the foundations of the revolutionary new concept of 'Inner Leadership' in the German Bundeswehr [armed forces]."[47]

This *Innere Führung* grew out of the military philosophy of General Wolf Graf von Baudissin in response to "the catastrophe of the Second World War during which the traditional German military . . . had willingly served the National Socialist dictatorship in a war of aggression and genocide."[48] General von Baudissin minced no words in explaining *Innere Führung* as the "demilitarization of the military's self-conception."[49] Scholar Jürgen Rose describes the new military culture of *Innere Führung* as striving "to overcome the suppression of human individuality that prevails

42. Rose, "Conscience in Lieu of Obedience," 177.

43. Rose, "Conscience in Lieu of Obedience," 177–78.

44. Rose, "Conscience in Lieu of Obedience," 178.

45. Rose, "Conscience in Lieu of Obedience," 179.

46. Rose, "Conscience in Lieu of Obedience," 180.

47. Rose, "Conscience in Lieu of Obedience," 180.

48. Rose, "Conscience in Lieu of Obedience," 180.

49. Rose, "Conscience in Lieu of Obedience," 181.

within a tightly regulated system rooted in strictly enforced order and obedience. At the same time, the role model of the *citizen in uniform* who is critically-minded, discriminating and has the courage of his or her convictions, is intended to banish a spirit of subservience once and for all from the military."[50] Astonishingly, "A German soldier who is confronted with a moral conflict and is able to explain it in a serious and credible manner need not obey orders, if, by executing them, he or she would be involved in legally 'grey area' activities. With its decision the Federal Administrative Court de facto reassigned the burden of proof. It is no longer the soldier who has to prove that his or her refusal to follow orders was required by law, but the government that must explain to the 'citizens in uniform' sent into battle that their mission complies with both international and constitutional law."[51] Simply put by the Court: "In case of a conflict between conscience and legal obligation the freedom of conscience is 'inviolable.'"[52]

The author I have been relying on in this appendix is Lieutenant Colonel Jürgen Rose, who himself became a test case of *Innere Führung* as selective conscientious objection when he declared to his superior office "that it goes against my conscience to support the operation of TORNADO weapon systems in Afghanistan, because . . . there are grave reservations with respect to constitutional, international, criminal and international criminal law. . . . I request to be exempted from all further tasks connected with 'Operation Enduring Freedom' in general, as well as from the deployment of the TORNADO weapons systems in particular."[53] His case was widely reported and debated in the German media. The result was that "the relevant military authorities promptly decided to move the objector to another division of his department, just as it was settled in the Federal Administrative Court's decision regarding the soldier's freedom of conscience. Apart from this, higher commands, including the Ministry of Defense, took no further action on this issue."[54] Lieutenant Colonel Rose concludes his article by quoting another selective conscientious objector, US Army First Lieutenant Ehren K. Watada, who refused to deploy to Iraq, but offered to deploy to Afghanistan or to resign: "To stop an illegal and unjust war, the soldiers

50. Rose, "Conscience in Lieu of Obedience," 181.
51. Rose, "Conscience in Lieu of Obedience," 187.
52. Rose, "Conscience in Lieu of Obedience," 188.
53. Rose, "Conscience in Lieu of Obedience," 188.
54. Rose, "Conscience in Lieu of Obedience," 191.

can choose to stop fighting it. . . . If soldiers . . . stood up and threw their weapons down—no President could ever initiate a war of choice again."[55]

This book began with the story of a German-speaking Austrian farmer, Franz Jägerstätter, who refused conscription into Hitler's army because he knew Germany's wars to be unjust and who refused to abandon his conscience by taking an oath of unconditional obedience to the Führer. It is fitting to bring this chapter toward closure with the story of a new German military culture that would honor such a witness. It is fitting to reflect on the story of a contemporary German officer who exercised *Innere Führung*, as did Jägerstätter, but who lived to tell the tale.

APPENDIX 5: SCO AS CIVIL DISOBEDIENCE

Strictly on grounds of moral argument, the right conscientiously to object to participation in a particular war is incontestable. I shall not argue the issue. The practical question before all of us is how to get the moral validity of this right understood and how to get the right itself legally recognized, declared in statutory law.

—JOHN COURTNEY MURRAY[56]

The wise man will wage just wars. . . . For, unless the wars were just, he would not have to wage them, and in such circumstances he would not be involved in war at all."

—SAINT AUGUSTINE[57]

---

55. Rose, "Conscience in Lieu of Obedience," 194. Lieutenant Watada's story did not end as happily as did that of Lieutenant Colonel Rose. He was court-martialed but eventually a mistrial was declared and Watada was given an "other-than-honorable discharge," the least favorable type of administrative discharge from the Army. The contrast between the German and American responses to Rose and Watada, respectively, demonstrates the differences in military cultures and their respect, or lack of it, for conscience. The most complete and straightforward account of Watada's story I have found is on Wikipedia, "Ehren Watada." For other stories of opposition to the Iraq war by members of the military, see Gutman and Lutz, *Breaking Ranks*. For an investigation of the extent of doubt about the justice of the war among those serving, see Minear, "Conscience and Carnage."

56. Murray, "War and Conscience," 25.

57. Augustine, *City of God*, 19.7.

Let's assume for the purposes of this final appendix to chapter 5 that Augustine's "wise man" refers both to the legitimate authority who has the right to declare war *and* to the warriors who would carry out that decision. Let's not assume, however, that authorities are always wise or wage only just wars, or that objectors are always sincere or correct in their assessment of the justice of a particular war.[58] What are the permutations of the relationship between them? What are the implications for the legalization of SCO? When does SCO become civil disobedience? I take it that "the primary distinction here is one of intent: the political objector aims through his civil disobedience to change policy; the selective conscientious objector aims to protect his own conscience."[59] As especially chapter 5 makes clear, this book is an argument for SCO as civil disobedience under the guidance of the just-war tradition of the Catholic Church. Can a society reasonably be expected to make legal allowances for SCO as civil disobedience, when the purpose of civil disobedience is to change policy, in this case, the decision to fight a war pursued by the legitimate authorities responsible for such a decision?[60] There are four main permutations of the basic dynamic between legitimate authority and personal conscience (in bold below), with the legal status of SCO adding further permutations to the basic four.

1. **Legitimate authority wages a just war. A sincere selective conscientious objector will not object.** There is no *present* need for legalization of SCO but there may be in the future. If SCO is not legal, there is no occasion for martyrdom, unless an objector mistakenly believes the war to be unjust (see #3). If we fight no unjust wars, we will have little if any SCO, so not on a scale that would be considered meaningful as civil disobedience.

2. **Legitimate authority wages an unjust war. A sincere SCO will object.** There is a practical need for legalization of SCO, a procedure that allows the objector to make his or her case; if judged to be sincere,

58. See Navin, "Sincerity, Accuracy."

59. Ellner, Robinson, and Whetham, *When Soldiers Say No*, 4. "The latter may, of course, also hope to change policy, and may therefore have two motives, but the second one is what defines his objection as conscientious." I am not sure that even with this qualification that a practitioner of civil disobedience such as Rev. Martin Luther King Jr. would allow conscience to be considered as somehow secondary. His commitment to changing policy was itself driven by conscience, and so then was his civil disobedience.

60. See Ellner, Robinson, and Whetham, *When Soldiers Say No*, which provides a diversity of perspectives on the question.

exemption or reassignment is granted. As retired Lieutenant Colonel Dan Zupan of the US Army has pointed out, "it is crucial that we recognize that nothing in a soldier's oath commits them to fighting unjust wars. . . . I can see no version of a social contract, agreed upon for the purpose of securing justice, that could bind me unknowingly to participate in the mass murder that is unjust war."[61] Legal recognition of SCO would effectuate Lt. Col. Zupan's insight.

If SCO is not legal, there is an occasion for martyrdom. Paradoxically that may make objection more dramatic: "As in the case of civil disobedience, change is more likely to result if resisters or objectors have to pay a high price for taking a moral stance. . . . A reduction of their personal sacrifice would diminish the meaning of their actions and with it their chances of affecting change."[62] But that is a strange argument for not legalizing SCO, since it honors the stance in principle but believes it should be punished in practice. If there is no legal recognition of the right to SCO, and if warriors in substantial numbers object to a particular war, in the thousands, it would create an administrative nightmare. That might be effective civil disobedience. If the numbers are small, in the dozens or scores, the administrative challenge might be manageable, and resistors would be subject to punishment. In the former case, SCO, even if *de jure* illegal, may be accommodated *de facto*, as seemed to be the case during the US war in Vietnam, when many objectors who were not pacifists were granted CO status.

It would seem that only a war believed to be unjust by a considerable number of warriors would provoke anything like a crisis. In which case, the objectors would have achieved their goal of provoking public debate on and even resistance to the war in question. If the number of objectors is small, the war may *not* be so manifestly unjust as to merit larger resistance. If SCO is legally recognized, it would probably encourage more warriors to question the justice of a particular war in which they are ordered to serve. It would also preclude the administrative difficulty of large numbers of courts-martial of SCOs. The granting of SCO status should not be intrinsically more difficult than

61. Zupan, "Selective Conscientious Objection," 92–93. Dan Zupan is Colonel, US Army (retired); before his retirement, he was head of the philosophy program at the US Military Academy, West Point. Ellner, Robinson, and Whetham, *When Soldiers Say No*, ix.

62. Ellner, Robinson, and Whetham, *When Soldiers Say No*, 247.

that of pacifist conscientious objection, when sincerity of conviction is decisive. Why should sincerity be limited to the absolute objector who will not defend his or her country under any circumstances by violent means but not be granted to the warrior who is willing to defend his country or justice or human life and rights at the possible cost of his or her own life—but who is not willing to be complicit in unjust wars of aggression or geopolitical reputation or the lust to dominate?

This is key: do we really fear that warriors, whether young enlistees or older officers, would refuse to defend their country if it were attacked unjustly? Do we really believe warriors knowledgeable of the just-war tradition and guided by the Catholic Church would regard the decision as akin to the "pick and choose" of a cafeteria line? It is an insult to the honorable consciences of warriors to suggest that SCO would express a mere preference, like choosing roast beef rather than fried chicken.

3. **Legitimate authority wages a just war. A sincere SCO mistakenly objects.** There is a need for an SCO system that allows the warrior to make his or her case; if judged to be sincere, exemption or reassignment is granted. The system has worked. If SCO is not legal, there is an occasion for martyrdom. In either case, the numbers objecting, mistakenly, would presumably be small, especially if the Catholic *ad bellum* court had not judged the war to be so unjust as to merit resistance.

4. **Legitimate authority wages an unjust war. An insincere SCO objects.** There is a need for an SCO system that allows the warrior to make his or her case; if judged to be insincere, exemption or reassignment is not granted and failure to deploy may be punished. This would also be the case of a just war and an insincere objector. If SCO is not legal, there is an occasion for martyrdom, although an insincere objector would not seem likely to take it.

I conclude that there is much to be gained and little to be feared from the legal recognition of SCO and much to be lost by maintaining the current legal situation. To refer to the previous appendix, I doubt that Germany, because of its legal recognition of *Innere Führung*, would be left undefended if it were unjustly attacked. I believe the establishment of a *jus ad bellum* court under Catholic auspices would allow Catholic warriors, and others, in all nations to make good on the promise of the just-war tradition to limit war to the necessary defense of innocent human life and rights. If unjust war is resisted within the aggressor nation, especially as a matter of substantial civil disobedience, there should be less need to fight a just war in response to injustice. Augustine's insight is true and cuts both ways. If there is not such internal resistance and the unjust war proceeds, the nation attacked has every right to defend itself.

6

Teaching and Forming
a Just War Conscience

The evaluation of the use of force in terms of just-war theory involves a mode of moral reasoning and assessment which is quite different from privatized and highly personalized conceptions of conscience in which a 'still, small voice' delivers absolute judgments for which no reason can be assigned.

—JOHN P. LANGAN, SJ[1]

Therefore, the final question may be whether there is abroad in the land a sufficient measure of moral and political discretion, in such wise that the Congress could, under safeguard of the national security, acknowledge the right of discretionary armed service. To cultivate this power of discretion is a task for all of us.

—JOHN COURTNEY MURRAY, SJ[2]

1. Langan, "Good of Selective Conscientious Objection," 95.
2. Murray, "War and Conscience," 30.

INTRODUCTION

IF SELECTIVE CONSCIENTIOUS OBJECTION is to become a social phenomenon on a wide enough scale to make a difference in our democracy's decisions about going to war, a cultural shift of considerable magnitude will be required, one reminiscent of shifts in attitudes toward slavery, women's equality, and environmental protection. A crucial element of that shift will surely be a new awareness on the part of ordinary citizens of the just-war tradition, including the post-Vietnam Christian endorsement of selective conscientious objection, as demonstrated by authoritative statements of the official leadership of the Catholic Church, as presented in chapter 2. Lay leaders will have a significant role to play in this shift, both in our nation's political life and within our military. The substance of that official teaching is articulated in the US bishops' 1983 pastoral letter, *The Challenge of Peace*, and its tenth anniversary follow-up, *The Harvest of Justice Is Sown in Peace*. It may be fervently hoped that new documents from national episcopal conferences and the Vatican will give heightened prominence to the Church's teaching on SCO. But how is such teaching to be received, learned, and embraced? What role, for example, do the more than 1,200 Catholic high schools and more than 200 Catholic colleges and universities in the US have to play? What might education on the just-war tradition look like? If conscience is at the heart of this ethical tradition, and if conscience is a judgment of practical reason (chapter 3), how might Catholic schools endeavor to form the consciences of their students?

This chapter explores the relationship between pedagogy for justice in Catholic higher education and student psychological development, as portrayed in David Moshman's overview of the relevant literature in *Adolescent Rationality and Development: Cognition, Morality, and Identity*.[3] I will rehearse key themes in the three domains of his subtitle, but will begin with the topic of the final chapter, "Adolescents as Young Adults," as the first question most postsecondary educators—and citizens generally—will ask is whether college students should be thought of as adolescents, and thus whether Moshman's book has any relevance to their thinking and practice as teachers. A related question has to do with public concern about the capacity of young people to enter into such complex questions as whether to go to war in particular circumstances. I conclude with seven summary

---

3. Moshman, *Adolescent Rationality*. Full disclosure: Professor Moshman was on my doctoral committee at the University of Nebraska-Lincoln.

theses and a case study of a university course on Christian Ethics of War and Peace.

COLLEGE STUDENTS AS ADOLESCENTS, ADOLESCENTS AS YOUNG ADULTS

Moshman's basic definition of adolescents is that they are "rational agents making progress toward more advanced forms and levels of rationality in multiple domains."[4] More particularly, "Adolescents are qualitatively and categorically distinct from children. There is no empirical support, however, for a state of rationality common to most adults but rarely seen in adolescents."[5] Adolescence "is best conceptualized not as the last stage of childhood, or even as an intermediate period between childhood and adulthood, but rather as the first phase of adulthood."[6]

This leads to a rousing defense of adolescents against the prejudicial stereotypes adults often apply to them:

> Adolescents often fail to reason logically, but the same is true of adults. Adolescents often fail to adequately test and revise their theoretical understandings, but adults fail in the same ways. Adolescents often show simplistic conceptions of knowledge and primitive forms of social and moral reasoning, but so do adults. Adolescent thinking is subject to peer pressure, emotional biases, cognitive distortions, and self-serving denial, but so is that of adults. . . . In summary, psychological research on adolescents clearly disconfirms adult stereotypes of adolescent irrationality and immaturity.[7]

But what about the oft-cited contention that adolescent brains are still developing? Moshman observes, "Popular assumptions notwithstanding, brain research has not shown an age-related maturation of brain structures and modes of functioning that generate new forms or levels of cognition or behavior."[8] He argues, "Brain changes are in large part the result of thinking, action, and experience [and are not merely biological]. Whatever the

---

4. Moshman, *Adolescent Rationality*, xv.
5. Moshman, *Adolescent Rationality*, xvi.
6. Moshman, *Adolescent Rationality*, xvii.
7. Moshman, *Adolescent Rationality*, 206, 214.
8. Moshman, *Adolescent Rationality*, 215.

problems of adolescence, waiting for adolescent brains to mature is not the solution."[9]

Developmentally, college students are more like their professors (and parents) than they are different. Thus, the research literature on adolescent development is relevant to theorizing about teaching the just-war tradition during the college experience. If we think of our students as rational agents and the just-war tradition as an "advanced form of rationality," what can we learn from the literature about development in the three domains of cognition, morality, and identity?

COGNITIVE DEVELOPMENT

Most basically, "rationality, in its oldest, broadest, and deepest sense, is a matter of having good reasons for one's beliefs and actions,"[10] and "reasoning may be defined as epistemologically self-constrained thinking . . . that is, thinking aimed at reaching justifiable conclusions."[11] Moshman observes that "what lies at the core of advanced cognitive development is the development of metacognition," or "cognition about cognition."[12] Of special concern is "epistemic cognition" or "knowledge about the fundamental nature and justifiability of knowledge and inference."[13] Epistemic cognitive development "proceeds from an objectivist epistemology to a subjectivist epistemology and ultimately, in some cases, to a rationalist epistemology."[14] "For the objectivist . . . truth and falsity are sharply distinct . . . on the basis of logic, evidence, and authority. . . . A subjectivist, in contrast, sees truth as relative to one's point of view."[15] A rationalist "construes rationality as metasubjective objectivity—a fallible quest for truth through reflection on and coordination of subjectivities."[16] A rationalist knows "we may have good reason to prefer some beliefs to others even if we cannot prove any of those beliefs true or false."[17]

9. Moshman, *Adolescent Rationality*, 216.

10. Moshman, *Adolescent Rationality*, 23.

11. Moshman, *Adolescent Rationality*, 26–27.

12. Moshman, *Adolescent Rationality*, 37, 38.

13. Moshman, *Adolescent Rationality*, 40.

14. Moshman, *Adolescent Rationality*, 43.

15. Moshman, *Adolescent Rationality*, 43.

16. Moshman, *Adolescent Rationality*, 45.

17. Moshman, *Adolescent Rationality*, 45.

Epistemic cognition is *constructed* as "individuals engage in an ongoing process of justifying their ideas, reflecting on their concepts of justification, and reconstructing those epistemic concepts as necessary."[18] Three factors are key: reflection, coordination, and peer interaction.[19] Consider Moshman's simple scenario.[20] Two children face each other across a table, with other items of furniture placed around the room. Asked to describe the room, each will do so from his or her particular point of view, describing these items as on the left or right, on this near side or that far side of the table. But if the children were to reflect on their two mirror-image descriptions, coordinate those two descriptions against each other, and interact with each other about these contrary but not false perspectives, they might come to understand that it is better to describe the room via the compass coordinates of north and south, east and west. They have transcended both an objectivist and a subjectivist rationality and arrived at a more developed form of rationality. The pedagogical payoff is straightforward:

> Rationality develops via processes of reflection, coordination, and peer interaction, not by learning facts and skills from someone who is already more rational. This does not mean, however, that you can do nothing to help [students] develop. At the very least, you may be able to facilitate their development by encouraging them to interact and reflect. Directly pointing out various systemic relationships—such as what's near to you is far to him—may play a positive role by providing additional bases for reflection and discussion. New terms and concepts you introduce—such as north, south, east, and west—may provide linguistic and intellectual scaffolding for the construction of new conceptual structures. . . . Ultimately, however, [students] must construct their own rationality.[21]

Moshman then contrasts **symmetric and asymmetric social interactions**, depending on whether levels of "knowledge, authority, and/or power" between those interacting are similar or different. "Symmetric social interactions are . . . especially likely to encourage individuals to reflect on their own perspectives and to coordinate multiple viewpoints." Because "peer interactions are more likely than adult-child or teacher-student interactions to approximate the ideal of symmetric social interactions," they

18. Moshman, *Adolescent Rationality*, 50.
19. Moshman, *Adolescent Rationality*, 54–55.
20. Moshman, *Adolescent Rationality*, 55–57.
21. Moshman, *Adolescent Rationality*, 59.

are likely to "play a critical role in fostering the autonomous processes of reflection and coordination that generate progress toward higher levels of objectivity."[22] The principal role of teachers will be to maintain "an environment in which students are free to express and discuss their ideas and to seek additional information."[23]

MORAL DEVELOPMENT

Moshman's exemplary scenario for this domain is significantly more arresting than that of two children describing a room and its furnishings from different perspectives. The question now is how to think about "female circumcision, also known as female genital mutilation," which "is practiced in more than 40 countries, mostly in Africa and the Middle East."[24] Moshman contrasts his own view of this practice—"There are evil things in the world, and this is one of them"—with that of a moral relativist, who would contend that Moshman has no rational basis for his reaction, since "what is moral is what is deemed moral within a given culture." From such a perspective, there is no "basis for any notion of moral development distinct from social learning," since "morality is cultural conformity" and "there is no internal force moving one toward greater morality."[25] Such a view is obviously deeply contrary to Catholic doctrine about the human person, as described in chapter 3.

If one agrees with Moshman about such an issue as female genital mutilation (or, in Catholic terms, insists there are universal, objective moral norms), the challenge is to develop a morally evaluative framework that transcends ethnocentrism. But is this possible and what would it look like? It looks like, Moshman suggests, the Universal Declaration of Human Rights, which claims that "everyone has the right to life, liberty, and the security of person" and that "no one shall be subjected to torture or to cruel, inhuman or degrading treatment,"[26] which would rule out genital mutilation, its culturally accepted practice notwithstanding. But what is the argument for such a universalist perspective, and what is the psychological

22. Moshman, *Adolescent Rationality*, 60.

23. Moshman, *Adolescent Rationality*, 61.

24. Moshman, *Adolescent Rationality*, 65.

25. Moshman, *Adolescent Rationality*, 66, 67.

26. Moshman, *Adolescent Rationality*, 68.

evidence that the development of such a perspective is possible for the individual?

To answer these questions, Moshman turns first to Jean Piaget, then to Lawrence Kohlberg, and finally to critiques of and developments beyond Kohlberg. Piaget "argued that genuine morality is not imposed by parents or other agents of culture but rather constructed in the context of peer interaction."[27] "Moral development comes about as children, in their interactions with other children, increasingly grasp 'the permanent laws of rational cooperation.'"[28] "Whereas Piaget emphasized childhood, however, Kohlberg's theory posits that moral development often continues through adolescence and well into adulthood" and does so through six stages: heteronomous morality, individualism and exchange, mutual expectations, social system, social contract, and universal ethical principles.[29] Moshman summarizes a massive amount of research by reporting that "the evidence has confirmed that males and females of all ages from diverse cultural and religious backgrounds can be classified into Kohlberg's stages and develop through those stages in the order postulated."[30] The descriptions of Stages 4–6 would seem to be particularly relevant to developing a personal commitment to just-war ethics generally and to SCO specifically.

In Stage 4 reasoning, the individual takes on the perspective of his or her society, such that "preserving that system is one's fundamental moral obligation. . . . In societies such as the United States, Stage 4 reasoning becomes increasingly common over the course of adolescence and is the predominant mode of moral understanding for most adults."[31] Stage 5 reasoning, however, "rather than [construing] moral issues exclusively from the perspective of the social system . . . involves the evaluation of social systems from a **prior-to-society perspective**." At this stage, "laws and entire social systems can . . . be morally evaluated on the basis of **postconventional moral principles**" (such as the principles found in the just-war tradition).[32] Postconventional reasoning is "most likely to develop in complex societies where there is a clash of cultures," as it "transcends

27. Moshman, *Adolescent Rationality*, 69.

28. Moshman, *Adolescent Rationality*, 70.

29. Moshman, *Adolescent Rationality*, 70–74.

30. Moshman, *Adolescent Rationality*, 71.

31. Moshman, *Adolescent Rationality*, 73.

32. Moshman, *Adolescent Rationality*, 73.

any particular culture and permits cross-cultural analysis."[33] Unfortunately, according to Kohlbergian research, such reasoning "is virtually never seen before adulthood and remains rare at any age." Stage 6 reasoning is even rarer: "Outside the abstruse realm of moral philosophy, and related areas such as law and theology, there is no evidence of human reasoning at this level."[34]

Mary Ann Glendon's masterful narrative of the creation of the UDHR[35] is an object lesson in the kind of reasoning Kohlberg evoked as Stage 6, but do only highly educated individuals such as the philosophers, theologians, and legal scholars who articulated the universal principles enshrined in the UDHR object to such practices as genital mutilation? Were those men and women who originated and led the movement for the abolition of slavery in the late eighteenth century, many of whom were well-educated but were not professional philosophers, simply freaks of nature? And what about the ordinary citizens, the housewives and even children, who rallied to the appeals of the abolitionists, even against appeals to their own self-interest and to the preservation and stability of the social order? In *Bury the Chains: Prophets and Rebels in the Fight to Free an Empire's Slaves*, Adam Hochshild argues that "to feel a just indignation" against slavery, it was empathy (not postconventional moral reasoning) that made the crucial difference and changed the most powerful empire on earth.[36] Postconventional moral reasoning may be rare, according to Kohlberg, but ordinary citizens in significant numbers embrace causes that embody such reasoning.

MORAL DEVELOPMENT BEYOND KOHLBERG

According to Moshman, robust empirical support for Kohlberg's account of moral development does not mean it is "correct and comprehensive."[37] As if to explain the phenomenon alluded to above—that children in early nineteenth-century England could understand why their mothers were not buying sugar produced by slaves—Moshman reports that "children as young as 3 or 4 years old, contrary to Kohlbergian expectation, already

---

33. Moshman, *Adolescent Rationality*, 74.

34. Moshman, *Adolescent Rationality*, 74.

35. Glendon, *World Made New*.

36. Hochshild, *Bury the Chains*, 366.

37. Moshman, *Adolescent Rationality*, 75.

distinguish morality from social convention."[38] "It is clear," he observes, "that Kohlberg's cognitive theory does not adequately consider the role of emotion and empathy in moral development."[39]

Moshman suggests that what's lacking in "Kohlberg's conception of morality as justice and respect for rights" can be identified in terms of three other conceptions of the moral domain: care and compassion, character and virtue, and moral foundations.[40] Carol Gilligan is famously responsible for arguing that Kohlberg's research was male-biased and that whereas an orientation toward justice is male, "care represents the female voice."[41] However, "systematic overviews of the vast literature on gender differences in moral development have not supported her categorical claims regarding male and female moralities."[42] Nonetheless, "Kohlberg himself came to see benevolence and justice as dual aspects of an underlying respect for persons."[43]

That takes us to a third conception of the moral domain, known as eudaimonism because of its origins in ancient Greek philosophy, especially the ethics of Aristotle (which Aquinas incorporated into his own ethics, so influential in Catholic tradition), which "highlights the moral relevance of character, virtue, and human flourishing [*eudaimon*]."[44] But because human flourishing is determined differently by different cultures, "it is not clear how a eudaimonist approach avoids relativism or establishes rationality."[45] However, since the rebirth of virtue ethics in the mid-twentieth century, much has been written on these questions, as exemplified by the title of a famous book, *Whose Justice? Which Rationality?*[46] I have attempted to appropriate the virtue tradition to Catholic social learning in my article, "Teaching Justice After MacIntyre: Toward a Catholic Philosophy of Moral Education."[47] Per the observation of Charles Curran et al., however, that

---

38. Moshman, *Adolescent Rationality*, 75.

39. Moshman, *Adolescent Rationality*, 76.

40. Moshman, *Adolescent Rationality*, 78.

41. Moshman, *Adolescent Rationality*, 79.

42. Moshman, *Adolescent Rationality*, 79.

43. Moshman, *Adolescent Rationality*, 80.

44. Moshman, *Adolescent Rationality*, 81.

45. Moshman, *Adolescent Rationality*, 83.

46. MacIntyre, *Whose Justice?*

47. Bergman, "Teaching Justice." See also chapter 3 of my book *Catholic Social Learning*.

"one of the underdeveloped aspects of Catholic social teaching is the role of the virtues," much more needs to be done.[48]

The fourth conception of the moral domain referenced by Moshman is the social-intuitionist moral foundations theory recently championed by psychologist Jonathan Haidt, most fully in his controversial book, *The Righteous Mind: Why Good People Are Divided by Politics and Religion.*[49] Moshman's own book appeared before Haidt's, so his critique is limited to previously published articles. Here is my own brief critique of moral foundations theory, with which Moshman, in a personal communication (February 12, 2016), has said he is in complete agreement:

> I don't believe all of Haidt's "moral foundations" are created equal. Fairness and caring are genuinely moral values . . . because they can be self-correcting. Especially if we think of fairness as justice and justice as respect for all persons, it seems hard to imagine having too much justice (or too much caring). One might misunderstand or misapply such a value, but in that case justice and/or caring would provide the needed corrective. But what about loyalty, authority, and sanctity or purity [the other moral foundations of Haidt's theory]? Christopher Browning's *Ordinary Men: Reserve Police Battalion 101 and the Final Solution in Poland* offers an admittedly extreme example of those values not being tempered by justice and caring.[50] That is, those values are not self-correcting, individually or in combination. Those "ordinary" men slaughtered thousands of Jews in cold blood because they were ordered to (authority), their comrades were doing it (loyalty or conformity to the group), and the Jews were portrayed as vermin (purity). Their scores on Haidt's instrument would have been, presumably, very high for those three values. . . . In more ordinary contexts, loyalty, authority, and sanctity might contribute to human flourishing—but not in the absence of the genuinely moral foundation of respect for all persons.[51]

Moshman's own conclusion is that justice and care "are deemed part of the moral domain by virtually all individuals, cultures, and theorists because they represent the core of any justifiable morality." Nevertheless, "ingroup loyalty, respect for authority, and disgust for impurity affect our

48. Curran, Himes, and Shannon, "Commentary," 430.

49. Haidt, *Righteous Mind.*

50. Browning, *Ordinary Men.*

51. Excerpted and slightly edited from a letter published in *Commonweal,* January 28, 2016.

behavior regardless of whether we deem these to be moral considerations and regardless of whether we have adequate reason to do so."[52] Being able to recognize when these values become disvalues would seem to be an important challenge for any moral tradition, such as just-war ethics, that has respect for human dignity at its core. How do the two genuinely moral foundations, justice and care, develop in adolescence, the first phase of adulthood? Moshman answers that "research and theory suggest three answers: principled reasoning, perspective taking, and moral identity."[53]

ADVANCED MORALITY: PRINCIPLES, PERSPECTIVE TAKING, EMPATHY

James Rest and colleagues have advanced what is known as "neo-Kohlbergian" theory, based on extensive research with the Defining Issues Test (DIT), which exposes subjects to moral dilemmas in a multiple-choice pen-and-paper questionnaire rather than a Kohlbergian interview format. In *Postconventional Moral Thinking*,[54] Rest et al. argue that "people (a) usually use multiple schemas rather than fit into a single stage [of moral reasoning] and (b) show gradual progress toward postconventionality rather than step up from one stage to the next." More importantly for the credibility of SCO, "in contrast to traditional Kohlbergian findings that postconventional moral reasoning is rare, DIT research across a variety of cultural contexts shows postconventional moral understanding to be common among adolescents and adults."[55]

Moshman argues that moral principles are best understood as "meta-rules" and that they serve "four fundamental purposes."[56]

> First, they can justify rules that do provide clear moral guidance in specific contexts. Second, they can serve as a heuristic for taking all perspectives into account in cases where it is not possible to consider every actual and potential perspective individually. Third, strict formal principles may direct our attention beyond those with whom we naturally empathize and may counteract the self-serving biases that render us less sympathetic to persons or

52. Moshman, *Adolescent Rationality*, 86.

53. Moshman, *Adolescent Rationality*, 89.

54. Rest et al., *Postconventional Moral Thinking*.

55. Moshman, *Adolescent Rationality*, 91.

56. Moshman, *Adolescent Rationality*, 91, 93.

viewpoints we find objectionable. And finally, principles can be made public and thus serve as a basis for explanation, discussion, and shared decisions and commitments.

The third and fourth purposes would seem to be especially relevant to Catholic Social Teaching, with its concern for the marginalized, the "other," those with whom we do not naturally empathize, and for political participation on behalf of the common good. Browning's "ordinary men" may have been acting according to certain values, but they weren't acting according to the principles of justice and care that seem designed to counter such "self-serving biases." Just-war tradition represents such an advanced morality and offers a set of principles that serve all four purposes identified by Moshman. Needless to say, Franz Jägerstätter embodied values and moral principles opposite those of Browning's "ordinary men," although in many ways Jägerstätter himself was quite ordinary, notably in his education.

Thus it is a short move from considerations of advanced morality as principled morality to advanced morality as advanced perspective taking. Drawing on the foundational research of Robert Selman, Moshman observes that "adolescents and adults often fail to reflect adequately on their relationships, but they are generally capable of third-party perspective taking, whereas children are not." Perspective taking "is both cognitive and emotional."[57] Kohlberg's ideal, universalizable moral principles are "precisely those that take all perspectives into account."[58] John Gibbs's "masterful theoretical synthesis," *Moral Development and Reality*,[59] which places perspective taking at the center of advanced moral functioning, draws on Kohlberg but also on the research of Martin Hoffman, who "saw empathy as the primary basis for morality and worked out a comprehensive theory of moral development centered on the development of empathy," the "emotional side of perspective taking."[60] Again, Jägerstätter is an exemplar, in this case of perspective-taking, as he was able to imagine fighting against Nazi Germany if he were a citizen of France.

In *Catholic Social Learning: Educating the Faith That Does Justice*,[61] I draw extensively on Hoffman's work to explain the moral experience

57. Moshman, *Adolescent Rationality*, 94.

58. Moshman, *Adolescent Rationality*, 95.

59. Gibbs, *Moral Development*. Moshman cites the second edition, which doesn't address the moral-foundations theory of Haidt as does the third edition cited here.

60. Moshman, *Adolescent Rationality*, 95.

61. Bergman, *Catholic Social Learning*.

of college students studying in the Dominican Republic for a semester, in close relationship with impoverished Dominicans and marginalized Haitian-Dominicans. According to Moshman, Hoffman argued that "principles . . . may expand our empathic reactions to those not present, but without empathy the principles would have no force."[62] CST principles are likely to have no force in our students' lives absent the experience of empathy for the marginalized, the oppressed, and the alleged enemy, in the case of unjust war. If the empirical research is right, this would be as true for Catholics in any of the diverse cultures of Africa, for example, as in the cultures of the United States. "Research on social cognition suggests that differences among individuals and social contexts within cultures are greater than differences between cultures."[63] Once again, the Universal Declaration of Human Rights may be lifted up as the preeminent example of a genuinely global ethic, and again, the affinity of the UDHR with CST can be celebrated.[64]

IDENTITY FORMATION

Erik Erikson, the founding theorist in our final domain, posited eight stages of identity development across the life span, from infancy to late adulthood, where the fifth stage, adolescence, is "the sensitive period." The ideal result of identity exploration during this period is "a sense of individuality, a role in society, an experience of continuity across time, and a commitment to ideals."[65] James Marcia is primarily responsible for advancing research and theory on identity development beyond Erikson. Marcia's theory depends on the concept of "identity commitments,"[66] of which there are four types. "Individuals entering into adolescence typically fall into one of two categories. The **identity-diffused** individual has no strong commitments and is not seeking any. . . . The **foreclosed** individual, by contrast, does have clear commitments . . . internalized from parents or other agents of culture; they are not self-chosen, in that no alternatives have been seriously considered."[67]

62. Moshman, *Adolescent Rationality*, 96.

63. Moshman, *Adolescent Rationality*, 100.

64. Glendon, "Sources of Rights."

65. Moshman, *Adolescent Rationality*, 121.

66. Moshman, *Adolescent Rationality*, 121.

67. Moshman, *Adolescent Rationality*, 121–22.

"It is possible, however, for an individual who is either foreclosed or identity-diffused to move into an **identity crisis**, which Marcia (1966) referred to as a state of **moratorium** . . . where one has no current identity commitments but is seeking to make such commitments. . . . The positive outcome [is] . . . the status known as **identity-achieved**."[68] Echoing Erikson, research in the Marcia tradition "indicates that the most active period for identity formation is the period from adolescence through early adulthood," the college years.[69] While "Marcia's scheme is widely accepted as a useful basis for understanding adolescent identity formation . . . what appears to be missing in the standard identity measures, according to influential researcher Augusto Blasi, is the basic identity question, 'Who am I?'"[70]

Moshman himself has contributed to this reconceptualization by devising "a brief definition of identity that captures most of the elements highlighted by most contemporary theorists and provides a useful framework for addressing the construction of identity in adolescence: *An identity is, at least in part, an explicit theory of oneself as a person*," as "a rational agent," and as "singular and continuous."[71] This singularity and continuity come together in what theorists "commonly call **narrative identity**, a personal life history that is deemed to define the self."[72] A sure marker of an effective CST educational program would be the extent to which students tell their life stories in terms of CST principles and the experiences, such as immersions, that shaped their commitments to these principles during their college years. Moshman captures this idea perfectly: "my compassion for victims of poverty . . . may be so central to my self and identity that I would see some hypothetical future version of myself who lacked such compassion as being a fundamentally different person than my present self, and I might be right."[73] As one of my own students put it so eloquently: "Living in solidarity with the poor is hard, but I can't imagine not trying."

---

68. Moshman, *Adolescent Rationality*, 122.

69. Moshman, *Adolescent Rationality*, 123.

70. Moshman, *Adolescent Rationality*, 125, 129.

71. Moshman, *Adolescent Rationality*, 130, 132, 133.

72. Moshman, *Adolescent Rationality*, 135.

73. Moshman, *Adolescent Rationality*, 137.

THE CONSTRUCTION OF RATIONAL MORAL IDENTITY

"To the extent that you come to see your rational agency as central to who you are, you have a **rational identity**."[74] Such individuals "are more likely to change their beliefs appropriately, in light of evidence and argument, because they see such change not as acknowledgement of a fundamental shortcoming but as an affirmation of themselves as rational agents."[75] Advancements in rationality and in identity seem to be mutually supportive. But how is rational identity related to morality? Moshman's "definition does not require a commitment to any particular set of moral beliefs, values, rules, or principles and is thus consistent with moral diversity among those who have strong moral identities."[76] Thus, we might say that a person who has fully embraced CST or SCO as a Catholic is likely to have a strong moral identity, but so might the non-religious individual, for example, who has embraced the moral teachings of humanism, as in the UDHR. To the extent that the Catholic and the humanist do indeed form their identities "on the basis of respect and/or concern for the rights and/or welfare of others," and to the extent that both are indeed willing "to change their beliefs appropriately, in light of evidence and argument," there should be opportunity and incentive for mutually corrective and creative dialogue.[77]

Such rational identities would seem to be presumed in the several dialogical imperatives of chapter 5 of Pope Francis's encyclical *Laudato Si'* (2015). It is hard to see how such dialogues could take place in the absence of strong but open rational and moral identities. The men (and one woman, Eleanor Roosevelt) who developed the UDHR represented diverse cultures and histories, although all shared a high degree of education and cross-cultural experience. Thus Moshman argues for a "pluralist rational constructivism," which is "open to both universals and differences."[78]

But "pluralist" has other meanings in this context. "Diversity may exist within individuals" as well as "across individuals and across groups."[79] Research demonstrates that "most people use a combination of justice, care, and virtue reasoning," which suggests that there is more than one way to be

74. Moshman, *Adolescent Rationality*, 175.

75. Moshman, *Adolescent Rationality*, 175.

76. Moshman, *Adolescent Rationality*, 177.

77. Moshman, *Adolescent Rationality*, 175.

78. Moshman, *Adolescent Rationality*, 188.

79. Moshman, *Adolescent Rationality*, 188.

an adherent of just-war thinking, even for the individual, and presumably more than one way to promote and form that adherence in higher education. If teachers of just-war ethics operate from a commitment to pluralist rationalist constructivism, they will be dissuaded from thinking of their pedagogies as mere training or indoctrination.[80]

IMPLICATIONS FOR EDUCATION

Moshman's argument for intellectual freedom is straightforward: if we believe the purpose of education is to promote rationality in cognitive, moral, and identity development, there can be no alternative to "the sort [of education] that respects students as persons," as rational agents.[81] To be a rational agent in a democracy means that citizens "be conscious of themselves as thinking, willing, active beings, bearing responsibility for their choices and being able to explain those choices by references to their own ideas and purposes."[82] To which the Catholic educator might add, *as critically informed by the values, vision, and virtues of CST, including the just-war tradition and SCO.*

Moshman sums up by observing, "What marks a rational constructivist approach is an overarching context of liberty, where students are free to disagree with what is presented and ultimately to decide for themselves what to believe."[83] Is there some risk in this approach that one generation will not be able to pass on to the next its own values and beliefs? According to Moshman, "If . . . we communicate the reasons for our commitments and encourage adolescents to form justifiable commitments of their own, much of what we value will endure."[84] If what we value most is the dignity of the human person, the foundational value of Catholic moral teaching, we can hardly hope to pass that value on without embodying it in our relationships with students. One teaches respect for human dignity by respecting the dignity, the rational agency, of the one being taught.

80. Moshman, *Adolescent Rationality*, 191.

81. Moshman, *Adolescent Rationality*, 195.

82. Moshman, *Adolescent Rationality*, 197.

83. Moshman, *Adolescent Rationality*, 201.

84. Moshman, *Adolescent Rationality*, 203.

CONCLUSION: SEVEN THESES

How might the research and theory reported by Moshman inform our pedagogical practice on behalf of SCO? Several key themes stand out, which I offer as a summary of this investigation:

1. High school and college students may be thought of as adolescents but as adolescents who are *young adults*, more like their teachers than like children. They have been young adults since leaving childhood at about age thirteen, so especially at ages eighteen to twenty-two they are not beginners.

2. Secondary and even more so postsecondary students are best thought of as *rational agents*, as reasoners, responsible for constructing and justifying their own beliefs and identities.

3. There is no one way to appropriate the values, vision, and virtues of Catholic moralitly, but *reflection, coordination, and symmetric peer interaction* in a context of intellectual freedom provide the practices most conducive to the development of advanced rationality in all domains.

4. An advanced morality such as represented by the just-war tradition *requires both principled reasoning and perspective-taking, both cognitive and emotional.* Tradition itself provides the principles but appropriating them authentically requires not only rational dialogue but also self-transcendence—and both as a matter of personal identity.

5. If we think of CST as doctrine, as in the *Compendium of the Social Doctrine of the Church*, we dare not think of Catholic social learning as *indoctrination*, the non-critical imposition of a particular morality or perspective, lest we undermine the foundation of that teaching in the dignity of the person as a rational agent.

6. Our classrooms, curricula, and campus communities should aspire to the kind of *intellectual and moral community* that gave rise to the Universal Declaration of Human Rights, with which CST has impressive affinity. A Catholic *ad bellum* court would represent such a community.

7. Finally, if we communicate effectively the reasons for our own commitments to the just-war tradition and encourage our students to form

justifiable commitments of their own, what we value about Catholic teaching will endure, and even prosper.

A CASE STUDY

Sic et Non: The Formation of Conscience as an Academic Enterprise: Teaching to Encourage Objection to Unjust War[85]

This final section describes an undergraduate course, "Christian Ethics of War and Peace," taught for more than two decades at a Catholic university. This 500-level course (which was available for graduate credit) introduces students to the development and application of Christian theological and ethical perspectives on the use of lethal force from the biblical period to the present day. Both just war and pacifism are considered in both Catholic and Protestant traditions. Special attention is given to the formation of personal conscience and the development of skills of practical reasoning in light of Christian tradition and in the context of US citizenship.[86] Students are asked to develop and articulate their own commitments in light of the long-standing tension between arguments for pacifism and for just war in Christian tradition. Borrowing from contemporary cognitive psychology, this task is described *to the students* as one of "reflective judgment" regarding an "ill-structured problem."

On the syllabus and throughout the semester, I refer the students to a historical precedent for what I am asking them to do. I quote historian David G. Hunter, who observes, "In the twelfth century, when Peter Abelard wished to exercise the theological ingenuity of his students, he presented them with a series of conflicting 'authorities,' the famous treatise *Sic et Non*. Included among the theses and antitheses was the proposition that 'Christians are not allowed for any reason to kill anyone, and the contrary [view].' Abelard knew, of course, that opinions could be adduced from Christian tradition to support both sides of the argument, and he set before his students the task, of resolving, if possible, the contradictions."[87]

Patricia King and Karen Kitchener, in their 1994 book *Developing Reflective Judgement: Understanding and Promoting Intellectual Growth*

---

85. A version of this section appeared as Bergman, "Teaching to Prevent Unjust War."

86. The full syllabus is available on request to rbjps@creighton.edu.

87. Hunter, "Decade of Research," 87.

and Critical Thinking in Adolescents and Adults, argue that the most mature form of cognition is the ability to deal not only with "well-structured problems" but with "ill-structured problems."[88] A well-structured problem "can be described with a high degree of completeness" and "can be solved with a high degree of certainty," so that "experts usually agree on the correct solution." An ill-structured problem, on the contrary, "cannot be described with a high degree of completeness" and "cannot be resolved with a high degree of certainty," so that "experts often disagree about the best solution, even when the problem can be considered solved." As Moshman put it, at this level of cognitive development, rational agents know "we may have good reason to prefer some beliefs to others even if we cannot prove any of those beliefs true or false."[89] If the problem is well-structured, the goal is to "learn to reason to correct solutions." If the problem is ill-structured, the goal is to "learn to construct and defend reasonable solutions."[90] The latter is clearly the harder task, and the one relevant to living out the just war perspective as an SCO.

King and Kitchener delineate three levels (and seven stages) of reflective judgment,[91] which correspond to the three levels of cognitive development described by Moshman as objectivist, subjectivist, and rationalist. At the highest cognitive achievement, Stage 7, the individual believes that "one can judge an argument by how well thought-out the positions are, what kinds of reasoning and evidence are used to support it, and how consistent the way one argues on this topic is as compared with other topics."

Peter Abelard was right: views on "the proposition that 'Christians are not allowed for any reason to kill anyone . . . could be adduced from Christian tradition to support both sides of the argument.'" Therefore, like Abelard, I set before my students "the task, of resolving, if possible, the contradictions." If the experts of the tradition disagree, the ethics of killing must be an ill-structured problem, and the educational goal must be developing a reflective judgment that can "construct and defend reasonable solutions." I ask them to attempt Stage 7 reflective judgment. I define this challenge, for the purposes of the course, as a matter of formation of

88. See especially "Problem Structure," in King and Kitchener, *Developing Reflective Judgment*, 10–13.

89. Moshman, *Adolescent Rationality*, 45.

90. All the quotations in this paragraph are taken from Table 1.1 in King and Kitchener, *Developing Reflective Judgment*, 11.

91. All quotations in this paragraph are taken from Exhibit 1.1 in King and Kitchener, *Developing Reflective Judgment*, 14–16.

personal conscience, which is highly valued in the Catholic intellectual tradition, as demonstrated in chapter 3 of this book, and in which conscience is understood as a judgment of practical reason.

I pursue this goal not only by teaching what some of the diverse authorities in the tradition have written, but also by asking the students to reflect personally on those writings. Course requirements include an almost weekly "workbook on conscience": ten personal reflections of one page each on the week's readings or class discussions. The second assignment is a final two-part paper directly inspired by Abelard's *Sic et Non*. I ask the students, first, to write a statement of conscience referring substantially to the readings, explaining why they adhere to either just war or pacifism—and how they negotiate the tension between those two perspectives. They are asked to address the strengths and weaknesses of the positions they adopt *and* reject, demonstrating that they understand the theological tension between (and within) the Christian realism of the just-war tradition and the Christian witness of pacifism, even as they stake out a defensible position on one side or the other.

Second, they are asked to apply what they have presented in the first part to one of the four wars of America that we have considered, however briefly, as case studies, which means contending with both pro and con perspectives on the justice, or lack of it, of the war in question. If a student stakes out a pacifist position, they are asked to use what they believe to be the least inadequate just-war perspective for their analysis. Together these two writing assignments, totaling at least twenty pages, count for one-half of the course grade.

I taught this course once a year for more than twenty years, refining it along the way, but I have attempted no systematic analysis of the students' final papers to determine what stages of reflective judgement they have demonstrated. But to varying degrees of excellence, of course, they engage this difficult assignment seriously, even relishing its intellectual and moral challenge. I offer one excerpt from a student's reflection about her statement of conscience, obviously not as evidence proving the course's effectiveness, but simply to give a flavor of how a student might come to appreciate the challenge of the assignment—of coming to terms personally with the ill-structured problem that is forming a Christian conscience on war:

> The best paper I have written during my college career relevant to
> Justice and Peace Studies was my term paper for Christian Ethics of
> War and Peace titled "What Difference Does It Make to the Dead?

A Case for Pacifism." Never have I been made to think harder in a rigorous format about a crucial, relevant, and personal moral issue than I was in writing this difficult paper. I literally lost sleep over deciding my ethical standpoint on just war versus pacifism and I am a better person for it . . . because of the way it challenged me to dig within some tension filled spaces. I think a paper that causes one to question one's assumptions, beliefs, values, and opinions is the definition of a good personal ethics paper. . . . Though I feel the arguments I made were for the most part sound, upon second and third reading and even as I was writing the paper, I found myself constantly questioning the conclusions I came to regarding my position for pacifism. I took and continue to take issue with my own points made in the paper. For that reason I have a greater appreciation for the many shades of grey and complexities of such difficult moral questions.

I am confident that the hundreds of young people who passed through this crucible of personal conscience formation are better equipped than they would be otherwise, and better equipped than most of their fellow citizens, to engage in public debate over the justice of future wars, some of which might even be stopped if a significant number of similarly morally serious citizens were to be formed. If, that is, personal conscience were assumed to be applicable to the decision to go to war and not just to its conduct, leaving the prior decision to rulers. And that is an imperative for moral educators in all faith traditions, in secular academies, and on every continent. Of course, it would be irresponsible to ask young people to achieve and act on this level of moral maturity as isolated individuals. Providing the supporting social framework for such fraught deliberations was the burden of the preceding chapter.

The final chapter puts the work of conscience in the context specifically of the *jus ad bellum* criterion of legitimate authority and puts that criterion in the context of Catholic theology. A case study of the US war in Vietnam places legitimate authority in a particular epochal historical context and dramatizes the necessity of the vigilant exercise of personal conscience of every citizen on behalf of the common good.

7

Presumptions and Eschatology

Legitimate Authority and Primacy of Conscience

Every ethic presupposes an eschatology, a goal for which we strive, a hoped-for future entailed in every decision.

—JAMES F. KEENAN, SJ[1]

THE CHALLENGE OF PEACE

THIS BOOK OPENED WITH an affirmation of the teaching authority of the Catholic Church in the US as demonstrated in their most famous pastoral letter. It will close likewise. The lengthy and transparent preparation and climactic publication, on May 3, 1983, of the US bishops' pastoral letter *The Challenge of Peace: God's Promise and Our Response* provoked not only vigorous public debate about US nuclear policy but also scholarly debate about the theoretical presumptions of the just-war tradition itself. The very idea that there *were* presumptions underpinning that tradition was something of an innovation, since the term itself, if not the conceptual reality pointed to, was not employed by Augustine or Aquinas. But it was not the innovative use of "presumption" *per se* that occasioned the strongest outcry

1. Keenan, "Moral Theology," 122.

from critics,[2] but rather the specific presumption the bishops derived from a foundational principle of all Christian ethics: "we should do no harm to our neighbors; how we treat our enemy is the key test of whether or not we love our neighbor; and the possibility of taking even one human life is a prospect we should consider in fear and trembling."[3] As Saint Paul sums up his discussion of the commandments in his *Letter to the Romans* (13:10): "You shall love your neighbor as yourself. Love does no evil to the neighbor; hence, love is the fulfillment of the law." Anthony F. Lang Jr. goes so far as to say that "using force was not considered to be a problem until Jesus' witness concerning matters of violence appeared."[4]

The formidable question arising from this starting point becomes obvious: "How is it possible to move from these presumptions to the idea of a justifiable use of force?"[5] The bishops answer by drawing on the seminal thought of St. Augustine, but using contemporary language: "Faced with the fact of attack on the innocent, the presumption that we do no harm, even to our enemy, yielded to the command of love understood as the need to restrain an enemy who would injure the innocent."[6] Notice that this is not an argument for or from self-defense but for defense of the innocent neighbor, which becomes the just-war criterion of defense of the common good, especially in Aquinas.[7]

2. Johnson, "Broken Tradition"; Weigel, "Moral Clarity."

3. NCCB, *Challenge of Peace*, #80.

4. Lang, "Just War Tradition," 203.

5. NCCB, *Challenge of Peace*, #80.

6. NCCB, *Challenge of Peace*, #81.

7. Aquinas, *Summa*, #II-II, Q. 40–42. Although Aquinas in defining just cause quotes Augustine's description of just war "as one that avenges wrongs, when a nation or state has to be punished, for refusing to make amends for the wrongs inflicted by its subjects, or to restore what it has seized unjustly" (Q. 40, First Article, "I answer that"), Aquinas himself is more likely to speak of just war as defense of the common good than of punishing or correcting wrongs. For example: "Such like precepts [not to resist evil] . . . should always be borne in readiness of mind, so that we be ready to obey them, and, if necessary, to refrain from resistance or self-defense. Nevertheless, it is necessary sometimes for a man to act otherwise for the common good" (Q.40, First Article, Reply to Objection 2). The first-named requirement of a just war, "the authority of the sovereign," is defined in terms of what thereby seems to be the more fundamental requirement, "the care for the common weal" and "defending the common weal against external enemies" (Q. 40, First Article, "I answer that"). Notice also his discussion of "Whether it is lawful for clerics and bishops to fight?": "wars are lawful and just in so far as they protect the poor and the entire common weal from suffering at the hands of the foe" (Q. 40, Second Article, Objection 1). Finally, so central is the common good to his understanding of just war

The perhaps non-controvertible enunciation of the basic presumption against doing harm becomes, for the bishops, a presumption against war, which is, for the critics, controvertible indeed. The bishops argue that "just war teaching has evolved . . . as an effort to prevent war; only if war cannot be rationally avoided, does the teaching then seek to restrict and reduce its horrors. It does this by establishing a set of rigorous conditions which must be met if the decision to go to war is to be morally permissible." But the bishops do not stop there: "Such a decision, especially today, requires extraordinarily strong reasons for overriding the presumption *in favor of peace* and *against war*."[8]

Their detractors argue, on the other hand, that if there *is* a presumption in the just-war tradition it is, not surprisingly, *in favor of justice* and *against injustice*—and since punishing or correcting injustice may require going to war, there can be no presumption against such a decision.[9] The bishops, however, claim to have Pope Pius XII on their side of the debate: "The Christian will for peace . . . is very careful to avoid recourse to the force of arms in defense of rights which, however legitimate, do not offset the risk of kindling a blaze with all its spiritual and material consequences."[10] The bishops then go on to explicate a "set of rigorous conditions which must be met if the decision to go to war is to be morally permissible." Here we get the well-known categories of *jus ad bellum* ("why and when recourse to war is permissible")[11] and *jus in bello* ("the conduct of war").[12]

In this context, a footnote points to scholarly articles by Ralph Potter, "The Moral Logic of War,"[13] and by James Childress, "Just War Criteria,"[14]

---

that Aquinas can justify rebellion against a tyrant, or not, depending on the effect on the common good: "A tyrannical government is not just, because it is directed, not to the common good, but to the private good of the ruler. . . . Consequently there is no sedition in disturbing a government of this kind, unless indeed the tyrant's rule be disturbed so inordinately, that his subjects suffer greater harm from the consequent disturbance than from the tyrant's government" (Q. 42, Second Article, Reply to Objection 3).

8. NCCB, *Challenge of Peace*, #83.

9. Johnson, "Broken Tradition"; Weigel, "Moral Clarity."

10. NCCB, *Challenge of Peace*, #83.

11. NCCB, *Challenge of Peace*, #84–85. Although these Latin terms are nearly synonymous with just war ethics today, they were a late development in that tradition. See Kolb, "Origin of the Twin Terms."

12. NCCB, *Challenge of Peace*, #101.

13. Potter, "Moral Logic."

14. Childress, "Just-War Theories." I am citing Childress's earlier version of the 1980 article cited by the bishops; it appeared in *Theological Studies* in 1978.

for "analysis of the content and relationship of these principles."[15] It is particularly from Potter that the bishops adopt the language of presumption: "Our common life is sustained by a strong moral and legal presumption against the use of force. . . . The logic generally applied by wise critics in thinking about right and wrong in the use of force is admirably simple in its basic structure. First, there is a presumption against the use of force. The burden of proof rests heavily upon anyone who would take arms against his neighbor. But secondly, it is conceded that certain exceptions must be made for the sake of the common good."[16]

The language of presumption provides a layperson's short-hand for Childress's philosophical argument for the *prima facie*[17] duty of nonmaleficence: "As individuals or members of institutions, we have a prima-facie duty not to injure others. . . . Insofar as an act injures another, it is prima-facie wrong and stands in need of justification. . . . [S]ome kinds of action (including killing) are 'intrinsically wrong,'" but (quoting William Frankena) "They may conceivably be justified in certain situations, but they always need to be justified."[18] Although Childress adopts this language from philosophical ethics (especially W. D. Ross),[19] he observes that "Christian theologians might derive this obligation not to injure or kill from the norm of agape" or from "the Fifth (or Sixth) Commandment . . . 'Thou shalt not kill.'"[20] Indeed, "The claim that injury and killing are prima-facie wrong is thus compatible with a number of philosophical and religious frameworks."[21]

But it is crucial to place this presentation of the presumption against war where the bishops do themselves. While contemporary scholars like Potter and Childress may provide them with an analytic language in which to present the just-war criteria that must be met if the presumption against war is to be overridden, the bishops rely less on such theoretical arguments than on the deep background of the Christian just-war tradition in Scripture. *The Challenge of Peace* begins not with ethical theory but with biblical revelation. Sections of chapter 1 address "Peace and the Kingdom"

15. NCCB, *Challenge of Peace*, n. 35.
16. Potter, "Moral Logic," 203, 205.
17. Literally, *at first face*, but colloquially, *at first sight*.
18. Childress, "Just-War Theories," 431.
19. Childress, "Just-War Theories," 430.
20. Childress, "Just-War Theories," 431.
21. Childress, "Just-War Theories," 431.

(#27–55), "Kingdom and History" (#56–65), and "The Moral Choices for the Kingdom" (#66–121), including sub-sections on "Peace and Fidelity to the Covenant" (#33–35) and "Hope for Eschatological Peace" (#36–38) in the Old Testament, and on "Jesus and the Reign of God" (#44–51) and "Jesus and the Community of Believers" (#52–54) in the New Testament (#39–55).

The bishops deliberately set the ethical question of war in the theological contexts of eschatology (kingdom or reign of God) and ecclesiology (covenant, community of believers). Stanley Hauerwas, a critic of the bishops' letter from a pacifist position, is correct: it all begins with how we understand the relationship of the kingdom of God—the central message of Jesus—to human history.[22] For the bishops, the most fundamental presumption is the inauguration of the kingdom of God in the birth, prophetic ministry, death, and resurrection of Jesus. Eschatology first, ecclesiology second, and ethics third. How do we understand the relationship of the kingdom of God to human history? Has it definitively arrived (Hauerwas) or is it yet to come in fullness (bishops)? How do we understand the role of the church in that tensive context? Enacting the peaceable kingdom here and now in communities of alternative vision (Hauerwas) or engaging the political world in hopes of nudging it toward the kingdom (bishops)? How do we understand the life and death decisions we make in light of the Church's relationship to history and kingdom? Christians may never kill (Hauerwas) or killing may sometimes be justified in order to defend the innocent and the common good (bishops)? See figure 1 for a chart I have used in the classroom to help students appreciate the differences among four representative perspectives on how Christian theologies shape Christian ethics of war and peace.

Figure 1. The Three E's of Christian Ethics of War and Peace

"The debate between pacifism and just war thinking is a theological issue of how we are to read and interpret history."[23]		
ESCHATOLOGY	ECCLESIOLOGY	ETHICS of war and peace
Relation of kingdom of God to history	Relation of church to world	Relation of disciple to state

22. Hauerwas, "Should War Be Eliminated?"

23. Hauerwas, "Should War Be Eliminated?" 52.

Christian Witness: Pacifism (Hauerwas)[24]		
Realized: the kingdom is here and now	Church lives God's reality over against the world	Conscientious objection

Christian Realism: Just War (Niebuhr)[25]		
Future: kingdom is yet to come	Christians seek approximation of justice in a sinful world	Just warrior

"Just War as Christian Discipleship" (Bell)[26]		
God sanctifies here and now	Church forms faithful disciples/soldiers	Faithful warriors if war is just

"The Challenge of Peace": Strict Just War (US Bishops)[27]		
"Already but not yet"	In the world but guiding, changing it	CO or just warrior (SCO)

As the influential Protestant ethicist Paul Ramsey put it, "Not for nothing did all the theologians of the past [before the sixteenth century] discuss the justice of war under the heading of charity and its subheading peace, which is a work of charity!"[28] This is the theological context in which the bishops place their understanding of the just-war tradition, which leads them to a particular and determinative eschatological perspective: "Christians are called to live the tension between the vision of the reign of God and its concrete realization in history. The tension is often described in terms of 'already but not yet': we already live in the grace of the kingdom, but it is not yet the completed kingdom. Hence, we are a pilgrim people in a world marked by conflict and injustice. Christ's grace is at work in the world; his command of love and call to reconciliation are not purely future ideals but call us to obedience today."[29] This call to love of neighbor and even enemy is why "the Church's teaching on war and peace establishes a strong presumption against war which is binding on all; it then examines when this presumption may be overridden, precisely in the name of preserving the kind of peace which protects human dignity and human

24. Hauerwas, "Should War Be Eliminated?"
25. Niebuhr, "Why the Christian Church."
26. Bell, *Just War as Discipleship*.
27. NCCB, *Challenge of Peace*.
28. Ramsey, *Just War*, 207.
29. NCCB, *Challenge of Peace*, #58.

rights."[30] This seems perfectly in line with the perspectives of Augustine and Aquinas. This bishops' fundamental perspective has not been formed by Potter and Childress, however helpful their meta-ethical analyses may be, but by fidelity to Christ and his proclamation of the kingdom of God within history.

I confess that when I first came across rejection of the bishops' language of presumption, I was incredulous. But in an attempt to get beyond sometimes sterile argument and counter-argument, I'd like to suggest (but not fully develop) another approach, one that I believe is true to the tradition and acknowledges the complexity of the question. I would return yet again to Aquinas, who relied so heavily on Augustine, and suggest that the schoolman provides what we might think of as the *three* presumptions of the just-war ethic—if we must have presumptions at all—the three criteria he articulated for a just war: legitimate authority, just cause, and right intention (peace)—although that hardly means forgetting the *ur*-presumption of the Gospel command to love even the enemy. But I would list them in the order used in *The Harvest of Justice Is Sown in Peace*, the tenth-anniversary commemoration of *The Challenge of Peace*. The bishops offer no explanation for this new ordering, but I would say again (see n. 7) that as the usually first-named requirement, legitimate authority, is defined in terms of responsibility for the common good and defense against injustice, the criterion of just cause logically comes first. But as all three criteria must be met, according to Aquinas and subsequent commentators—they are a package deal—it is probably beside the point to argue which is most important or primary. I would observe, nonetheless, that in Aquinas's account, legitimate authority is not absolute or total. If a ruling authority trespasses egregiously against the common good, and so loses its legitimacy, the people may be justified in rebellion.[31] On the other hand, the presumptions for justice and for peace are as absolute as they can be *in tandem*. One may never act against justice or peace except in the name of peace or justice. There's the rub. This side of the eschaton, justice and peace may not always kiss (Ps 85:11).

PERSONAL CONSCIENCE AND VIETNAM

In the context of this book and its focus on the primacy of personal conscience, the criterion of legitimate authority must be given special attention.

30. NCCB, *Challenge of Peace*, #70.

31. *Summa Theologiae*, II-II, 41.2. See especially the Reply to Objection 3.

I propose doing so less by theoretical discourse than by investigating its practice in the major international conflict of my lifetime, the American War in Vietnam (the War in Iraq being a close second as a possible case study of the problem of legitimate authority).[32] It may be that my interest in writing this book was germinated as an undergraduate during crucial years of that war, 1966–70. Because I was a college student, I was deferred from the draft; because I was a student at a land-grant university—Kansas State was the first institution of higher learning established by the Morrill Act in 1863—as an able-bodied male I was required to take two years of military training. I completed the freshman and sophomore years in the Reserved Officer Training Corps. But as I learned more about the war, I became increasingly uncertain of its legitimacy. Although I had been an active member of a mainstream Protestant church all my young life, and although I had a solid education in a good public-school system, I had been taught nothing of the just-war tradition. And as my much older half-brother had graduated from K-State and its ROTC program and then served in combat in World War II in Europe, I grew up with little if any skepticism of the justice of America's wars. I had no reason to think I would have done differently than did my brother, had I been born twenty-seven years earlier, as that was clearly a war with a just cause. I knew nothing of pacifism, nor of the almost 2,000 years of Christian tradition on the question of war. And yet, public debate, as I experienced it in the national media and on campus, was all about the justice of this war. The looming draft made that debate very personal.

I decided not to continue into the final two years of ROTC. As I recall, only one other sophomore cadet in my immediate cohort of forty made that decision, which meant that upon graduation we would be eligible for the draft. Thirty-eight of my peers thought it better to serve as an officer

32. For an illuminating analysis of "The Iraq War and Political Lying," among similar topics, see DeCosse, "Authority, Lies, and War," 380–86. Also see *Uncovered: The War on Iraq*, a 2004 documentary film (available on YouTube) directed by Robert Greenwald that includes interviews with more than two dozen intelligence professionals from the State Department, CIA, and Pentagon, as well as weapons inspectors, ambassadors, journalists, and politicians, all of whom speak to the claims of the George W. Bush administration that Iraq possessed weapons of mass destruction and had links to Al-Qaeda, and that these claims were known to be false within the intelligence community before the invasion of Iraq in 2003. For more recent reporting on deception and the war in Afghanistan, see Gibbons-Neff, "Documents Reveal": "Prominent American officials concealed pessimistic assessments about the long-running military campaign in Afghanistan, according to thousands of pages of documents published by *The Washington Post*."

than as a private, and to pick up financial help for the last two years of college. It is the great irony of my political life that President Nixon, whom I campaigned against in 1968 (even though I was too young to vote) and voted against in 1972, made the issue vanish for me, if not for most of my peers, by instituting a lottery system intended to do away with class bias— no more educational deferments. An official reached into a large glass jar containing capsules representing all the days of the year. Men born on the first 195 days drawn out one by one became eligible for conscription. A second lottery determined the order of conscription for men sharing each birthday. My birthday, November 3 (which I much later learned to be the feast day of Saint Martin de Porres, patron of those working for social justice), came up on the 320th selection. Perhaps not surprisingly, my memory of the event has been of a drum being spun—like the wheel of the goddess of chance, luck, and fate, Fortuna, or like a prize wheel at a carnival. I got lucky. Won the prize. Most did not.

I don't know who was more relieved, myself or my mother, in whose living room I had watched the nightly news with its body counts and footage of protests all around the country and even the world—and where I watched that exercise of chance back in Washington DC. I went off to graduate school instead of basic training—or alternative service, or incarceration. Had I not been so fortunate, I would have had to apply for conscientious objection status, although I would have had to do so as a *selective* CO, although I didn't know the terminology at the time. That position was not officially recognized as qualifying for exemption, but it is my impression that in fact many draft boards allowed it in practice, given the growing opposition to the war and the many young men who objected, even if they were not pacifists. Fifty years later, here's the book those anxious years provoked.

THE AMERICAN WAR IN VIETNAM AND THE CRITERION OF LEGITIMATE AUTHORITY: A CASE STUDY BASED ON THE PENTAGON PAPERS

It makes no sense to say that we have grounds for presuming that the cause our own government commands us to support is just. The presumption is all the other way; and if to formal considerations we add the evidence of history, then the doctrine that we have a duty to presume that our own

government is in the right in the matter of war and peace looks like a piece
of insanity.

—J. M. CAMERON[33]

What caused the disastrous defeat of American policies and armed
intervention [in Vietnam] was indeed no quagmire . . . but the willful,
deliberate disregard of all facts, historical, political, geographical, for more
than twenty-five years.

—HANNAH ARENDT[34]

Introduction

In mid-1967, Secretary of Defense Robert S. McNamara commissioned a
history of United States involvement in Indochina from World War II to
the present. The thirty-six authors—military and civilian professionals in
the Departments of Defense and State—worked for a year and a half to produce "approximately 3,000 pages of narrative history and more than 4,000
pages of appended documents—an estimated total of 2.5 million words"
comprising forty-seven bound volumes.[35] The study was meant by McNamara to be top-secret but became ironically so when "people in the White
House, in the Department of State, and in the Defense Department apparently ignored the study," even to the point "that those who should have been
most concerned with what the study had to tell never set eyes on it."[36] The
irony sharpens further upon realization that "the people who read these
documents in the [New York] Times were the first to study them."[37] That became a possibility thanks to one of the authors, Daniel Ellsberg, who leaked
photocopies of most of the massive study to the press precisely because it

33. Cameron, "Foreword," xiii.
34. Arendt, "Lying in Politics," 32.
35. *New York Times, Pentagon Papers*, ix–x.
36. Arendt, "Lying in Politics," 30.
37. Arendt, "Lying in Politics," 31 (quoting Tom Wicker).

was not being taken seriously by the authorities responsible for US foreign and military policy.[38] What deepens even that irony is that "the Pentagon Papers revealed little significant news that was not available to the average readers of dailies and weeklies."[39] In other words, "the public had access for years to material that the government vainly tried to keep from it."[40] This lapidary history of the provenance of *The Pentagon Papers* embodies a pattern the history recorded therein plays out over and over again: willful ignorance of the best intelligence available and deliberate deception of the public by democratically elected and therefore legitimate public authorities responsible for the common good of the nation. A few examples will make the point that the conduct of legitimate authority must be viewed with a deliberate skepticism even in a democratic republic.

A Pattern of Denial and Deception

Hannah Arendt points out "the strange fact that the mistaken decisions and lying statements [of successive administrations] consistently violated the astoundingly accurate reports of the intelligence community."[41] In his introduction to the Bantam edition, Neil Sheehan, whose investigative reporting is singled out as the basis for the newspaper's publication of *The Pentagon Papers*, and who was also one of the four *New York Times* journalists to write commentaries that comprise the ten chronologically delineated

---

38. Arendt, "Lying in Politics," 44.

39. One revelation, however, stands out: "in late 1945 and early 1946, Ho Chi Minh wrote at least eight letters to President Truman and the State Department requesting American help in winning Vietnam's independence from France. . . . The analyst says he could find no record that the United States ever answered Ho Chi Minh's letters. Nor has Washington ever revealed that it received the letters" (*New York Times, Pentagon Papers*, 26). The specific help Ho proposed was that the United States support Vietnamese independence "according to the Philippines example." The Treaty of Paris (1898) had transferred sovereignty from Spain to the United States. The revolution against Spain then, in effect, continued against the US, ending unsuccessfully in 1902. The US did not grant the Philippines independence until 1946. It is astonishing that Ho Chi Minh would propose anything like such a process for gaining Vietnamese independence from France. Of course, not only did the US not respond to Ho's request, it took over the role of the re-colonizer, at least from the Vietnamese perspective. The nation's independence and unification then played out in the war against the United States.

40. Arendt, "Lying in Politics," 45.

41. Arendt, "Lying in Politics," 14.

chapters of the Bantam edition, summarizes one major instance of this pattern of ignoring intelligence and deceiving the public:

> The Johnson Administration, though the President was reluctant and hesitant to take the final decision, intensified the covert warfare against North Vietnam and began planning in the spring of 1964 to wage overt war, a full year before it publicly revealed the depth of its involvement and its fear of defeat.
>
> This campaign of growing clandestine military pressure through 1964 and the expanding program of bombing North Vietnam in 1965 were begun despite the judgment of the Government's intelligence community that the measures would not cause Hanoi to cease its support of the Vietcong insurgency in the South, and that the bombing was deemed militarily ineffective within a few months.[42]

But the pattern was set by earlier administrations. Hedrick Smith, writing about "The Overthrow of Ngo Dinh Diem: May-November, 1963," observes that

> the early months of 1963 were a season of bullish public pronouncements about the war. In his State of the Union address on Jan. 14, President Kennedy declared that the "spearpoint of aggression has been blunted in Vietnam," while Adm. Harry D. Felt, commander in chief of Pacific forces, predicted victory within three years. Although this reflected the view prevailing among the policy makers, a national intelligence estimate on April 17 offered a less glowing picture. Provided that outside help to the Vietcong was not increased, the intelligence paper estimated that the guerrillas could be "contained militarily" but added that there was still no persuasive evidence that the enemy had been "grievously hurt" by the allied war efforts. Conclusion: "The situation remains fragile."[43]

Of course, the most famous example of this pattern of deception is the Gulf of Tonkin incident. Forty-one years later, on December 1, 2005,

> The National Security Agency . . . released hundreds of pages of long-secret documents on the 1964 Gulf of Tonkin incident, which played a critical role in significantly expanding the American commitment to the Vietnam War. . . . The most provocative document is a 2001 article in which an agency historian argued

42. *New York Times, Pentagon Papers*, xi.
43. *New York Times, Pentagon Papers*, 164.

that the agency's intelligence officers "deliberately skewed" the evidence passed on to policy makers and the public to falsely suggest that North Vietnamese ships had attacked American destroyers on Aug. 4, 1964. Based on the assertion that such an attack had occurred, President Lyndon B. Johnson ordered airstrikes on North Vietnam and Congress passed a broad resolution authorizing military action.[44]

The agency historian, Robert J. Hanyok, "wrote that 90 percent of the intercepts of North Vietnamese communications relevant to the supposed Aug. 4, 1964, attack were omitted from the major agency documents going to policy makers. 'The overwhelming body of reports, if used, would have told the story that no attack had happened.'"[45]

A year later, as reported by Fox Butterfield in "The Buildup: July, 1965–September, 1966,"

> Gen. William C. Westmoreland's troop requests jumped from a total of 175,000 men in June, 1965, to 275,000 that July, to 443,000 in December and then to 542,000 the following June. Neither the requests of the American commander in Vietnam nor President Lyndon B. Johnson's rapid approval of all but the last of them was made public.

At the same time, the study says, the Johnson Administration's continual expansion of the air war during 1965 and 1966 was based on a "colossal misjudgment" about the bombing's effect on Hanoi's will and capabilities.

> A secret Defense Department seminar of 47 scientists—"the cream of the scholarly community in technical fields"—concluded in the summer of 1966 that the bombing of North Vietnam had had "no measurable effect" on Hanoi.[46]

Smith quotes one of the analyst's judgment that North Vietnam

> was an extremely poor target for air attack. The theory of either strategic or interdiction bombing assumed highly developed industrial nations producing large quantities of military goods to sustain mass armies engaged in intensive warfare. NVN, as U.S. intelligence agencies knew, was an agricultural country with a

44. Shane, "Vietnam War Intelligence," 1.
45. Shane, "Vietnam War Intelligence," 2.
46. *New York Times, Pentagon Papers,* 459, 462.

rudimentary transportation system and little industry of any kind.[47]

After dramatically intensifying the bombing campaign and increasing the number of troops on the ground in the mid-sixties, no one among the policy-makers or military brass was prepared for the enemy's display of viability in early 1968. As E. W. Kenworthy recounts in "The Tet Offensive and the Turnaround," the Pentagon study

> says that the offensive [which began on January 31, 1968] took the White House and the Joint Chiefs "by surprise, and its strength, length and intensity prolonged this shock." For the President, the study makes plain, the shock and disappointment were particularly severe, because throughout much of 1967 he had discounted "negative analyses" of United States strategy by the Central Intelligence Agency and the Pentagon offices of International Security Affairs and Systems Analysis. Instead, the study says, Mr. Johnson had seized upon the "optimistic reports" from General Westmoreland to counteract what many Pentagon civilians sensed was a growing public disillusionment with the war.[48]

Only four days before the Tet offensive began, Gen. Westmoreland had stated, "The year ended with the enemy increasingly resorting to desperation tactics in attempting to achieve military/psychological victory; and he has experienced only failure in these attempts."[49] However, "the study sums up the lesson of the Tet offensive" as having "imposed itself finally upon President Johnson and led him to accept the view of those civilian advisers and the intelligence community that he had so long resisted in his search for 'victory.'" On March 31, 1968, a chastened President delivered a nationally televised address in which he announced severe restrictions on the bombing campaign, smaller than anticipated troop increases, and that "I shall not seek, and I will not accept the nomination of my party" for a second term.[50]

---

47. *New York Times, Pentagon Papers,* 469.
48. *New York Times, Pentagon Papers,* 592.
49. *New York Times, Pentagon Papers,* 593.
50. *New York Times, Pentagon Papers,* 611.

Image, Dominos, Consequences

Perhaps there would have been no need for a Vietnam Memorial on the mall in Washington if the five administrations, both Democratic and Republican, that prosecuted the American war in Vietnam had heeded the consistent intelligence gathered and reported by their own professionals. Perhaps those five administrations would then not have had need to deceive the American public about our growing involvement over three decades. North Vietnam unified the country at the cost of perhaps two million Vietnamese lives, but the nations of southeast Asia did not begin falling to Communism like dominoes, as had been incessantly and alarmingly foretold. In 1954 President Eisenhower had approved a National Security Council paper that "predicted that the 'loss of any single country' in Southeast Asia would ultimately lead to the loss of all Southeast Asia, then India and Japan, and finally 'endanger the stability and security of Europe.'" According to the Pentagon study, "The domino theory and the assumptions behind it were never questioned."[51] But that's overstated according to the study itself. Neil Sheehan reports in "The Covert War and Tonkin Gulf: February-August, 1964" that the President submitted a formal question to the CIA in June: "Would the rest of Southeast Asia necessarily fall if Laos and South Vietnam came under North Vietnamese control?" According to Sheehan, recounting the Pentagon study, "The agency's reply on June 9 challenged the domino theory, widely believed in one form or another within the Administration":

> "With the possible exception of Cambodia," the C.I.A. memorandum said, "it is likely that no nation in the area would quickly succumb to Communism as a result of the fall of Laos and South Vietnam. Furthermore, a continuation of the spread of Communism in the area would not be inexorable, and any spread which did occur would take time—time in which the total situation might change in any number of ways unfavorable to the Communist cause."[52]

Sheehan further summarizes the Pentagon study's references to ignored intelligence reports by recounting, "As in the case of earlier C.I.A. analysis stating that the real roots of the Vietcong strength lay in South Vietnam, the study shows that the President and his senior officials were not inclined

51. *New York Times, Pentagon Papers*, 7.
52. *New York Times, Pentagon Papers*, 253–54.

to adjust policy along the lines of this analysis challenging the domino theory."[53]

In one of the most often cited passages of *The Pentagon Papers*, Sheehan reports that

> behind these foreign-policy axioms about domino effects, wars of liberation and the containment of China, the study also reveals a deeper perception among the President and his aides that the United States was now the most powerful nation in the world and that the outcome in South Vietnam would demonstrate the will and the ability of the United States to have its way in world affairs. The study conveys an impression that the war was thus considered less important for what it meant to the South Vietnamese people than for what it meant to the position of the United States in the world.[54]

John T. McNaughton, Assistant Secretary of Defense for International Security Affairs, "would later capsulize this perception in a memorandum to Mr. McNamara seeking to apportion American aims in South Vietnam":

> "70 pct.—To avoid a humiliating U.S. defeat (to our reputation as a guarantor).
>
> "20 pct.—To keep SVN (and then adjacent) territory from Chinese hands.
>
> "10 pct.—To permit the people of SVN to enjoy a better, freer way of life."[55]

Even though the domino theory continued to be the public rationale for US involvement in Vietnam[56] (even though this theory was challenged by the intelligence community), it may actually have been less a factor in policymaking at the highest level than was a concern to avoid injury to the image of the US as the most powerful nation in the world. I leave the final words on what can be learned from *The Pentagon Papers* about the exercise of "legitimate authority" during the US war in Vietnam to Hannah Arendt:

---

53. *New York Times, Pentagon Papers*, 254.

54. *New York Times, Pentagon Papers*, 255.

55. *New York Times, Pentagon Papers*, 255.

56. See President Johnson's address before the National Legislative Conference on September 29, 1967, for an example of this public rationale: https://millercenter.org/the-presidency/presidential-speeches/september-29-1967-speech-vietnam.

The ultimate aim was neither power nor profit. Nor was it even influence in the world to serve particular, tangible interests for the sake of which prestige, an image of the "greatest power in the world," was needed and purposefully used. The goal was now the image itself, as is manifest in the very language of the problem-solvers [Arendt's term for McNamara, McGeorge Bundy, and other policy-making officials in the Kennedy/Johnson administrations], with their "scenarios" and "audiences," borrowed from the theater. . . . Image-making as global policy—not world conquest, but victory in the battle "to win the people's minds"—is indeed something new in the huge arsenal of human follies recorded in history.[57]

CONCLUSION: RETHINKING LEGITIMATE AUTHORITY

David DeCosse argues "that democratic theory should be more fully integrated into Catholic thought on war and peace and, in particular, into the just war criterion of legitimate authority."[58] He offers six steps toward this integration, two of which are especially pertinent to the argument of this chapter, and indeed of the book as a whole:

> Third . . . Catholic thought should be more bold in assessing claims to go to war made by government leaders and more inclined to view such claims from the perspective of the possibly deceived. Fourth, the criterion of legitimate authority should specifically include a requirement for truthful speech to citizens about going to war.[59]

These recommendation about skepticism regarding leaders' claims said to justify going to war and truthfulness as a requisite of legitimate authority resonate deeply with the patterns of willful ignorance and deliberate deception during the American war in Vietnam as revealed in *The Pentagon Papers*. If Arendt is right, and I believe the historical analyses of Halberstam, Sheehan, and perhaps McMaster would concur, that "what caused the disastrous defeat of American policies and armed intervention was indeed

---

57. Arendt, "Lying in Politics," 17–18. Other valuable and in-depth studies of the US decision-making process during the Vietnam War include Halberstam, *Best and the Brightest*; Sheehan, *Bright Shining Lie*; and McMaster, *Dereliction of Duty*.

58. DeCosse, "Authority, Lies, and War," 393.

59. DeCosse, "Authority, Lies, and War," 393–94 (emphasis added).

no quagmire . . . but the willful, deliberate disregard of all facts, historical, political, geographical, for more than twenty-five years,"[60] then such skepticism is not only a right but a duty, a moral responsibility of the citizen and the citizen-soldier.

This book has argued that personal conscience, as formed by Catholic just-war ethics and as informed, potentially, by the expert deliberations of persons of authoritative knowledge regarding that tradition and all the disciplines that would bear on the decision to go to war, assembled by the Church to deliberate and judge on its behalf, could and should become a formidable bulwark against unjust war. Saint Augustine said it best: "The wise man will wage just wars. . . . For, unless the wars were just, he would not have to wage them, and in such circumstances he would not be involved in war at all."[61]

I have argued that the problem is not the just-war tradition but the unjust-war tradition, specifically the conventional view that warriors have no responsibility to judge the justice of the wars they are asked to fight. I presented the story of Blessed Franz Jägerstätter as an example of solitary *selective* conscientious objection in his refusal to participate in Hitler's unjust wars. Sociologist Gordan Zahn's analysis of how Jägerstätter conformed his conscience to the early Christian martyrs rather than the politically compliant Catholic hierarchies of Germany and Austria points the way to a more robust ecclesial counterpoint to the machinations of "legitimate authority." I then traced the evolution of Catholic thinking on conscientious objection from Augustine in the early fifth-century to the US bishops in the late twentieth-century to John Paul II in the early twenty-first, such that Jägerstätter's example can now be said to be in full conformity with magisterial teaching (or is it the other way around?). Because conscience is at the heart of this book, I outlined Thomas Aquinas's influential account of the structure and primacy of personal conscience, as reflected in the *Catechism of the Catholic Church*. I then investigated the phenomenon of combat-induced moral injury as an assault on conscience, as exemplified in five US warriors' diverse experiences in WWII, Vietnam, and Iraq, and argued that exposing warriors to such injury, especially the ultimate moral injury of being ordered to fight in an unjust war, raises the stakes for decision-making in a democratic society even higher than we might otherwise have imagined. I explored Augustine's wrestling with the dilemma of the just judge

60. Arendt, "Lying in Politics," 32.

61. Augustine, *City of God*, 19.7.

in an unjust justice system and compared that to a present-day military interrogator's moral injury from his deeply conflicted experience in Iraq.

The heart of my proposal to heighten the role of personal conscience in public debates about particular wars is philosopher Jeff McMahan's vision of a trans-national *jus ad bellum* court. I suggested how that could be accomplished by and within the Catholic Church, as the necessary structure to make selective conscientious objection a possibility for more warriors, and citizens generally, at least among Catholics, beyond the heroic example of a martyr like Franz Jägerstätter. Five appendices followed that chapter, each suggesting that proposing such a role for the Church and for the warrior's conscience is not entirely new with this book. I advanced the perspective that psychological science gives ample warrant for thinking that even young citizens and warriors have the capacity to deliberate as adults on the justifiability of particular wars, but that like all of us, their consciences need an appropriate formation, authoritative guidance, and social support.

Finally, I put the argument of the book in the context of debates provoked by *The Challenge of Peace* on the presumptions and eschatology of the just-war tradition, and especially the *jus ad bellum* criterion of legitimate authority, the debate partner, as it were, of personal conscience. The Vietnam War, as portrayed in *The Pentagon Papers*, was presented as a case study of legitimate authority gone profoundly awry. The need for a "second opinion" on the part of citizens and soldiers could hardly be made more plain. I wish to close this book on preventing unjust war, with its heavy toll of lives and souls and minds, with a reflection on the most compelling and even haunting portrait of conscience of which I am aware, Seamus Heaney's poem, "From the Republic of Conscience." A transcendent but deeply humane utopia gets the last word and draws us forward.

Epilogue

From the Republic of Conscience

I HAVE COME TO think of this book as an extended meditation on the quotations from Augustine and Aquinas that appear as epigraphs. Their writings on just war and Aquinas's writing on conscience (chapter 2) are foundational to the Catholic tradition and central to my argument. My Excursus on Augustine's wise judge and his wounded conscience is yet one more indication that the term moral injury may be new but the phenomenon not. Yoking the Catholic traditions on just-war ethics and personal conscience ever more tightly through the establishment of a Catholic *ad bellum* court has been the burden of this book. The exemplary conscience of Franz Jägerstätter and his reliance on the early martyrs as his reference group has been the inspiration for this proposal. To the existentially and ethically determinative question, To whom do you belong? Franz answered, the one true church of the martyrs. Had he had the opportunity, he might have answered, "I belong to the Republic of Conscience, indeed, I am an Ambassador."

From the Republic of Conscience was written by the Irish poet Seamus Heaney, recipient of the Nobel Prize for Literature in 1995, at the request of Amnesty International Ireland to commemorate International Human Rights Day in 1985. Amnesty International's highest award, Ambassador of Conscience, takes its name from this poem. Heaney said about it,

> I took it that Conscience would be a republic, a silent, solitary place where a person would find it hard to avoid self-awareness and self-examination; and this made me think of Orkney [Island].

I remembered the silence the first time I landed there. When I got off the small propeller plane and started walking across the grass to a little arrivals hut, I heard the cry of a curlew. And as soon as that image came to me, I was up and away, able to proceed with a fiction that felt workable yet unconstrained, a made-up thing that might be hung in the scale as a counterweight to the given actuality of the world.[1]

Colm O'Gorman, writing on behalf of Amnesty International, recipient of the Nobel Prize for Peace in 1977, paid tribute to the poet on the day of his death, August 30, 2013: "Seamus was a magnificent man. He was a true ambassador of conscience, a man whose empathy for the powerless and the marginalized was matched by his magnificent capacity to construct language which demanded a deep reflection on what it means to be human."[2]

From the Republic of Conscience

I

When I landed in the republic of conscience
it was so noiseless when the engines stopped
I could hear a curlew high above the runway.

At immigration, the clerk was an old man
who produced a wallet from his homespun coat
and showed me a photograph of my grandfather.

The woman in customs asked me to declare
the words of our traditional cures and charms
to heal dumbness and avert the evil eye.

No porters. No interpreter. No taxi.
You carried your own burden and very soon
your symptoms of creeping privilege disappeared.

II

Fog is a dreaded omen there but lightning
spells universal good and parents
hang swaddled infants in trees during thunderstorms.

Salt is their precious mineral. And seashells
are held to the ear during births and funerals.
The base of all inks and pigments is seawater.

1. Heaney, [remarks on" From the Republic of Conscience"].
2. O'Gorman, "Remembering Seamus Heaney."

Their sacred symbol is a stylised boat.
The sail is an ear, the mast a sloping pen,
the hull a mouth-shape, the keel an open eye.

At their inauguration, public leaders
must swear to uphold unwritten law and weep
to atone for their presumption to hold office—

and to affirm their faith that all life sprang
from salt in tears which the sky god wept
after he dreamt his solitude was endless.

III

I came back from that frugal republic
with my two arms the one length, the customs woman
having insisted my allowance was myself.

The old man rose and gazed into my face
and said that was official recognition
that I was now a dual citizen.

He therefore desired me when I got home
to consider myself a representative
and to speak on their behalf in my own tongue.

Their embassies, he said, were everywhere
but operated independently
and no ambassador would ever be relieved.[3]

The Republic of Conscience functions like one of Jesus's parables of the kingdom: it is both familiar and strange, intimate and distant, calm and demanding, as ordinary as salt and as dramatic as lightning, requiring both humility and magnanimity, empathy and courage. It is indeed "*a silent, solitary place where a person would find it hard to avoid self-awareness and self-examination.*" It is "at hand" (Mark 1:15), "already but not yet" (*The Challenge of Peace*), waiting for its realization. It is "*a made-up thing that might be hung in the scale as a counterweight to the given actuality of the world.*" If we were centered in that kind of gentle yoking of opposites, would we not be better equipped to enact the humanizing, conscience-driven vision of Catholic teaching on justice even in war? Would we not be better able to pursue both justice and peace?

The wise man will wage just wars. . . . For, unless the wars were just, he would not have to wage them, and in such circumstances he would not be involved in war at all.

—SAINT AUGUSTINE, *CITY OF GOD*, 19.7

There are two reasons why men especially deviate from justice. The first is because they defer to important persons. The second is because they defer to the majority.

—SAINT THOMAS AQUINAS, *COMMENTARY ON THE BOOK OF JOB*, 34.2

Those who want to find the right way to eternal well-being should not walk with the majority of people who are usually timid about making sacrifices, and they should not entrust themselves to leaders whose actions differ from their words.

—FRANZ JÄGERSTÄTTER[4]

4. Putz, *Franz Jägersttätter*, 215.

Acknowledgments

LYNN SCHNEIDERMAN, INTERLIBRARY LOAN Specialist at Creighton University's Reinert-Alumni Memorial Library, has done exceptional work procuring materials needed for the research that informs this book. I marvel that a request for an obscure article can be made via email one day and it shows up in my inbox the next, from halfway across the continent. Thank you, Lynn!

Cathy Laake at the Kroc Institute for International Peace Studies at the University of Notre Dame retrieved from the archives there the otherwise unpublished Working Paper by John Howard Yoder that informs Appendix 2. I am grateful.

Former colleagues at Creighton University who have contributed in some way to this project have been cited within the text, but I'd like to thank them again here: Olaf Bolke, Julia Fleming, John O'Keefe, Nicolae Roddy. I also express my gratitude to Dean Bridget Keegan of the Creighton College of Arts & Sciences, and Dr. Laura Heinemann, then Chair of the Department of Cultural & Social Studies, for supporting my application for Emeritus status, which has made all the difference. I would not otherwise have had access to Interlibrary Loan and other Creighton University resources, which has made this book possible.

Editors at various periodical publications not only published my articles but granted permission for their use in this book, as cited within the text. I appreciate this support even though in most cases no legal permission was required. It was Bernard Prusak of the journal *Expositions* whose inclusion of the article that became chapter 5 elicited Drew Christiansen's interest and encouragement. I am especially grateful to Fr. Christiansen, SJ, for agreeing to write the foreword.

I am grateful to Farrar, Strauss, & Giroux for granting permission to use Seamus Heaney's *From the Republic of Conscience* in the epilogue. That magnificent poem and parable enriches this book considerably.

Needless to say, this book depends on the intellectual endeavors of many, from Augustine and Aquinas to McMahan, Moshman, and Zahn, to name only the most obvious. Perhaps my singular contribution has been to bring their thinking into conversation with each other in what I hope readers will consider a coherent argument. Any faults of this book are the responsibility of the author, not his esteemed sources or consultants.

And I am grateful to Wipf and Stock Publishers for taking on this book. The editors I have worked with, Charlie Collier, Chelsea Lobey, and Matthew Wimer, have been both personable in their communications and expert in their editing and publication management. Thank you.

Bibliography

[Note: The documents of the Catholic bishops of the United States are listed below under three organizational titles: National Conference of Catholic Bishops, Unites States Catholic Conference, United States Conference of Catholic Bishops. These variations have no bearing on the authority of the documents themselves.]

Ackerman, Peter, and Jack DuVall. *A Force More Powerful: A Century of Nonviolent Conflict*. New York: St. Martin's, 2000.

Allen, John L. *All the Pope's Men: The Inside Story of How the Vatican Really Thinks*. New York: Doubleday, 2004.

Amery, Carl. *Capitulation: The Lesson of German Catholicism*. New York: Herder and Herder, 1967.

Aquinas, Thomas. *Truth*. Vol. 2, *Questions X–XX*. Translated by James V. McGlynn. Chicago: Henry Regnery, 1953.

Arendt, Hannah. "Lying in Politics." In *Crises of the Republic*, by Hannah Arendt, 1–48. San Diego: Harcourt Brace, 1972.

Augustine. Letter 229.2, to Darius (excerpt). In *The Early Fathers on War and Military Service*, by Louis J. Swift, 115. Wilmington, DE: Michael Glazier, 1983.

"Augustine's Bible." Reprinted from a Friends of Augustine bulletin: http://www.augnet.org/en/life-of-augustine/augustine-in-general/1302-augustines-bible/.

Bauman, Zygmunt. *Modernity and the Holocaust*. Ithaca: Cornell University Press, 1989.

Bell, Daniel M., Jr. *Just War as Christian Discipleship: Recentering the Tradition in the Church Rather than the State*. Grand Rapids: Brazos, 2009.

Benbaji, Yitzhak, and Naomi Sussman, eds. *Reading Walzer*. London: Routledge, 2014.

Benestad, J. Brian, and Francis J. Butler, eds. *Quest for Justice: A Compendium of Statements of the United States Catholic Bishops on the Political and Social Order 1966–1980*. Washington, DC: National Conference of Catholic Bishops/United States Catholic Conference, 1980.

Bergman, Roger. *Catholic Social Learning: Educating the Faith That Does Justice*. New York: Fordham University Press, 2011.

————. "Conscientious Objection to Unjust War: From Augustine to John Paul II." *Journal of Religion and Society* Supplement 14 (2017) 28–43. https://dspace2.creighton.edu/xmlui/bitstream/handle/10504/109258/2017-7.pdf.

————. "Jesus, Scripture, and the Ethics of War." *Creighton Magazine* (Summer 2003) 30–35.

————. "Jettisoning Just War Endangers Just Peace." *National Catholic Reporter*, September 12, 2016. https://www.ncronline.org/news/justice/jettisoning-just-war-endangers-just-peace.

————. "Journey Into Shame: Implications for Justice Pedagogies." *Engaging Pedagogies in Catholic Higher Education*, 1.1, Article 2 (2015). https://digitalcommons.stmarys-ca.edu/epiche/vol1/iss1/2.

————. "Preventing Unjust War: The Role of the Catholic Church." *Expositions: Interdisciplinary Studies in the Humanities* 12 (2018) 8–19. https://expositions.journals.villanova.edu/issue/view/159.

————. "Teaching Justice After MacIntyre: Toward a Catholic Philosophy of Moral Education." *Catholic Education: A Journal of Inquiry and Practice* 12.1 (2008) 7–24.

————. "Teaching to Prevent Unjust War." *Journal of Peace and Justice Studies* 28 (2019) 81–88.

————. "Toward a Sociology of Conscience: The Example of Franz Jägerstätter and the Legacy of Gordon Zahn." *Journal for Justice and Peace Studies* 23 (2014) 73–97.

————. "'You say Tertullian, I say Augustine': An Essay on Intra-Catholic Dialogue on War, Justice, and Peace." *Expositions: Interdisciplinary Studies in the Humanities* 14/2 (expected fall 2020).

Boudreau, Tyler. "The Morally Injured." *Massachusetts Review* 52.3/4 (2011) 746–54.

Brackley, Dean. *The Call to Discernment in Troubled Times*. New York: Crossroad, 2004.

Brennan, Thomas J., and Finbarr O'Reilly. *Shooting Ghosts: A U.S. Marine, a Combat Photographer, and Their Journey Home from War*. New York: Viking, 2017.

Brock, Rita Nikashima, and Gabriella Lettini. *Soul Repair: Recovering from Moral Injury after War*. Boston: Beacon, 2012.

Browning, Christopher R. *Ordinary Men: Reserve Police Battalion 101 and the Final Solution in Poland*. New York: HarperPerennial, 1992.

Butler, Joseph. *Five Sermons*. Edited by Stephen L. Darwall. Indianapolis: Hackett, 1983.

Cameron, J. M. "Foreword to Carl Amery." *Capitulation: The Lesson of German Catholicism*. New York: Herder and Herder, 1967.

Capizzi, Joseph E. "Selective Conscientious Objection in the United States." *Journal of Church and State* 38.2 (1996) 339–63.

Caputo, Philip. *A Rumor of War*. New York: Henry Holt, 1977.

Carnahan, Kevin. "Perturbations of the Souls and Pains of the Body." *Journal of Religious Ethics* 36.2 (2008) 269–94.

Catechism of the Catholic Church. "On Moral Conscience." Part Three, Section One, Chapter One, Article 6. Mahwah, NJ: Paulist, 1994. https://www.vatican.va/archive/ccc_css/archive/catechism/p3s1c1a6.htm.

Cavanaugh, William T. "At Odds With the Pope: Legitimate Authority & Just Wars." *Commonweal*, May 23, 2003. https://oldarchive.godspy.com/faith/At-odds-with-the-pope-legitimate-authority-and-just-wars.cfm.htm.

Childress, James F. "Just-War Theories: The Bases, Interrelations, Priorities, and Functions of Their Criteria." *Theological Studies* 39.3 (1978) 427–45.

Curran, Charles, ed. *Conscience*. Readings in Moral Theology 14. New York: Paulist, 2004.

Curran, Charles E., Kenneth R. Himes, and Thomas A. Shannon. "Commentary on *Sollicitudo rei socialis.*" In *Modern Catholic Social Teaching: Commentaries & Interpretations,* edited by Kenneth R. Himes, 415–35. Washington, DC: Georgetown University Press, 2005.

DeCosse, David E. "Authority, Lies, and War: Democracy and the Development of Just War Theory." *Theological Studies* 67 (2006) 378–94.

Dorn, A. Walter, David R. Mandel, and Ryan W. Cross. "How Just Were America's Wars? A Survey of Experts Using a Just War Index." *International Studies Perspectives* 16 (2015) 270–85.

Drinan, Robert. *Vietnam and Armageddon: Peace, War, and the American Conscience.* New York: Sheed & Ward, 1970.

Dubik, James M. "Foreword: Expanding Our Understanding of the Moral Dimension of War." In *Afterwar: Healing the Moral Wounds of Our Soldiers,* by Nancy Sherman, xi–xvii. Oxford: Oxford University Press, 2015.

Duffey, Michael K. "The Just War Teaching: From Tonkin Gulf to Persian Gulf." *America* 164 (February 2, 1991) 83–89.

Edmonds, Bill Russell. *God Is Not Here: A Soldier's Struggle with Torture, Trauma, and the Moral Injuries of War.* New York: Pegasus, 2015.

Ellner, Andrea, Paul Robinson, and David Whetham, eds. *When Soldiers Say No: Selective Conscientious Objection in the Modern Military.* Farnham, UK: Ashgate, 2015.

Ellsberg, Robert. "St. Martin of Tours." In *All Saints: Daily Reflections on Saints, Prophets, and Witnesses for Our Time,* by Robert Ellsbert, 288–89. New York: Crossroad, 1997.

Ford, John C. "The Morality of Obliteration Bombing." *Theological Studies* 5 (1944) 261–309.

Forest, Jim. "Introduction." In *Franz Jägerstätter: Letters and Writings from Prison,* edited by Erna Putz, ix–xxx. Maryknoll, NY: Orbis, 2009.

Francis, Pope. *Laudato Si': On Care for Our Common Home.* Vatican City: Vatican Press, 2015.

———. "Nonviolence: A Style of Politics for Peace." World Day of Peace Message of January 1, 2017. https://w2.vatican.va/content/francesco/en/messages/peace/documents/papa-francesco_20161208_messaggio-l-giornata-mondiale-pace-2017.html.

Frank, Tenney. "The Import of the Fetial Institution." *Classical Philology* 7 (1912) 335–42.

Genovesi, Vincent J. "The Just-War Doctrine: A Warrant for Resistance." *The Thomist* 454 (1981) 503–540.

Gibbons-Neff, Thomas. "Documents Reveal U.S. Officials Misled Public on War in Afghanistan." The New York Times, December 9, 2019. https://www.nytimes.com/2019/12/09/world/asia/afghanistan-war-documents.html?searchResultPosition=6.

Gibbs, John. C. *Moral Development and Rationality: Beyond the Theories of Kohlberg, Hoffman, and Haidt.* 3rd ed. Oxford: Oxford University Press, 2014.

Glendon, Mary Ann. "The Sources of Rights Talk: Some Are Catholic." *Commonweal* 128 (October 12, 2001) 11–13.

———. *A World Made New: Eleanor Roosevelt and the Universal Declaration of Human Rights.* New York: Random House, 2001.

Gray, J. Glenn. *The Warriors: Reflections on Men in Battle.* 2nd ed. New York: Harper & Row, 1973.

Gutman, Matthew, and Catherine Lutz. *Breaking Ranks: Iraq Veterans Speak Out against the War*. Berkeley: University of California Press, 2010.

Haidt, Jonathan. *The Righteous Mind: Why Good People Are Divided by Politics and Religion*. New York: Pantheon, 2012.

Halberstam, David. *The Best and the Brightest*. Greenwich, CT: Fawcett Crest, 1972.

Häring, Bernard. *Embattled Witness: Memories of a Time of War*. New York: Seabury, 1976.

Hauerwas, Stanley. "Should War Be Eliminated?" In *Against the Nations: War and Survival in a Liberal Society*, by Stanley Hauerwas, 169–208. Minneaplis: Winston Press, 1985.

Heaney, Seamus. "From the Republic of Conscience." In *Opened Ground: Selected Poems 1966–1996*. London: Faber & Faber, 1998.

———. [remarks on "From the Republic of Conscience"]. https://genius.com/Seamus-heaney-from-the-republic-of-conscience-annotated.

Hehir, J. Bryan. "The U.S. Catholic Bishops and Selective Conscientious Objection: History and Logic." In *Selective Conscientious Objection: Accommodating Conscience and Security*, edited by Michael F. Noone Jr. Boulder, CO: Westview, 1989.

Hersh, Seymour. "Overwhelming Force: What Happened in the Final Days of the Gulf War?" *The New Yorker* (May 22, 2000) 49–82.

Himes, Kenneth R. *Christianity and the Political Order: Conflict, Cooptation, and Cooperation*. Maryknoll, NY: Orbis, 2013.

———. *Drones and the Ethics of Targeted Killing*. Lanham, MD: Rowman & Littlefield, 2016.

Hochshild, Adam. *Bury the Chains: Prophets and Rebels in the Fight to Free an Empire's Slaves*. Boston: Houghton Mifflin, 2005.

Hodgson, Timothy J., and Lindsay B. Carey. "Moral Injury and Definitional Clarity: Betrayal, Spirituality and the Role of Chaplains." *Journal of Religion & Health* 56 (2017) 1212–28.

Holmes, Arthur F., ed. *War and Christian Ethics: Classic and Contemporary Readings on the Morality of War*. 2nd ed. Grand Rapids: Baker Academic, 2005.

Hoffman, Tobias. "Conscience and Synderesis." In *The Oxford Handbook of Aquinas*, edited by Brian Davies and Eleonore Stump, 255–64. Oxford: Oxford University Press, 2012.

Hogan, Linda. "*Synderesis, Suneidesis* and the Construction of a Theological Tradition." *Hermathena* 181 (Winter 2006) 125–40.

Hovey, Michael. "A Man of Peace: Gordon C. Zahn, 1918–2007." *Commonweal* 135.3 (2008) 6.

Hunter, David G. "A Decade of Research on Early Christians and Military Service." *Religious Studies Review* 18 (1992) 87–94.

John XXIII, Pope. *Pacem in Terris*. In *Catholic Social Thought: The Documentary Heritage*, edited by David J. O'Brien and Thomas A. Shannon, 137–70. Maryknoll, NY: Orbis, 2010.

John Paul II, Pope. *Centesimus Annus*. In *Catholic Social Thought: The Documentary Heritage*, edited by David J. O'Brien and Thomas A. Shannon, 471–523. Maryknoll, NY: Orbis, 2010.

Johnson, James Turner. "The Broken Tradition." *The National Interest* 45 (1996) 27–36.

———. *Ideology, Reason, and the Limitation of War: Religious and Secular Concepts*, by James Turner Johnson, 1200–740. Princeton: Princeton University Press, 1975.

Kaveny, Cathleen M. "Intrinsic Evil and Political Responsibility." In *Voting and Holiness: Catholic Perspectives on Political Participation*, edited by Nicholas P. Cafardi, 126–34. Mahwah, NJ: Paulist, 2012.

Keenan, James F. "Moral Theology Out of Western Europe." *Theological Studies* 59 (1998) 107–13.

———. "Ten Reasons Why Thomas Aquinas Is Important for Ethics Today." *Blackfriars* 75.884 (July/August 1994) 354–63.

King, Martin Luther, Jr. "Letter from Birmingham Jail." In *A Testament of Hope: The Essential Writings and Speeches of Martin Luther King, Jr.*, edited by James M. Washington. New York: HarperCollins, 1986.

King, Patricia M., and Karen S. Kitchener. *Developing Reflective Judgment: Understanding and Promoting Intellectual Growth and Critical Thinking in Adolescents and Adults.* San Francisco: Jossey-Bass, 1994.

Kolb, Robert. "Origin of the Twin Terms jus ad bellum/jus in bello." *International Review of the Red Cross* 320 (October 31, 1997) https://www.icrc.org/en/doc/resources/documents/article/other/57jnuu.htm.

Lang, Anthony, Jr. "The Just War Tradition and the Question of Authority." *Journal of Military Ethics* 8 (2009) 202–16.

Lang, Daniel. *Casualties of War.* New York: Pocket, 1969. Originally published in *The New Yorker*, October 18, 1969.

Langan, John. "The Elements of St. Augustine's Just War Theory." *Journal of Religious Ethics* 12.1 (1984) 19–38.

———. "The Good of Selective Conscientious Objection." In *Selective Conscientious Objection: Accommodating Conscience and Security*, edited by Michael F. Noone Jr., 89–106. Boulder, CO: Westview, 1989.

Lewy, Guenter. *The Catholic Church and Nazi Germany.* N.p.: Da Capo, 1964.

Lifton, Robert J. *Home from the War: Vietnam Veterans: Neither Victims nor Executioners.* New York: Touchstone, 1973.

Linn, Ruth. "Conscience at War: On the Relationship Between Moral Psychology and Moral Resistance." *Peace and Conflict Studies* 7 (2001) 337–55.

———. "The Moral Judgment, Action, and Credibility of Israeli Soldiers Who Refused to Serve in Lebanon (1982–1985)." In *Selective Conscientious Objection: Accommodating Conscience and Security*, edited by Michaael F. Noone Jr., 129–51. Boulder, CO: Westview, 1989.

Litz, Brett T., et al. "Moral Injury and Moral Repair in War Veterans: A Preliminary Model and Intervention Strategy." *Clinical Psychology Review* 29 (2009) 695–706.

MacIntyre, Alasdair. *Whose Justice? Which Rationality?* Notre Dame: Notre Dame University Press, 1988.

MacNair, Rachel M. "Perpetration-Induced Traumatic Stress." In *Peace Movements Worldwide.* Vol. 2, *Players and Practices in Resistance to War*, edited by M. Pilisuk and M. N. Nagler, 263–70. Santa Barbara, CA: ABC-CLIO/Praeger, 2011.

Marin, Peter. "Living in Moral Pain" *Psychology Today* (November, 1981) 68–80.

Markus, R. A. *Saeculum: History and Society in St. Augustine's Theology.* Cambridge: Cambridge University Press, 1970.

———. "Saint Augustine's Views on the 'Just War.'" *The Church and War* 20 (1983) 1–13.

Marlantes, Karl. *What It Is Like to Go to War.* New York: Grove, 2011.

McMahan, Jeff. "Foreword." *When Soldiers Say No: Selective Conscientious Objection in the Modern Military*, edited by Andrea Ellner, Paul Robinson, and David Whetham. Surrey, UK: Ashgate, 2014.

———. *Killing in War*. Oxford: Oxford University Press, 2009.

———. "The Prevention of Unjust Wars." In *Reading Walzer*, edited by Yitzhak Benbaji and Naomi Sussman, 233–55. London: Routledge, 2014.

McMaster, H. R. *Dereliction of Duty: Lyndon Johnson, Robert McNamara, the Joint Chiefs, and the Lies That Led to Vietnam*. New York: HarperPerennial, 1997.

Meager, Robert Emmet, and Douglas A. Pryor. *War and Moral Injury: A Reader*. Eugene, OR: Cascade, 2018.

Messer, Lynne C. "Natural Experiment." *Encyclopedia Britannica*. https://www.britannica.com/science/natural-experiment.

Minear, Larry. "Conscience and Carnage in Afghanistan and Iraq: US Veterans Ponder the Experience." *Journal of Military Ethics* 13.2 (2014) 137–57.

Monteith, Robert. *Discourse on the Shedding of Blood and the Laws of War*. London: Kegan Paul, Trench & Co, 1885. Kissinger Legacy Reprints.

Morris, David J. *The Evil Hours: A Biography of Post-Traumatic Stress Disorder*. Boston: Mariner, 2016.

Moshman, David. *Adolescent Rationality and Development: Cognition, Morality, and Identity*. 3rd ed. New York: Psychology Press, 2011.

Mott, Stephen C. "After All Else—Then Arms?" In *Biblical Ethics and Social Change*, by Stephen C. Mott, 143–64. Oxford: Oxford University Press, 1982. A revised edition was published in 2011.

Murray, John Courtney. "War and Conscience." *A Conflict of Loyalties: The Case for Selective Conscientious Objection*, edited by James Finn. New York: Pegasus, 1968.

———. *We Hold These Truths: Catholic Reflections on the American Proposition*. Kansas City: Sheed & Ward, 1960.

National Advisory Commission on Selective Service. *In Pursuit of Equity: Who Serves When Not All Serve?* Published by the Commission, 1967.

National Conference of Catholic Bishops [NCCB]. *The Challenge of Peace: God's Promise and Our Response*. Washington, DC: United States Catholic Conference, 1983. [Also in O'Brien and Shannon, *Catholic Social Thought*, 689–806.] http://www.usccb.org/upload/challenge-peace-gods-promise-our-response-1983.pdf.

———. *Economic Justice for All: Pastoral Letter on Catholic Social Teaching and the U.S. Economy*. Washington, DC: United States Catholic Conference, 1986. [Also in *Catholic Social Thought: The Documentary Heritage*, edited by David J. O'Brien and Thomas A. Shannon, 604–88.] http://www.usccb.org/issues-and-action/human-life-and-dignity/war-and-peace/nuclear-weapons/upload/statement-the-challenge-of-peace-1983-05-03.pdf.

———. *The Harvest of Justice Is Sown in Peace*. Washington, DC: United States Catholic Conference, 1993. http://www.usccb.org/beliefs-and-teachings/what-we-believe/catholic-social-teaching/the-harvest-of-justice-is-sown-in-peace.cfm.

Navin, Mark. "Sincerity, Accuracy and Selective Conscientious Objection." *Journal of Military Ethics* 12 (2013) 111–28.

Nazarov, A., et al. "Role of Morality in the Experience of Guilt and Shame within the Armed Forces." *Acta Psychiatrica Scandinavica* 132 (2015) 4–19.

Niebuhr, Reinhold. "Why the Christian Church Is Not Pacifist." In *War and Christian Ethics*, edited by Arthur F. Holmes, 301–13. Grand Rapids: Baker Academic, 2005.

New York Times. The Pentagon Papers. Toronto: Bantam, 1971.

Newman, John Henry. "A Letter Addressed to His Grace the Duke of Norfolk on Occasion of Mr. Gladstone's Recent Expostulation." In *Conscience, Consensus, and the Development of Doctrine.* New York: Doubleday, 1992.

O'Brien, David J., and Thomas A. Shannon, eds. *Catholic Social Thought: The Documentary Heritage.* Expanded ed. Maryknoll, NY: Orbis, 2010.

O'Connell, Timothy E. "Understanding Conscience." In *Conscience,* edited by Charles E. Curran, 25–38. Readings in Moral Theology 14. Mahwah, NJ: Paulist, 2004. [Also as "Conscience," In O'Connell, *Principles for a Catholic Morality,* chapter 9. Rev. ed. San Francisco: HarperCollins, 1990.]

O'Gorman, Colm. "Remembering Seamus Heaney." Amnesty International, August 30, 2013. https://www.amnesty.org/en/latest/campaigns/2013/08/remembering-seamus-heaney/.

Palmer-Fernández, Gabriel. "White Flags on the Road to Basra: Surrendering Soldiers in the Persian Gulf War." *Journal of Social Philosophy* 32 (2001) 143–56.

Pax Christi International. "An Appeal to the Catholic Church to Re-Commit to the Centrality of Gospel Nonviolence." May 17, 2016. https://nonviolencejustpeace.net/2016/05/17/an-appeal-to-the-catholic-church-to-re-commit-to-the-centrality-of-gospel-nonviolence/.

Peters, Edward. *Torture.* Expanded ed. Philadelphia: University of Pennsylvania Press, 1996.

Pius XII, Pope. "Communism and Democracy." In *The Major Addresses of Pope Pius XII,* Vol. 2, *Christmas Messages.* St. Paul: North Central Publishing, 1961.

Pizan, Christine de. "War and Chivalry." In *The Ethics of War: Classic and Contemporary Readings,* edited by Gregory M. Reichberg, Henrik Syse, and Endre Begby, 210–26. Oxford: Blackwell, 2006.

Pontifical Council for Justice and Peace. *Compendium of the Social Doctrine of the Church.* Washington, DC: United States Catholic Conference, 2004.

Potter, Ralph. "Conscientious Objection to Particular Wars." In *Religion and the Public Order: Number 4,* edited by Donald A. Gianella, 44–99. Ithaca, NY: Cornell University Press, 1968.

———. "The Moral Logic of War." Department of Church and Society, Board of Christian Education, 1969. Reprinted in *War in the Twentieth Century: Sources in Theological Ethics,* edited by Richard B. Miller, 198–214. Louisville: Westminster John Knox, 1992.

Potts, Timothy C. *Conscience in Medieval Philosophy.* Cambridge: Cambridge University Press, 1980.

Powers, Brian S. "Moral Injury and Original Sin: The Applicability of Augustinian Moral Psychology in Light of Combat Trauma." *Theology Today* 73 (2016) 325–37.

Press, Eyal. "The Wounds of the Drone Warrior." *The New York Times Magazine* (June 17, 2018) 30–49.

Prusak, Bernard. "A Right Not to Fight: Making the Case for Selective Conscientious Objection." *Commonweal* 144.19 (December 1, 2017) 13–15.

Putz, Erna, ed. *Franz Jägerstätter: Letters and Writings from Prison.* Translated by Robert A. Krieg. Maryknoll, NY: Orbis, 2009.

Ramsey, Paul. *The Just War: Force and Political Responsibility.* New York: Scribner's, 1968.

Reichberg, Gregory M., Henrik Syse, and Endre Begby, eds. *The Ethics of War: Classic and Contemporary Readings.* Oxford: Blackwell, 2006.

Reid, Charles J., Jr. "John T. Noonan, Jr., on the Catholic Conscience and War: *Negre v. Larsen*." *Notre Dame Law Review* 76 (2001) 881–959. http://scholarship.law.nd.edu/ndlr/vol76/iss3/5.

Rest, James, et al. *Postconventional Moral Thinking: A Neo-Kohlbergian Approach.* Mahwah, NJ: L. Erlbaum, 1999.

Rose, Jürgen. "Conscience in Lieu of Obedience." In *When Soldiers Say No: Selective Conscientious Objection in the Modern Military*, edited by Andrea Ellner, Paul Robinson, and David Whetham, 177–94. Burlington, VT: Ashgate, 2014.

Schorr, Yonit, et al. "Sources of Moral Injury among War Veterans: A Qualitative Evaluation." *Journal of Clinical Psychology* (2018) 1–16.

Shane, Scott. "Vietnam War Intelligence 'Deliberately Skewed,' Secret Study Says." *The New York Times,* December 2, 2005. https://www.nytimes.com/2005/12/02/politics/vietnam-war-intelligence-deliberately-skewed-secret-study-says.html.

Shay, Jonathan. *Achilles in Vietnam: Combat Trauma and the Undoing of Character.* New York: Scribner, 1994.

———. "Moral Injury." *Psychoanalytic Psychology* (April 2014) 1–20.

———. *Odysseus in America: Combat Trauma and the Trials of Homecoming.* New York: Scribner, 2002.

Sheehan, Neil. *A Bright Shining Lie: John Paul Vann and America in Vietnam.* New York: Random House, 1988.

Sherman, Nancy. *Afterwar: Healing the Moral Wounds of Our Soldiers.* Oxford: Oxford University Press, 2015.

Smith, Robert J. *Conscience and Catholicism: The Nature and Function of Conscience in Contemporary Roman Catholic Moral Theology.* Lanham, MD: University Press of America, 1998.

Somme, Luc-Thomas, OP. "The Infallibility, Impeccability and Indestructability of Synderesis. *Studies in Christian Ethics* 19.3 (2006) 403–16.

Swift, Louis J. "Augustine on War and Killing: Another View." *Harvard Theological Review* 66 (1973) 369–83.

———. *The Early Fathers on War and Military Service.* Wilmington, DE: M. Glazier, 1983.

Tessman, Lisa. *Burdened Virtues: Virtue Ethics for Liberatory Struggles.* Oxford: Oxford University Press, 2005.

Tick, Edward. *War and the Soul: Healing Our Nation's Veterans from Post-Traumatic Stress Disorder.* Wheaton, IL: Quest, 2005.

United States Catholic Conference [USCC]. "Declaration on Conscientious Objection and Selective Conscientious Objection." October 21, 1971. http://www.usccb.org/issues-and-action/human-life-and-dignity/war-and-peace/declaration-on-conscientious-objection-and-selective-conscientious-objections-1971-10-21.cfm.

———. "Human Life in Our Day: Chapter II, 'The Family of Nations." In *Quest for Justice: A Compendium of Statements of the United States Catholic Bishops on the Political and Social Order 1966–1980*, edited by Brian J. Benestad and Francis J. Butler. Washington, DC: National Conference of Catholic Bishops/United States Catholic Conference, 1980.

———. "Statement of the American Bishops on Peace November, 1966." In *Vietnam and Armageddon: Peace, War, and the American Conscience*, by Robert Drinan, appendix D. New York: Sheed & Ward, 1970.

———. "Statement on the Catholic Conscientious Objector." October 15, 1969. http://www.usccb.org/issues-and-action/human-life-and-dignity/war-and-peace/

statement-on-the-catholic-conscientious-objector-division-of-world-justice-and-peace-1969-10-15.cfm.

———. "Statement on Registration and Conscription for Military Service." February 14, 1980. http://www.usccb.org/issues-and-action/human-life-and-dignity/war-and-peace/statement-on-registration-and-conscription-for-military-service-1980-02-14.cfm.

United States Conference of Catholic Bishops [USCCB]. *Forming Consciences for Faithful Citizenship.* November 2019. http://www.usccb.org/issues-and-action/faithful-citizenship/forming-consciences-for-faithful-citizenship-title.cfm.

———. *The Harvest of Justice Is Sown In Peace.* http://www.usccb.org/beliefs-and-teachings/what-we-believe/catholic-social-teaching/the-harvest-of-justice-is-sown-in-peace.cfm.

———. "Statement on Iraq." November 13, 2002. http://www.usccb.org/issues-and-action/human-life-and-dignity/global-issues/middle-east/statement-on-iraq.cfm.

Vatican Council II. *Gaudium et Spes.* In *Catholic Social Thought: The Documentary Heritage*, edited by David J. O'Brien and Thomas A. Shannon, 174–250. Maryknoll, NY: Orbis, 2010. http://www.vatican.va/archive/hist_councils/ii_vatican_council/documents/vat-ii_cons_19651207_gaudium-et-spes_en.html.

Verkamp, Bernard J. *The Moral Treatment of Returning Warriors in Early Medieval and Modern Times.* Scranton: University of Scranton Press, 2006.

Walters, LeRoy. "A Historical Perspective on Selective Conscientious Objection." *Journal of the American Academy of Religion* 41 (1973) 201–11.

Walzer, Michael. *Just and Unjust Wars: A Moral Argument with Historical Illustrations.* New York: Basic Books, 1977.

Watson, Alan. *International Law in Archaic Rome: War and Religion.* Baltimore: Johns Hopkins University Press, 1993.

Weigel, George. "Moral Clarity in a Time of War." *First Things* 139 (February 2003) 20–27. https://www.firstthings.com/article/2003/01/001-moral-clarity-in-a-time-of-war. Reprinted in *War and Christian Ethics*, edited by Arthur F. Holmes, 373–90. 2nd ed. Grand Rapids: Baker Academic, 2005.

Wicker, Brian. "The Significance of Franz Jägersttätter." *New Blackfriars* 89 (2008) 385–88.

Wikipedia. "Ehren Watada." https://en.wikipedia.org/wiki/Ehren_Watada.

Williams, Rowan. "War and Statecraft." *First Things* 141 (March 2004). https://www.firstthings.com/article/2004/03/war-amp-statecraft. Reprinted in *War and Christian Ethics*, edited by Arthur F. Holmes, 391–99. 2nd ed. Grand Rapids: Baker Academic, 2005.

Wood, David. *What Have We Done: The Moral Injury of Our Longest Wars.* New York: Little, Brown, 2016.

Wynn, Phillip. *Augustine on War and Military Service.* Minneapolis: Fortress, 2013.

Yoder, John Howard. *David Urquhart: Knight Errant for the Just War Tradition in the Age of Empire.* Working Paper Series 3: WP:8. University of Notre Dame: Joan B. Kroc Institute for International Peace Studies, 1993.

———. *When War Is Unjust: Being Honest in Just-War Thinking.* 1996. Reprint, Eugene, OR: Wipf & Stock, 2001.

Zahn, Gordon. *German Catholics and Hitler's Wars.* New York: Dutton, 1962/1969.

———. "He Would Not Serve." *America* 99.14 (1958) 888–90. Included as the first part of "Conscientious Objection in Nazi Germany: Martyrdom in 1943." In *War, Conscience and Dissent*, by Gordon Zahn, 177–83. New York: Hawthorne, 1967.

————. "In Celebration of Martyrdom." *America* 170.6 (1994) 8–10.

————. *In Solitary Witness: The Life and Death of Franz Jägerstätter.* Rev. ed. Springfield, IL: Templegate, 1986.

————. *War, Conscience and Dissent.* New York: Hawthorne, 1967.

Zupan, Dan. "Selective Conscientious Objection and the Just Society." In *When Soldiers Say No: Selective Conscientious Objection in the Modern Military*, edited by Andrea Ellner, Paul Robinson, and David Whetham, 89–96. Burlington, VT: Ashgate, 2014.

Index

Tables in the text are indicated in italics.

CPSIA information can be obtained
at www.ICGtesting.com
Printed in the USA
LVHW022247170722
723718LV00002B/336